A GUIDE TO IRISH ROOTS

by

William and Mary Durning

Dedicated to everyone whose
roots go back to the soil of
IRELAND

*Collected from oral tradition and
ancient records during visits to
Ireland, other parts of Europe
and North America.*

Cover Design by Clayton Clark III
Artwork by Wendi Fitzpatrick

Irish Family Names Society
P.O. Box 2095
La Mesa, California 92044-0600
1986

Library of Congress Catalogue Number 84-62760
International Standard Book Number 0-9601868-1-6
Printed in the United States of America
Original Printing 1986
Second Printing 1987
3rd Printing May. 1989

Published directly from the authors manuscript by:
The Irish Family Names Society
P.O. Box 2095
La Mesa, California 92044-0600

THE ORIGIN OF THE IRISH RACE

Table of Contents

Preface vii

Introduction ix

PART I

PART II

PART III

INDEX TO SURNAMES

SAINT MARY'S ABBEY, TRIM, COUNTY MEATH

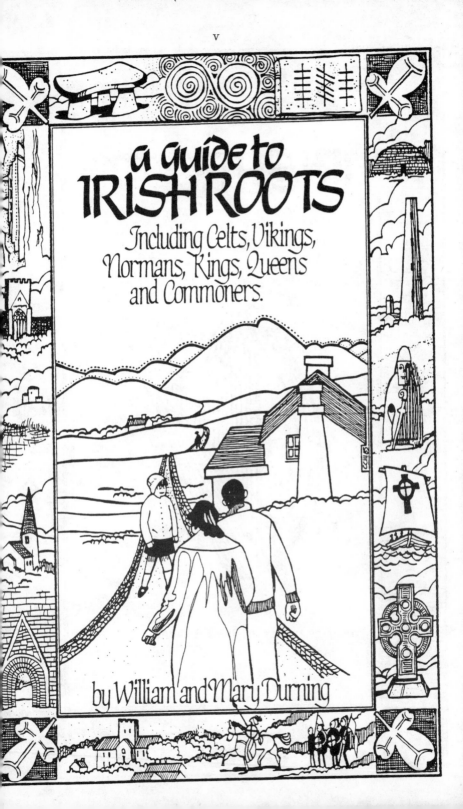

a guide to
IRISH ROOTS
Including Celts, Vikings, Normans, Kings, Queens and Commoners.

by William and Mary Durning

IRISH ROOTS

THE HARP, OLDEST HERALDIC SYMBOL OF IRELAND

PREFACE

"A Guide to Irish Roots," like its predecessor, "If You're a Wee Bit Irish," is a collection of traditional Irish family relationships presented in chart form. The arrangement of families follows as nearly as possible the oral tradition of the ancient Starai (Historian) or the Seanchai (Storyteller) as they related the ginealach (Genealogy) of Saints and heroes.

The "Guide" is divided into three parts to fulfill this purpose. The first part is the traditional history of the Irish people: this section begins with the origin of those who became the Gaels, and concludes with the Famine. Many persons in this section are keyed to the charts showing their place in traditional Irish history.

Part two is the charting of Irish families: the Irish were ardent genealogists from very early times. This part has as its base those families who made a place for themselves in Irish history. In Ireland, one could achieve recognition by being born into a noble family, holding a position in the church or by making an important contribution to an art, craft or the military. During the period of English rule one could also become part of a historical record by going to jail!

Traditionally, most Irish families sprang from a small number of Irish chiefs. As families multiplied each person was required to know his or her relationship to the ruling family. From this system developed the most comprehensive pattern of family relationships to be found in Western Europe. The charts trace these intertwining branches down to the period when Irish names were translated into English. The oldest Irish names were personal names which later became surnames resulting in confusion, since several widely separated and independent families may have the same surname. If this should be the case with your family, you will need to know the county of family origin. Cromwell shipped many people to Connacht during his invasion. Other attempts have been made to transplant families, none the less, many have remained in the same region for 300 years or longer. The charts are not a genealogy of Irish people but rather a family road map designed to aid those who may wish to do more detailed research.

Part three is an index to family names. First is
listed the most common English form of the original
Irish name. Next follows the Gaelic which is
written the way it was spelled for the authors
which is often an older form of Gaelic. The older
spelling was chosen as an aid to those researchers
who may wish to consult historical documents of an
early period. Next follows one or more variations
of the English name. Only those variations are
included which were given by persons who furnished
information. The study of names is a subject in
its own right. Surnames in the index are keyed to
the page where that name appears in the charts.
From that point, one can trace a traditional family
line **backward** through time by following the lines
connecting the names withing that family as it
joins others toward the front of the book. Names
are also keyed to counties on the maps as a guide
to the location of the family for an extended
period. It is hoped that this book will shorten
research time for those interested in their origins
as well as provide a traditional background for
those who would like to know more about kings,
queens, heroes and commoners who have gone before
them.

"A Guide to Irish Roots" has been prepared for
members of The Irish Family Names Society and other
interested persons. It has been printed directly
from the authors' manuscript, a collection of
thirty-five years.

WYNNE'S CASTLE - COUNTY KERRY

INTRODUCTION

From time to time, historians of various persuasions and nationalities have endeavored to explain the nature and origin of our Irish ancestors. The only universal conclusion: "The Irish are a different sort of folk." In this they agree with Irish tradition. Our most noted ancestors, the Gaels, believed their original homeland to have been the grasslands of Central and Eastern Europe. Their earliest progenitors a cattle herding folk. These early people based their entire civilization on oral tradition without the need for written records. A strong family relationship was the basic unit of their society. Each person was required to memorize his or her lineage up to that of the local king. At one time there were more than 150 separate kingdoms in Ireland. Thus developed in Ireland a complex system of genealogical relationships.

The Irish were not invaded by the Romans and so were able to maintain their original culture much longer than many of their Continental neighbors.

When Christianity came the people embraced it without bloodshed. The kings, wishing to have copies of the Bible for themselves, encouraged the art of writing. So it was that the "Green Island" became the School House of Europe during the Dark Ages.

In the 800's A.D., Viking raids destroyed many of Ireland's religous and educational institutions. The Viking occupation sent forth a stream of church men who crossed to the mainland. There they contributed much to the revival of religion and learning.

In 1169 an Irish king invited in a small group of Norman Knights. These aggressive folk, discovering the riches of the country, summoned reinforcements and carved out a kingdom for themselves. Their attempt to extinquish Irish culture failed. In time, through intermarriage with the natives, the Normans became solidly Irish.

In still later times, English kings and Cromwell's Parliament planted the land with Scotch and English farmers. They, in turn, were joined by the Huguenots and others from the mainland.

From this combination of sturdy blood lines have come our ancestors who found their way to the New World. Many of these folk, with little prospect of ever being able to return to the "Homeland", wiped all thought of it from their memory. They passed on very few family traditions to their children. Fortunately for those of us who would like to learn something of our past, many of the older folk still living in the West of Ireland possess a lively knowledge of the Ireland of old. It was from them, and a few old manuscripts that most of this book was collected.

It is to the more than 50,000,000 North Americans of Irish descent that this book is dedicated. It represents one important part of the complex and exciting inheritance which belongs to everyone who is "A Wee Bit Irish."

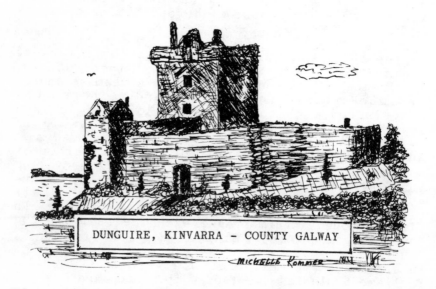

DUNGUIRE, KINVARRA - COUNTY GALWAY

MICHELLE KOMMER

IRISH ROOTS

part

one

LYONS, NEWCASTLE - COUNTY DUBLIN

IRISH ROOTS

The language and customs of our Irish ancestors
have joined together to create one of the most
interesting, ancient and exciting civilizations in
the West of Europe. Over the centuries, Ireland
has been populated by a variety of peoples. Of
these, our Gaelic speaking ancestors left the most
complete tradition of their origin and
civilization.

The first speakers of the oldest form of the Gaelic
language are believed to have reached Ireland two
milleniums before Christ. Another 900 years would
pass before the nomadic folk, called the "Gaels,"
voyaged to the "Green Island."

Little is known of the first residents, but the
Gaels have passed down to us a lively oral
tradition. The early Christian missionaries were
so fascinated by the stories of these people that
they wrote down the traditions as they heard them
told by the SEANCHAI (the ancient story telling
ones).

So durable were the tales of heroes, love affairs
and battles that respected story tellers living in
Ireland's Western Counties still tell them today.
The Authors listened to many of these gifted people
as well as visiting the national libraries of
Ireland, Scotland, Denmark, Norway and the British
Museum in search of the heritage of themselves and
other Irish families.

The Irish, an island folk, were spared many of the
cultural misfortunes of their Continental
neighbors. When the Romans extended their
occupation from the Continent to Britain, they
quickly learned to respect the aggressiveness of
their new neighbors on the "Green Island." Unlike
the settled folk whom the Romans easily subdued,
the Irish were a nomadic, aristocratic, independent
and aggressive people. Their regular raids on
Britain and the Continent impressed the Romans.
From these and other contacts it was deemed
inadvisable to attempt an invasion of the"Green
Island."

This bit of good luck permitted the Irish to
retain their customs, laws and traditions down to
recent times. Among the Western nations, only the
Irish have preserved for us so large a collection

of customs and laws. They portray a people whose origin was pastoral rather than the settled life with which we're most familiar.

To gain a real understanding of our roots, it's necessary to go back to a time before recorded history. A time when learning was passed directly from mouth to ear, from face to face.

In old Ireland, the story teller was a highly respected man or woman, one with a special position in Irish society. The whole community knew which home the "seanchai" would visit on a given evening. From his place by the fire, he conjured up visions of heroes spanning a thousand years. His tales made genealogies a personalized family history because those present were woven into the lineage of some long dead hero.

Fortunately, a few of these skilled individuals still live along the Western shores of Ireland. From their lips a visitor may learn about the adventures of a remote ancestor. The lucky may be treated to a traditional history of the nation, replete with legends filled with heroes like Maeve and Finn Mac Cool. The bonified oral historian carefully separates fact from fiction so there is no conflict between the two.

In days gone by, the seanchai frequently began the evening with the legend of PARTHALON (page II-3). Parthalon was a nomadic cattle herder, turned farmer. He was the first speaker of old Gaelic to visit Ireland. He came about 2,000 B.C. while Ireland was still recovering from the ice age. Rivers were changing course and new lakes being formed.

Today, the story teller may preface tradition with a knowledge of geology and archeology. It's an old Irish custom to make ancient history relevant to the listener.

IN THE BEGINNING

The ice age ended about 10,000 B.C. By 8500 B.C. the receding ice bared fertile land. Hardy plants like rhododendron, stunted birch and arctic willow sprang from the fecund soil. The warming trend continued. Wind and birds brought many new plant seeds from Britain and the Continent. Soon oak, hazel and pine joined the sturdy birch. Some animals may have survived the ice age. It's also probable that land and ice connected Ireland with the Continent making animal passage possible. Undoubtedly, man during his visits in later times, introduced some new species. By 7000 B.C., Ireland was once more covered with forest and populated with living creatures.

Archeologists believe that humans occupied Britain by 7500 B.C. If true, another 1,500 years would pass before their arrival in Ireland. Flint tools and the remains of camp fires betray their presence on the beaches of Antrim and Down. These finds date from about 6000 B.C.

One Irish legend gives evidence of early occupation of the island. The story tells how Noah's granddaughter and fifty maidens visited Ireland before the flood! Tales like this, when removed from their original context, led historians of the new scientific era (the 1700 and 1800's) to summarily reject many of Ireland's oldest legends. Nowadays we're developing a better understanding of what the ancients were attempting to tell us. We are learning how to interpret the real message of oral tradition and how it differs from the way ideas are presented in the written language of today.

ORIGINS

A detailed study of humanity reveals a variety of social classifications. Our Gaelic ancestors preferred a nomadic society based on language and tradition. A study of language is one way to trace the progress of our earliest ancestors through time and the migration of our ancestors on their way to and in Ireland.

Most dictionaries have a language chart beginning with an unknown mother tongue called "INDO-EUROPEAN". The children of this ancient language are those spoken by most Europeans today plus old Hittite, Iranian and Sanskrit. These variations became a new dialect when isolated groups, speaking the old language, added new words to their old vocabulary.

Our ancestors believed three original races peopled Europe. Along the shores of the

Mediterranian lived a short, dark, quick, intelligent, curly haired folk. The climate was warm and they discovered that cool caves made ideal homes. Their diet consisted of fish, fruits, nuts and occasional small animals. Living habits led to a closely knit communal society. As their numbers grew, the available caves proved too small to house the expanding population. The more innovative began to construct rectangular dwellings outside, which were similar in shape to their cave homes. Later on, crude stone walls were added around the dwellings to protect the inhabitants from wolves and other preditors.

The importation of bronze tools formed the foundation from which grew trade with their neighbors. Using iron tools, artisans created magnificent buildings of stone, the ruins of which can still be seen. These ancestors of ours were the first European merchants and engineers.

In the tree covered hills north of the sea, lived a different kind of people. They were of medium height, heavy set, straight haired with brown to grey eyes. These were casual, lumbering, easygoing folk who didn't mind doing repetitive tasks. Their food supply consisted of roots, nuts, berries, vegetables and slow moving animals. They practiced limited agriculture in the clearings. Home was a lean-to of branches and twigs in summer. In the winter they lived in pits dug in the ground.

Depletion of soil mandated movement from clearing to clearing. A bright member of this community was the inventor of one of the most important tools devised by the early human race - the stone ax! Clumsy as this tool appears to be, it changed hunters to farmers and made settled life possible. With it, the forests of Europe were felled. These inventive ancestors made axes by the million and exported them all over Europe. They were the first mass producers.

Commerce developed between the Mediterranians and the mountain folk. Both began to live in large, settled communities exchanging people and products. Later, two important inventions were imported from Africa and the East. These were writing and mathmatics, a combination which made the civilizations of Greece and Rome a possibility. From these peoples came the written accounts of life and traditions which we call Ancient European History.

There was, however, another society to which almost half the Continental population belonged. They were the nomads of the north and east, who lived upon the grasslands joining Europe to Asia. These folk were a conglomerate of peoples with a bond of cattle herding and common language.

Their lifestyle was quite different from that of the settled folk. In their society cattle represented both food and wealth. The nomads lived on the produce of their cattle which resulted in a diet of milk, butter and cheese. An occasional treat, a strong drink, was brewed from fermented mare's milk.

Early nomadic dwellings were devised from sheets of felt draped over low trees. As the trees disappeared from the grasslands, portable dwellings took their place. These were round imitations of the felt draped trees. In time, the wealthier individuals mounted portable huts on huge wagons, some up to thirty feet long. These were the first mobile homes!

The nomads were a transient people. They were also unique and imaginative artists. Art may have been a substitute for a lack of variety in their lives. The mountain people had changing landscapes and a diverse animal and bird life. The nomad saw only endless plains covered with grass and grazing cattle. As compensation, the nomadic artist chose vivid colors with intricate design and fantastic creatures. Each person in the clan strove for personal identity in dress, manner and property.

The nomads created a viable civilization without the need to reduce any part of it to writing. Their customs, laws and genealogy were common knowledge required of every member of the clan. It was their custom to gather at specified times to settle disputes, enact laws, arrange weddings and renew communal ties. The civilization of the nomad was as successful in its environment as was the better known culture of the settled people.

Most of what we know of the nomads of Europe comes from the Gaelic Irish who claim them as ancestors and the Greek historian HERODITUS who visited them about 400 B.C.

One important difference in custom between the settled folk and the nomad was the use of land. The settled folk planted crops which took time to mature. Around this necessity developed the idea of private land ownership. The migratory nomad looked at land use quite differently. His cattle needed to roam across open space in search of grass. He considered land to be public property for the use of all. Imagine the conflict when a nomad's cattle chanced upon a farmer's field. The farmer would obviously be upset if cattle devoured the crops he had faithfully tended. Not so with the nomad. He saw no harm in cattle eating whatever fodder they chanced upon. It's interesting that the use and ownership of land remains an important question even in our day.

THE SCYTHIANS

No one knows who invented the Indo-European tongue. Some think it was the nomadic band whom the Greeks called the Scythians (page II-3). When the ancient Irish (after they became Christians) were writing their genealogies, they included the Scythians in their lineage. The Irish Christians believed the Scythians to be descended from MAGOG, grandson of NOAH (page II-2). The Greeks believed them to be children of the Greek god ZEUS and the goddess BORYSTHENESE (page II-3).

The Scythians were a widely traveled and powerful people. At various times they migrated into Italy, Greece and as far as Egypt. They were a large and diverse population. The nucleus of the tribe was a clan of royal Scythians, to whom the other clans paid homage. As the family clans grew in size, some members broke off to form new clans. The largest continental group, called the KELTI or CELTS, are known to us from Roman records. Another branch took up residence in Turkey. They were called Galatians after the province they occupied. A mysterious tribe called the HYKSOS (page II-2) probably was a mixture of Scythians and Semitic peoples.

According to Irish tradition, all of these interesting and diverse folk were connected in some way with our Irish heritage.

The first of these ancients to visit Ireland descended from a king named FATHOCHTA (Page II-3).

THE SCYTHIAN IRISH

A legendary nomadic king named SCYTHES (page II-3) had five sons. Two of these were destined to figure in Irish pre-history. Fathochta was an ancestor of the first people to visit Ireland. BAATH was the progenitor of the second clan. This latter family, after many generations and wanderings, became the tribe known as the Gaelic Irish.

Five generations after Fathochta, one of his line named PARTHALON, was born. Parthalon's father was called "The Syrian," perhaps meaning that this branch of the family had migrated to that distant land. It also could mean that the dialect spoken by the father was closer to Syrian than Scythian. This son married a young lady from Sicily named DEQLGNAIT. Tradition says that he murdered his father and mother which was a reprehensible act even in early times. The clan rose against him, forcing Parthalon, along with his brother STERN (page II-3), to flee the country with their clans. They compounded the felony by stealing ships for their escape. Sailing toward the west they reached Ireland after numerous adventures. The island was uninhabited at the time. The clan prospered in Ireland until a plague, probably brought by sea going visitors, vanquished them all, save one. The survivor was TUAN, son of Stern. Tuan eventually died but was immediately reborn, as a bird, then an animal and finally as a salmon (which represents knowledge). He was caught and eaten by the wife of Mac Carrill, later to be reborn as TUAN MAC CARRILL (page II-98), in the time of the Saints. Thus, he was able to relate to church scribes the early history of Ireland!

At first glance this story is a fanciful bit of nonsense. In reality, it's a nomadic teaching tool. It points out that tradition requires a direct connection between past and present. The stories of one's ancestors must be retold to every generation. It also makes it clear that the ancients believed in transmigration and reincarnation.

THE STORY OF NEMEDIUS

NEMEDIUS (page II-4), came to Ireland about 300 years after Parthalon, accompanied by his two wives: MACHA, "the red head," who would be the ancestral mother of the FIR BOLG and the TUATHA de DANANN and REILBHO, from whom would come clans of Wales, the Isle of Man, the early inhabitants of Scotland and BRIOTAN MAOL (page II-6), the ancestor of SAINT PATRICK (II-6).

Both Parthalon and Nemedius were bedeviled by the dread FOMORIANS (page II-2). These sea pirates were an otherwise unknown people. One may speculate, however, that they were the forerunners of the Phoenicians. They were said to have come from the north coast of Africa. Many historians believe them to be an imaginary people, due to outlandish descriptions of them in Irish literature. Reality comes only when it's understood that oral tradition is usually exaggerated history: exaggeration is a device used to aid memory.

The Fomorians became oppressive masters, forcing the Nemedians to rebel. Some returned to their homeland in Greece, others crossed to the mainland and a remnant remained under bondage to the Fomorians. Those who returned to Greece were treated harshly by their relatives. They were given poor land which they tried to improve by hauling in fresh soil in leather bags. They grew into three clans, the most prominent being the Fir Bolg, "men of the leather bags." All three clans eventually found their way back to Ireland.

One branch chose to wander across Europe. They mixed with the mountain people we have already mentioned and with others in the far north. They became a quick witted people, learning many new techniques of metal smelting, agriculture and government. They also embraced a new religion, becoming followers of the goddess DANU. Thus, they acquired a new tribal name, the TUATHA de DANANN (page II-5).

RETURN OF THE TUATHA de DANANN

Messengers from Ireland informed the Tuatha that the Fir Bolg had returned to the "Green Island." The Tuatha decided they would return also. The clan brought symbols of their new culture, a caldron of plenty, representing their mastery of agriculture, a broad pointed spear and a "talking" sword, representing the mastery of metal. Most interesting of all was "the stone of truth" called the Lia Fail. It was said to make a sound when a true king stood upon it. It became a fixture in crowning ceremonies of future Irish kings. Some say the stone can still be seen on Tara hill along side the statue of Saint Patrick. Others say it was sent to Scotland for the crowning of an Irish king who set up a kingdom there. Eventually, the stone found its way to the church of Scone in Scotland, later to be taken by an English king. Now this stone is in the coronation chair in Westminister Abbey!

Family quarrels are part and parcel of Irish history. When the Tuatha returned to Ireland, they laid down a challenge to their relatives, the Fir Bolg. In the battle which followed, NUADA (page II-5), king of the Tuatha, lost an arm. Since only those in physically perfect condition could hold the title of king, Nuada was disqualified. But this wasn't the end of Nuada! Among his servants was a very clever and knowledgeable silver smith. The smith went to work at once and fashioned a fully functional silver arm for him. In this story our ancestors have preceded both H.G. Wells and present day fiction writers. Nuada was the first bionic man!

This and other wonders credited to the Tuatha have caused some historians to summarily reject their existence as humans and label them as demigods or figments of Irish imagination. If viewed from the standpoint of the Irish story teller, it's not difficult to understand that this is the story of a technically advanced race who may have mastered the smelting of iron as well as copper. One which had made advances in agriculture and who created mechanical devices to aid the disabled.

Whatever the truth, a truce was eventually reached with the Fir Bolg and the two co-existed until the arrival of the Gaels.

THE GAELS

Baath (page II-8) was the brother of

Fathochta. Baath had a son named FEINIUS FARSAIDH.
Feinius remained in the homeland and was a Scythian
king.   He was gifted with a broad based
understanding of language. He spoke not only his
own dialect but was fluent in the languages of the
settled tribes surrounding his kingdom. Some old
historians credit him with the creation of the
Celtic language. In his time, this new language
was understood by many different tribes because of
the loan words it contained.

In the mid 1700's B.C., a mysterious folk
called the HYKSOS (page II-2) invaded Egypt. They
were successful in part because they employed the
horse-drawn chariot, while the Egyptians fought on
foot. Some researchers credit the Scythians as the
first users of this weapon. The Hyksos may have
been a Semitic tribe who joined the Scythians.

As conquerors, the Hyksos were both plunderers
and businessmen. They studied the Egyptian
navigation of the Nile and saw the expansion of
shipping in the Mediterranian as opportunity for
immense profits. One problem was the fact that
Egyptian sailors were not familiar with European
languages. One of the Hyksos kings was aware of
Feinius' talent with language and sent a messenger
to him asking that someone of equal skill be sent
to teach the European language to their sea
captains. Feinius' son, NUIL "of the languages"
was selected to go to Egypt. His mission was so
successful that the Pharoah gave this prince his
daughter, SCOTA, in marriage. Their first son was
named GADEL. His skill in language was so great
that it became the name of a people who eventually
found their way to Ireland.

The Hyksos, like most nomadic peoples, abhored
physical labor. Egyptians were left in charge of
most of the routine tasks. Skilled persons were
imported as needed and slaves were often purchased
to perform physical labor. It's quite possible
that the Hebrew named JOSEPH (Genesis 37:12-36) was
sold into Egyptian slavery at this time.

The Hyksos remained in Egypt about 150 years.
Eventually the Egyptian princes gained sufficient
strength to buy off the Hyksos. Their band of
240,000 were paid to retreat to what is now
Palestine. There they melded into the general
population who in latter times would be called the
Canaanites or Phoenicians.

Among the projects of the new native Pharaohs was the construction of many cities. Apparently both native Egyptians and Hebrews, were conscripted for this task. It seems the Gaels remained some time in Egyptian controlled territory. Indications are that they departed or were expelled between the departure of the Hyksos and the exodus of the Hebrews.

Leaving the African continent, the Gaels sailed across the Mediterranian where they were rejected by relatives in Scythia. Eventually, the clan migrated to Spain, establishing a homeland and once more began to practice their age old profession of cattle herding.

In Spain, the usual territorial conflict between nomad and settled population erupted. The Gaelic hero of this period was MILE (also called Gallam and Milesius) whose title was "Mileg Espaine" - Mile, the soldier of Spain (page II-8). Mile's first wife was SEAUG who died shortly after the birth of their second child. Shock of this loss caused Mile to wish to return to the clan's ancient homeland. Fortunately, word of his exploits in Spain had come to the attention of numerous rulers around the Mediterranian. Visiting Scythia, he was welcomed and appointed general of the armies by the king. His success brought him to the attention of the current pharaoh in Egypt. Traveling to Egypt he again found himself head of an army. Once more proving his military leadership, the pharaoh rewarded Mile with the hand of his daughter, SCOTA (second of this name in Irish history). Mile traveled the Mediterranian visiting the Phoenicians at the site of a newly founded city, later known in history as Carthage. Eventually, he returned to Spain where his six children were born.

THE DRUIDS

The Druids had a highly secretive organization. It's difficult, if not impossible, to discover their origins. The best guess is that they were a nomadic cast originating in central Europe. They divided into two branches, one remaining with the Celts, the other finding its way to the Middle East. Little of their rituals are known for it was their custom to commit all their knowledge to memory and to pass it from generation to generation orally. Both men and women, particularly in Ireland, practiced this art. Their duties covered a wide spectrum of knowledge including religion, astronomy, law, rituals, genealogy and basic science.

They seem to have existed detached from clan rulers but were always advisors to the king. It was the custom of the druids to hold councils of their own with no outside interference. They read and wrote Greek as well as mastering the languages of their own and surrounding tribes. When in the presence of others they employed a sign language among themselves. Characters were formed by placing the hands across the chest. Opening and closing the fingers formed letters. All that is known of this hand language is found in medieval histories and Ogam inscriptions on tomb stones. (Morse used a system derived from Ogam for his telegraph code.)

The Druids who came to Ireland with the Gaels probably belonged to the middle eastern branch. In Persia, during the time of Christ, they were called the Magi. The word magi really means "the learned one," however, we derive the word magic from it and often mistakenly link the Magi with magicians.

It's human nature to revere or appreciate anything which is rare. With this in mind, one could guess that at least some druidical practices originated in an arid, treeless country. The Irish had a particular reverence for trees (each letter in the old Gaelic alphabet was named for a tree).

They also treasured water wells, possibly due to lack of water in a previous home land. Part of the druidic art was the observation of star patterns in the sky. This practice also points to origins in a clearer, dryer land.

The costume of the Irish druid carried hints of the Middle East. They were said to have worn cone shaped hats with flaps down over the ears and a tie under the chin. We don't know their hair style, but it may have been long and curled up, Scythian style, under the cone shaped hat.

The druid had four ritual uniforms, each identified a different function. During religious ceremonies and advisory councils, his white robe represented purity. When acting as an observer during a battle, a bull's hide coat and feathered headdress were worn. In council, at banquets or when reciting the genealogies, the uniform was a coat of six colors. When acting as judge, a collar of gold was added to the coat.

Aspiring to become a druid meant a long period of training. By the 200's A.D., the druid's tasks were divided. Except for the poetic class, most of the druidic duties remain shrouded in mystery. The DRISEG or beginning poets were required to master twenty well known epics and be able to recite them with expression and feeling.

The FOCLAIC class consisted of students considered to be advanced beginners, usually age 15 or 16 who were required to recite 30 tales perfectly before a critical audience.

The CILI were so called because they were able to hold the attention of large audiences with a repertoire of nearly 100 stories.

The ANRAID were highly skilled individuals whose training would correspond to a masters degree. This poet was usually a musician with military as well as poetic experience. He could captivate his audience with 175 tales of heroes, recite lengthy poems and sing songs of love and battle.

The OLLOMH held the highest poetic rank. He was the doctor of literature who knew the genealogy of all the clans and was a master of satire. Kings could rise or fall based upon his judgement of their performance. Kings both sought his advice and feared his satire.

The ancient Irish were a highly romantic and imaginative people. They were more capable than most, of visualizing objects, people and places from poetic description. A person with this mental capacity learns and understands more readily from oral description, than from the written word. The nomadic concept of the world may be quite different from that of the settled person.

Spiritual understanding came more easily to the nomad. This may explain why the Irish are said to have been the only western nation to become Christian without violent bloodshed.

It's obvious that the poet wielded enormous power over the community. It's said that the poets often used their position to secure justice for the less fortunate. Obviously, this power could also be misused. In the time of SAINT COLMCILLE (Columba, page II-68), minor poets became so numerous and their satire so objectionable that the kings were on the verge of expelling them from the country. Colmcille, himself a poet, returned from Iona, an isle off the coast of Scotland, to plead their case. So eloquent was his defense that he convinced the kings to allow the poets to remain with activities restricted.

The spirit world was very real to our Irish ancestors. Their strong belief is part of the reason fragile monuments in the form of standing stones, forts, tombs and castles, some well over 2,000 years old, still remain. They believed everything had personality, inanimate objects as well as living things. Thus, on occasion they would talk to a stone or a stream as if it were a person.

Some present day archeologists believe that circles of standing stones found in various parts of Ireland, are druidic calendars used as observatories determining positions of the sun and moon at rising above the horizon. Plotting sun and moon positions enabled the Druid to figure seasons and feast days. The moon was ideal for charting long periods as well as monthly cycles. They discovered a long cycle during which the moon returned to the same spot on the horizon every 19 1/2 years. The sun provided a short day/night cycle, a seasonal cycle and a long cycle of 30 years. The druids called this latter period an "age." From it we get our genealogical "generation."

It's abundantly clear that our ancestors were highly intelligent people. They adjusted to the needs of their age and were prepared in all repects to meet the challenges of the time in which they lived. The druids were progressive educators, meeting with their counterparts all over Europe. Just prior to the Church Age they were exchanging Greek texts among themselves.

THE GAELIC MIGRATION TO IRELAND

Researchers interested in tracing climatic

changes of the past tell us that in the 1,000's B.C., southern Europe suffered a long, hot, dry climatic change. Irish tradition places Mile in Spain during this period. The old records say that the heads of the Gaelic clans were called together and the seriousness of the situation discussed as many of their cattle were dying for lack of grass. A decision was reached that they should undertake a move to the "Green Island."

The Druids had predicted for several generations that the Gaels would have a homeland on an island far to the west. The trip wasn't as formidable as one would suspect. It's believed that the Phoenicians of the period made regular trading visits to Ireland and as far north as the Scandanavian countries. A warm current flows north-west out of the Bay of Biscay. Following this current, ships would pass south and west of Ireland. Skirting the coast of Spain and France as far as present day Brest, a ship could probably make the south coast of Ireland in four or five days from the French coast. Nevertheless, it was not without the hazard of adverse winds and occasional storms.

While the planned move progressed, Mile died. In a meeting the chiefs decided that Scota, wife of Mile, should lead the invasion. Although Scota probably came from the settled culture, she had speedily adapted nomadic ways. The evidence being her willingness to assume the responsibilities reserved only for men in most settled cultures. Nomadic women often assumed leadership, even in battle.

The Milasians were a numerous host and a fleet of ships was required to transport them and their chattel. As the expedition approached the Irish shore, turbulent wind and waves beset the armada. The old texts give credit to the Druids of the Tuatha de Danann in hampering their landing. What ever the cause, many people and goods were lost. Once on shore, the Gaels were attacked in force by the Tuatha de Danann. Queen Scota was killed in this battle. The Gaels were fierce and determined fighters, eventually gaining victory over the Tuatha. In making peace after the battle, the Tuatha agreed to live in the underground shelters which they normally occupied in winter. The surface land was to belong to the Gaels. This arrangement gave rise to the stories of "the little people" of Ireland.

Only three of Mile's sons survived the landing. They were HEREMON, HEBER and IR, along with LUGHAID, son of their uncle ITH (page II-8). The Gaels held council and divided Ireland between them. Heremon chose the Northern half, a portion of which was granted to the family of his brother Ir. The southern half of the island went to Heber. He in turn, granted the southwest corner of his territory to his cousin Lughaid. The artisans who came with them from Spain were divided equally between north and south.

In Spain, genealogies were determined by a father/son relationship. Wave and war had so disrupted the community that an additional form of relationship was devised From the migration forward, a genealogical relationship to a king could be established by living for a time in a particular king's territory.

The first traditional Irish history was probably written down by foreign Christian missionaries serving in Ireland who were fascinated with Irish tradition. Unfortunately, we know little about the large numbers of people brought in from England and the Continent as slaves nor of the foreigners who came to school in Ireland during the dark ages. Only now and then does history mention outsiders. The PICTS (page II-2) are a case in point. Originally they came from Thrace, a territory north of Greece. A large number of them arrived on the south Irish coast looking for a place to found a colony. At that time Ireland was being invaded by the people of Wales. The Picts aided the Gaels in driving off the invaders. Asked if they could remain, the Gaels gently refused but informed them that the land to the north, now called Scotland, was uninhabited. The Irish further offered their women as wives, providing the kingly line pass via the women instead of the men. This agreement was kept down to historical times. From this story it may be assumed that the ancient Picts spoke some form of the old mother language, similar to Gaelic.

THE CLANS

The clan system in Ireland developed from the extended family. The oldest, brightest or most aggressive male was considered the leader of five generations. With the sixth generation a new family group was formed. This usually occured upon the death of the leading male. As the number of family groups increased, one branch generally gained dominance over the family clan.

Eventually these related families became large enough to form a petty kingdom. At one time, more than 150 independant kingdoms existed. Thus the saying, "Every Irishman has a King or Queen for an ancestor." The extent of family interest in government went no further than the petty king. This king, however, had a genealogical relationship to the kings who were his neighbors. This relationship could be traced back to the original division of the country into four provinces. Each province had its oldest or royal clan. The petty kings in convention chose a provincial king from this family line.

From time to time a very strong provincial ruler arose. He received attention because of superior character or force of arms. This man, with his army, visited his neighbors in other provinces. If accepted by a sufficient number of petty kings (which involved paying tribute or giving hostages) he would be declared "high king" (Gaelic = Ard Ri).

Becoming high-king was not so much a matter of election to political power as a submission of the less powerful kings. Each three years the high king called a meeting of important persons from each of the provincial kingdoms. Entertainment for the guests was provided at the high king's expense. The genealogies were reviewed, confirming the rights of succession. Agreements were reached and disputes settled. The rights of kings, officers and citizens were codified as the BREHON LAWS.

Since Irish families were large, prospective leaders within the royal families were numerous. Leadership at all levels required intelligence, physical fitness and most of all military prowess. The system of selection invited competition and often led to disagreements. Since cattle were the recognized medium of exchange, a favorite sport of would-be leaders was the theft of livestock from a neighboring kingdom. The natural result was continual skirmishing between neighboring clans.

The annals are filled with descriptions of these activities.

The annalists have given us a distorted view of Irish history. They deemed it necessary to report only the unusual. If the annalists accounts are considered to be a complete history, it could be assumed that the Irish spent most of their time warring with each other. If the time periods are added during which nothing is reported happening in a particular part of the country, it is evident that the general population enjoyed peaceful persuits much of the time.

The life of the lowly Irish was "no bed of roses," but in all probability the poorest enjoyed more freedom and lived better than did a person of like status under European feudalism.

The Irish social system permitted even those in poverty or slavery to advance in rank. A slave could become a freeman. A freeman could borrow cattle from the local king to start his own herd. The large cattle owner could join the kings court. The apprentice in all trades could advance to business ownership. Finally, the brightest could be fostered to a druid and become part of the educated class.

CLIMBING THE LADDER

One characteristic of all nomadic peoples of the ancient world was a high degree of personal liberty. The greatest hope of the common man was to advance from his menial task of drawing water, sawing wood or herding cattle to that of cattle ownership.

An individual, if qualified, could enter the military at age seven or begin training in one of the skills required by the community. A child of that age was well on his way to manhood. He had already discovered the necessity of surviving on his own. From that time, he was in an atmosphere of intense competition. First with his own brothers and sisters, (Irish history reveals that women were almost as competitive as men) then with his neighbors. Surviving to age seven required skill, agility, sharp native instincts and a knowledge of the social structure of the community.

An Irishman enjoyed his greatest freedom in his own community. The Continental peasant was bound to the soil on which he was born. The Irishman, by right, could wander anywhere he wished within his local kingdom. His right to travel was permitted outside if he could recite his relationship to the provincial king. Travel outside his own province was more restricted, often permitted only when special events were declared by the high-king. There were exceptions as one climbed the social ladder. A poet, harper or druid was permitted free and protected travel anywhere in the land, as were the high-king's tax collectors.

Roads were few and travel not always safe. Nevertheless, with his native skills an individual could make his way almost anywhere.

Hospitality is an old Irish custom. The king was required to extend hospitality to anyone who came to his door. In later times, travelers became so numerous that the kings established hotels wherever roads crossed in their kingdom. The meager fare and poor quarters didn't invite lengthy stays, but the service was free to all. Possibly the best example of this kind of hospitality was provided by the large universities which sprang up during the dark ages. Foreign students by the thousand came to Ireland. The only requirement was a willingness to learn and possession of writing material. All else was free.

Private ownership of land by the Gaels didn't take place until a very late date. Initially, families lived well on the produce of their cattle and the gathering of fruits and native plants. As their numbers grew, the local king assigned family plots. These were rotated from time to time so each family could have use of the best land in turn. The poorer and mountainous land was reserved for community grazing.

Before monasteries were built, the king's personal fort served all the functions of a town. It was a storehouse, court and place of exchange. The artisans lived in close proximity and provided all the needed services. From this beginning grew the cottage industries which still survive in Ireland.

Historians like to point out that there were no towns in Ireland at this time. To put it quite simply, there was no need. Given the rather small population and rural atmosphere, the cottage industries, supplied all the necessities of a free and imaginative people.

THE HEROES

The heroic age in Ireland extended from about 250 B.C. to the fall of Emain Macha (the northern capitol), in 450 A.D. This was an age of leisure for the ruling class. The provincial kings maintained order with a small standing army whose members were quartered on the inhabitants of the province. Slaves performed the menial tasks. Traders brought luxury goods, seeds and plants not previously found in Ireland. Food was abundant. Ireland exported three items which were in great demand, cattle, horses and the famous Irish Wolf Hound. It was a period of temperate weather. The green pasturelands produced fat cattle. The limited farming then being practiced, more than fulfilled the needs of the entire population.

Poets and artists contested with each other to prove their skills. Metal smithing became an art. Much of the fine art produced by metal workers dates from this period. Fairs and contests drew large crowds. Poets and harpers traveled about the nation and were always welcomed by the local chiefs.

The war chariot, probably a Scythian invention, was a favorite of the Irish military. This was the time of Finn Mac Cool, Fearghus and Cu-Chulainn. Military heroes traveled from province to province seeking contests and all attended the high-kings tri-annual gathering.

During the reign of high-king Conor Mac Nessa (about 1 A.D.), a giant hall was built at Tara which had at least 14 doors and could accomodate perhaps a thousand people. It was, in its time, the largest building in Western Europe.

Since cows were used as money, the Irish ate less meat than other Europeans. At the kings gathering, his generosity was demonstrated by an abundance of meat. It was a long standing rule that the choice cut should go to the greatest hero. To prove themselves before the king, several heroes might claim to be the greatest. Brawls were common, but the high-king mandated that all weapons should be gathered and stored in a separate building, reminiscent of a custom later practiced in our old western towns.

During this period, Ireland has often been pictured as a very backward nation. This was far from the true condition of our ancestors. They were, if anything, more efficient in the use of their resources and certainly healthier than their Continental equivalents. The Druids had for centuries written in Greek for their own benefit. As early as 350 A.D., histories and genealogies were written down at the kings command, as well as the recording of ancient laws. The demand for written documents became so great that the Druids began to teach writing in their schools. Although this learning was not available to the general population. It's said that many offensive books were destroyed by the clergy when the Church Age dawned.

So the stage was set for the entry of Christianity. It would be a new way of understanding life and its time had come.

THE CHURCH AGE

There is evidence that representatives of Irish culture made their appearance on the Continent long before Christianity came to Ireland. One example being CELESTIUS, a brilliant lawyer of Irish descent.

It's believed that some, perhaps many, of the slaves brought to Ireland were Christians. As time passed some gained a measure of freedom. They called for a minister to be sent to them. Their request fell on sympathetic ears and a missionary named PALLADIUS came to their aid. Unfortunately, he had been trained in the gruff autocratic manner of the continental Romanized church. He appears to have been rejected by the "Irishized" slaves and refuted totally by the natives. He returned to the Continent and died soon afterwards.

It was an Irish king in search of slaves who unwittingly laid the foundation for the church age in Ireland.

In the year 388 or 389 A.D., KING NIALL (page

II-45-53) led his men on a raiding expedition to the big island and the Continent. Included in the unfortunates captured were a number of young adults, one a teenager named SUCCAT (meaning "clever in war") who would be destined to fight a spiritual battle.

He was given to a gruff but kindly chieftian named MILIUE whose kingdom lay in what is present day County Antrim. Succat came from a Christian family and it's said he prayed often while herding the chieftians animals. During long days with other Irish herders, he must have absorbed a goodly portion of the Irish "nature." After seven years he was sufficiently familiar with the country, the people and the language to plan his escape. Sailing from an Irish port, Succat found his way back to his family. This was the beginning of a journey which would bring him back to Ireland years later.

There is another old saying, "Once you have visited Ireland, you will always be a "A wee bit Irish." This proved true for Succat. He is said to have had a vision of the Irish calling him to return as their minister. When news of the failure of the mission of Palladus reached the small mission at Auxerre, where he was then in residence, his wish to return to Ireland was intensified. Some say the Pope consecrated him an Archbishop and gave him a new name: PATRICIUS. He became the world famous SAINT PATRICK (page II-6).

Patrick was more than forty years old when he returned to Ireland. His method of announcing his arrival is a story in itself.

The Druids believed in four prime elements of nature, these were: air, water, earth and fire. Some think that the druidic cast in Europe originated as a result of their learning the art of creating fire.

It was a practice among the Druids in Ireland to require that all fires be extinguished each year on a given day. Then, at a certain time in the evening, the chief druid ascended a hill near the king's residence where he lighted a huge bonfire. Other druids throughout the country were also stationed on the highest hills in their territory. As each saw the fires from the direction of the king's residence, it was a signal to restart their own. To this local fire, all the people in the neighborhood would come to buy coals to restart their home fires.

Patrick was aware of this ceremony and considered it an excellent way to announce his return. On the day the fires were to be extinguished, he and twenty companions stationed themselves atop the hill of Slane, a spot which was plainly visible from the High King's residence at Tara, then capitol of Ireland. Patrick and his assistants set off a magnificent blaze just before the chief druid kindled his. This act was strictly forbidden. King LAOGHAIRE (page II-63) was greatly agitated by this breach of conduct and immediately sent his soldiers to investigate. Patrick and his party dressed in their ecclastical robes and bound with chains, were brought before the king. This was the opportunity Patrick was seeking. He explained why he had come and gave the king his testimony. The king did not become a Christian (although members of his household did), however, he granted Patrick permission to pursue his mission throughout the land.

The church age gave Ireland a new direction and life. It marked the beginning of Irish influence upon the outside world. More than 300 of Irelands first saints were foreigners, but the Irish for their part, plunged wholeheartedly into the work of the Church. Soon they were sending missionaries of their own to the Continent.

The monasteries in Ireland replaced the king's residence as the center of non-governmental activity. It served as church, school, patron of the arts, storehouse and hotel. The monastic community began to offer the same services as the medieval towns on the mainland.

From earliest times, the Irish have been quick to learn. The new schools offered many disciplines not previously available. Students flocked in. Books by the thousands were written by students and teachers. This was an opportunity for the talented to display their mastery of word and picture. The church age made the Irish rich in mind and spirit.

The old Irish were extremists by nature, so some of the saints found monastic life too soft. They withdrew to remote spots and purposely lived a meager existence, free from outside interference.

Others chose to go where few had been before. They colonized Iceland long before the arrival of the Vikings. SAINT BRENDAN (page II-45) made numerous trips into the wild Atlantic. Many think he reached the shores of the New World. A viking historian says that on one of their visits to the mainland of America, they discovered white men, marching in procession and waving flags.

Many of the reclusive saints were the most talented. In the 500's A.D. lived a saint named KEVIN. He was a handsome fellow but chose to resist the advances of Irish maidens in favor of a solitary life in the Church. As penance for worldly thoughts he took up residence in a hollow tree. Soon he was discovered and dashed away to a cave in a secluded valley. His solitude didn't last long as students eager to absorb his knowledge of reading, writing and self-discipline flocked to his hiding place. Thus, the famous monastery of GLENDALOUGH was founded.

Ireland gave birth to a number of famous monasteries because of a personal desire for solitude. One of the most famous was CLONMACNOIS. The crumbling walls of the abandoned churches and toppling ancient grave stones visable today are but a shadow of an institution which grew from thirteen dedicated Church men to a community of 15,000! Of these, 5,000 were students. It's said that this school was the first in Ireland, and possibly in Europe, to have an endowed professor. The endowment came from High-King Roderic O'Connor. It's also the burial place of this much maligned king.

Adventuresome Irish clerics scattered across Europe. SAINT VERGILIUS went to France in 741. He spent some time in the court of PEPIN le BREF, the father of the famous Charlemagne (page II-139). Later he became archbishop of Salzburg. GILLA ne NAEMH LAIGHEN found his way to Wursburg. SAINT FURSEY spent much time in France while others ventured as far south as Italy and to the Holy Land.

So, the early Irish Churchmen spread beyond the confines of their small island, eventually reaching most parts of the explored world.

THE VIKINGS

The Vikings were the most adventuresome people in early European history. Their homeland was Denmark, Norway and Sweden. Tradition and fact combine to tell us that they were a mixture of hardy peoples.

From Ireland comes the story of the seamen called FOMORIANS. They may have been viking ancestors and were probably early Phoenicians from Carthage. The Fomorians made their home on Tory Island off Irelands north-west coast and on islands off Scotland, which would later be the home of the Viking clans.

Viking religion was a combination of ancestor and fear worship. It may have originated as veneration of ODIN (page II-106), an ancient ancestor. It's said that he migrated from Troy with 600 followers to the site of present day Denmark.

The Vikings, like the Irish, were a hardy people used to hardships, quick tempered, strong and virile. Before initiating the raiding of neighbors, these Northmen lived so distant from events in Southern Europe that they were able to maintain their customs, traditions and religion unchanged by Christianity. They might not have entered Irish history at all except for the hand of fate.

We're not sure of the exact reason why the north men began to "go Viking." Some traditionalists think that the combination of a cold weather cycle and poor land made it difficult for the country to support a growing population. Others believe that it was because of the encroachment of Christianity, a religion to which they were violently opposed. As often happens, the unexpected gave them an opportunity to visit Ireland.

In the late 700's a brilliant shipbuilder, plying his trade in a little shop just south of present day Oslo, Norway, had a revolutionary idea. The result was a unique sailing vessel capable of withstanding the turbulent Atlantic Ocean. The secret of its success was an extended keel, flared sides and flexible wood construction. Smaller versions for sixteen men were light enough to be carried by the crew. Ocean going models required from thirty to sixty oarsmen, as well as a sail.

Testing their new ship, the Vikings hugged the coasts and occasionally ventured into the open sea. Moving ever south, they visited the Scottish coast and its numerous islands. It was in Ireland that they found the really big prize.

Except for coastal skirmishes, the Irish had been free from invaders for nearly 400 years. The country was blessed with natural resources including alluvial gold. Much of this wealth found its way to the monasteries. The Irish were completely unprepared for the vicious onslaught which befell them. In 795, the missions on the islands off Irelands north coast fell to the raiders. The Vikings were astonished at the ease with which booty came into their hands. Word of the treasures soon reached their homeland and the invasion of Ireland began in earnest.

The Viking was a formidable foe, partly because of his religious beliefs. His greatest after-life reward came when he died in battle. Another reason for their success was due to the ferocity with which they attacked an unsuspecting prey. Approaching shore, a volunteer among them ate an hallucinatory mushroom. In moments, the warrior became so wild that he had to be tied to the mast. Ashore, it took four men to hold him. Given an ax and pointed toward the enemy, his violence was sufficient to put all but the most valiant to flight. When the plundering was finally put down by the Irish, the Vikings brought their families and settled at the mouths of Ireland's rivers. So, it was the Vikings, not the Irish, who built the first towns in Ireland.

The Vikings had great plans and Ireland was just a way station on their path of conquest. They rolled out of the north like a great wave. The Isle of Man was occupied and a kingdom carved out in the in the center of England. They navigated most of the rivers in Europe, founded a kingdom in Russia and another in Sicily. Their stay in France will be detailed in a later chapter.

Two hundred years after the invasion began, Ireland had her strongest High-King whose name was BRIAN BORU (Brian Boroime, page II-19-20). in the year 1014, he defeated the Vikings at CLONTARF.

Although Brian died in the battle, the Vikings were so thoroughly vanquished that those able to leave, left Ireland for good. The few remaining took Irish names and melded into the general population.

A hundred years would pass before Ireland would again be faced with a similar danger.

HIGH-KING RODERICK O'CONNOR

Roderick was the last high-king of Ireland. The Norman invasion began in 1169 during his reign. He was also the grandfather of the first DHUIRNIN (page II-90), progenitor of the Durning family.

This King has often been blamed for the disasters which befell Ireland during his reign. Perhaps it was just his fate to have been in a place of leadership during one of the most trying times in ancient Irish history.

All of Europe was in the throws of dramatic change when he became king. It was the time of the Crusades. a time of pestilence, wars and generally unsettled conditions. TOIRDHEALBHACH MOR, Rodericks father, proved himself an exceptionally strong High-King. Next to Brian Boru, he came closest to creating a united Ireland. Perhaps too much was expected of his son, Roderick.

From the beginning of his reign, Roderick could not secure the submission of all the provincial kings. The loyalty of some kings and the Viking city of Dublin had to be purchased. Roderick was a well educated man and appears to have been more interested in peaceful pursuits than border clashes. He endowed the first professorship at the Irish University of Clonmacnois. He arranged for a resumption of the gathering of Clan leaders at TELTOWN. This parliament had not functioned for many years. Roderick re-instituted the national olympics. The regional fairs with their match-making and displays of foreign merchandise by Dublin merchants once more took place. Given time, his government might have followed the settled pattern already established by some nations on the Continent.

Roderick was not well versed in foreign affairs. Neither was he responsive to criticism of the Mother Church regarding the independant course of Irish Christianity. More importantly, he didn't understand the power of the Church to force compliance.

It must be further admitted that Roderick wasn't an astute military strategist. The national army in those days was a temporary one and Levys were called to service for short periods. Only the professional soldiers employed by the various kings were fully equipped. The ordinary soldiers equipment was little more than a saffron shirt and a farm tool. All, of course, were barefoot. They were ill trained, if at all. Their reason for volunteer service was meat provided by the king and a chance to share in booty.

This was the extent of Irish military preparedness when the Normans invaded in 1169.

THE VIKINGS AND THE NORMANS

The Vikings were an amazingly energetic people. Swedish Vikings colonized Russia while other Northmen raided the island in the Seine (now the heart of Paris).

A Viking chief named HROLF or ROLLO (page II-112) was a particularly aggressive fellow. He caused so much trouble for the French king that he was granted, along with his followers, a territory now called Normandie. In exchange, he agreed to stop raids on other parts of the kingdom. Rollo's descendants were called NORMANS. Five generations after Rollo, WILLIAM (called "the conqueror") was born. He was the son of ROBERT I (page II-113). This William was destined to change the future of both Britain and Ireland. William's exploits in Britain are well-known. Less is known of his relatives and others who came with him on the invasion of Britain. Following the feudal custom, William proceeded to parcel out lands on the big island to his relatives and friends.

The Welsh king RHYS ap TEWDOR (page II-114) was not pleased with the presence of Norman Barons in his kingdom. Never the less, an agreement of sorts was reached culminating in the espousal of Rhys daughter NESTA to William's son, HENRY I. Nesta would have two other husbands: STEPHEN of Cardigan (page II-116) and GERALD of Windsor (page II-115). It was the military prowess of Nesta's children and Norman relatives which would make the invasion of Ireland a success. At this point in history, Ireland's fate was, in part, again determined by a woman.

DIARMUID MacMURROUGH

In the late 1100's, Mac MURROUGH (page II-97) was king of Linster. He was a course, rough talking individual, not well liked by his own people. History tells us that the old rascal (he was over sixty) had an eye for DEARBFORGAL (she over forty-five) wife of TIGERNAN O'RUAIRC (page II-84). Tigernan was king of Breifne, a territory north of County Roscommon. While he was away on a religious pilgrimage in the north of Ireland, Diarmuid snatched Dearbforgal (Dirvilla) and took her back to his castle. Tigernan was justly insulted when he returned to discover Diarmuid's dirty trick. Not so much because of the loss of his wife as the injury to his honor and pride. In old Ireland one could legally collect for injury to one's honor. Tigernan immediately appealed to High-King Turlough O'Connor. The High-King agreed to raise an army and invade Linster. Tigernan recovered Dearbforgal, chasing her with scorpions according to tradition.

Thirteen years later Roderic O'Connor, then the High-King, and O'Ruarc drove Mac Murrough out of Ireland.

Diarmuid went to England looking for HENRY II (page II-113) seeking his help in regaining his kingdom. Henry was at war on the Continent but gave Diarmud authority to recruit in the city of Bristol. The Normans in Wales were experiencing difficulty in pacifying the Welsh, from whom they had taken lands. As a result, many were in debt to King Henry. One such was RICHARD Fitz GILBERT de CLARE (page II-118). He was called "strong bow" because he had mastered that strong Flemish weapon.

Although Strong Bow is given much of the credit for the successful Norman invasion, Nesta's descendants actually preceded him. He followed later and consolidated their gains. The first Norman contingent invaded Ireland in May of 1169.

The Normans took some smaller towns founded by the Vikings. This gave them rations and supplies.

When they arrived outside the Viking city of Dublin, many of the inhabitants fled.

Learning that the Normans had taken the city, High-King Roderick belatedly took action. He raised a large army and could have retaken the city. One can only guess why he decided against assault, choosing instead to blockade the invaders. Rations almost gone, the Normans decided upon a mounted attack outside the gates. Luck was with them. Roderick was bathing in the Liffey and narrowly escaped capture. The Irish army was caught unprepared for battle and easily routed. Most kept running until they reached home.

The conflict between Feudal and Gaelic law surfaced early. Strong Bow arrived about a year after the first invaders. He immediately married Eva, daughter of Mac Murrough. According to Norman law, he would thus gain control of Mac Murrough's kingdom upon Mac Murrough's death. This was illegal under Gaelic law since all property belonged to the Clan, not the king. With the help of De LACY, FITZGERALD and FITZSTEPHEN (page II-115-116-117) the Normans rapidly took over large portions of the Island. Henry II (page II-113) fearing loss of control over his Norman knights, planned his own invasion. Henry arrived with the blessings of the Church in October of 1171 accompanied by a military force of 4,500.

The Irish kings respected superior military strength. Believing that Henry would protect them from further intrusions by his knights, several Irish kings signed agreements paying homage to Henry. They apparently didn't realize that by signing a written agreement they were in fact transferring Ireland to the English king. Irish kings were accustomed to using oral agreements among themselves. These agreements ended when either party failed to live up to them. Not so with the written documents of the Normans. Under their laws, all property belonged to the king. If the kings tenant failed to live up to the written agreement, the king could repossess the land and everything upon it. As might be expected, the two systems of law met head on.

Although King Roderick had been granted the right to his own province of Connacht and was allowed to remain titular head of the Irish kings, he soon gave up politics and retired to the

Monestary of Cong. He died there at the advanced age of 98.

Despite the fact that a Norman knight named JOHN de COURCY invaded their territory, the Northern Irish kings refused immediate allegiance to Henry. They were to retain much of their sovereignty to the 1600's.

Although we have made it clear that civilizations usually progress from nomadic to settled status, there are notable exceptions. In Ireland the Vikings eventually became absorbed by the Gaels. Their descendants, the Normans, followed the same course. After initial invasion and plunder, the Normans began to speak the Gaelic language, adopt Irish clothing styles and enjoy the company of poets and harpers. The English, fearing the loss of their hold on the Island, adopted numerous suppressive measures over the years. In the late 1500's and early 1600's, the decision was reached to repopulate Ireland with outsiders. This was the plantation period.

THE PLANTATION

The English are a tenacious people and have demonstrated on many occasions an ability to "hang in there," not giving up in the face of near insurmountable odds. For four hundred years, down to the time of QUEEN ELIZABETH I, the Irish continued to resist English rule with their two-fold weapons; absorption and gorilla warfare. Yet, the invaders persisted.

At last, legalism coupled with unrelenting military suppression, broke the power of the Northern Chiefs. In the early 1600's they left Ireland forever and the Clans disintegrated, having become leaderless.

JAMES of SCOTLAND was now JAMES I of ENGLAND. It was said that in the process of gaining the kingship, he became obligated financially to some of his powerful fellow Scots. Now that the Irish leaders were gone, what better way to repay his debts than with Irish land? The king had two additional problems; much was owed to the companies in London who had supplied the establishment with goods and services and along the border of England

and Scotland lived many impoverished people who were near riot.

To solve these problems, SIR ARTHUR CHINCHESTER and SIR JOHN DAVIES acting on behalf of the king, had the counties of ARMAGH, CAVIN, DERRY, DONEGAL, FERMANAGH and TYRONE divided into parcels of 2,000, 1,000 and 1,500 acres. These were passed out to debtors and unpaid military men with the provision that they would clear the land of Irish tenants and bring in Scotch and English "Planters."

Most who agreed to come were poor Protestant farmers expecting a better life. The plan didn't work well. Many Irish tenants remained until later years. The planters did became successful farmers competing with English grown products. This brought restrictions on their exports. Upheavals in Europe sent a flood of French-German Protestants to Ireland. Ultimately, armed conflict broke out between the native Irish and the new population. On the surface, these disagreements could be viewed as religious or economic. However, the real conflict was the continued clash of two diverse cultures, settled and nomadic.

It was economic oppression by the English against the planters which, within three generations, caused many of the newcomers to move on to the colonies in the New World.

CROMWELL

Little of permanence is gained by war, secular or religious. The human race has often disgraced itself by engaging in such fruitless pursuits. CROMWELL's activities in England may have had some moral justification in the beginning, but by the time his forces reached the small, downtrodden country of Ireland, little benefit can be seen in the behavior of his troops.

Cromwell, like almost every other administrator from the settled society, misunderstood the Irish. Any city populated by rational settled people of the 1600's would have come to terms with any commander standing before its gates with a cannon, the newest tool for mass destruction. Not so with the Irish. Cromwell asked too much. Property loss was one thing, but requesting an abandonment of both custom and religion was unthinkable. He, in turn, responded with the only weapon he fully understood: crushing, unyielding, brute force. In the year following his arrival, more than three-fourths of Ireland's men of fighting age perished or left the country.

Most European wars were followed by the plague. Ireland was desolated in 1652-53. At its end a few older men, women and teen-age children were all that remained of a once great Gaelic civilization. In September of 1653, Parliament ordered many of those still alive to be driven to the province of Connacht.

The fortunate ones were those fighting men who left Ireland and settled in Europe. Their talents were greatly prized. They rose to positions of high rank in France, Austria, Poland, Portugal and Spain. Much less fortunate were Irish citizens convicted of minor misdeeds. They were shipped as virtual slaves to the Colonies and the islands of the Carribean.

In many ways the experiences of the Irish parallel the history of the Jews. Both peoples sprang from nomadic roots. In every case, the countries to which they were banished have profited greatly by their presence. In the U.S., many of our Irish ancestors were familiar with a sign in the shop window saying, "No Irish Need Apply." Yet, somehow our ancestors survived. Today, more than a third of the largest U.S. corporations are headed by persons of Irish descent. Everyone knows of Irish American contributions to government.

All of these events had suppression of liberty as the catalyst for spreading the Irish around the globe. The final great disaster faced by our ancestors sent forth the largest migration of all.

THE FAMINE

Millions of words have been written in an attempt to explain the famine. It's probable reason was an attempt to change the economic pursuits of a nation from a pastoral base to one of agriculture. The problem was further aggravated by charging the tenant farmer for the use of the land whether it produced or not.

The lowly potato added to the problem. It usually grew a bountiful crop on small acreage. In order to pay his rent, the Irish tenant planted most of his land in a saleable grain crop. In the process of dining primarily on the potato, the Irish farmer came to prefer it over other produce. When the potato crop failed, the farmer was less insistent than he otherwise might have been on keeping some of the grain for himself.

The horrors of the famine have been documented in other literary works and can be studied therein.

IRISH NAMES IN FOREIGN LANDS

In the beginning, family names were chosen from the personal name of an ancient hero or person within the family who had performed some outstanding deed. In old Ireland all citizens living within one of the petty kingdoms were considered related to the king. Thus the old genealogists, prior to the coming of the Normans, closely linked place of residence and family with the king.

The coming of the Normans and later the English, caused the displacement of many families. Some lost their identity, others connected themselves to the king of the new territory in which they found themselves. Some took the surname of one of the invaders. In England many families didn't have a surname. They were known only by a first name coupled with a descriptive term and the name of the land on which they lived. This naming system came to Ireland with the influx of large numbers of people from England. During the Plantation Period, Scotch and French names came to Ireland along with some German, Flemish and Dutch. To further complicate the naming pattern, Irish names were transliterated into English. A few Norman and English families took Irish names.

Fortunately, oral tradition remained alive during this time and many of the older folk continued to memorize the family genealogy. Some family names were confused and the precise lineage may never be discovered, nevertheless Irish genealogies furnish a great body of literature which are the bones of a once lively system of family relationships.

THE FINAL SEARCH

As our ancestors moved to other nations, they tended to be submerged in the new culture. Again, Irish names were translated into the new language. Immigration officers made errors as well, often totally mispelling a name. Some of these mispellings are close enough to the original so they can be recognized: "O" and "Mac" also caused problems. For example: O'Donnell and Mac Donnell are two distinct families, yet in the U.S. and Canada some of these families exchanged prefixes, others disposed of them all together.

The final problem results from the destruction of many records in Ireland which would be of use to the genealogist.

For these reasons a person wishing to search for relatives overseas will be asked by a researcher to provide information which may not be available. Such requests may include:

Name of the ship in which an ancestor arrived in the New World.
Home community of the ancestor in Ireland (County, Parish and Townland).
Religion of the ancestor.
Year and port of departure from Ireland.

Fortunately, those families who were in Ireland after 1650 tended to remain in the same communities for a relatively long period.

The purpose of this book is not to solve these problems but to provide a foundation upon which one can trace an ancestor and his traditional line through the course of Irish history and literature. In the process many interesting discoveries will be made, possibly relating to ones own family traditions.

Thus armed, one will be better prepared to do the research necessary to lay a foundation for further investigation. Finally do visit the Homeland! The remains of that little cottage where relatives once lived may still be standing!

There is no feeling compared with the thrill of planting one's feet on ground once trod by those who have gone before. As we become familiar with the trials and tribulations through which they passed, we can better appreciate the good life which we now enjoy as a result of their sacrifices.

DUNGANSTOWN CASTLE - COUNTY WICKLOW

KILCASH CASTLE - COUNTY TIPPERARY

IRISH ROOTS

BLARNEY CASTLE. BUILT BY THE MAC CARTHYS

GLENDALOUGH, COUNTY WICKLOW

PERSONS OF NOTE

The lusty realism of ancient Irish tradition was created through a unique combination of persons, places and events. Our ancestors seldom destroyed any structure which had once been an habitation or grave. The traveler in Ireland can still see ancient mounded tombs which were built more than 2,500 years ago. The graves of Saints a mere 800 to 900 years of age dot the landscape. Ruins of Gaelic and Norman castles are everywhere, more than 10,000 of them. All these are reminders of the personalities with whom they were associated. With a local story teller as a guide, every tree, stream or standing stone evokes memories of some long dead individual whose personality and the object join to produce some deed worth remembering.

The scope of this book must be limited to the origin of our family names, but personality and names cannot be separated. On the following pages will be found numerous heroes and saints together with a brief description of their activities and their place in the charts. The tracing of a surname will usually pass through one or more of these interesting characters. Undoubtedly, you will wish to know more about these ancients than is found here in. Visit your nearby college or university library and look for these books:

The Annals of Lock Ce', O'Curry's Lectures, The Annals of the Kingdom of Ireland by The Four Masters or the Atlas and Cyclopedia of Ireland by P.W. Joyce, 1914. Using these will make the charts come alive.

IMPORTANT PERSONS

The following personalities have their place in Irish history. The Irish, upon becoming Christian, naturally wished to connect their genealogies with those found in the Bible, so it's appropriate that important personalities in the Bible are also listed here.

ABRAHAM 2180 B.C.   page II-1
This Old Testament hero gave up a wealthy and comfortable life to become a nomadic wanderer. His father, Terah, was an idol worshiper. Abraham sought the Spirit of God.

ADAM   page II-1
The Biblical ancestor of the human race.

AESCWINE 530 A.D.   page II-106
King of the East Angles.

AETHELBEORATH (Ethelbert) page II-106
First Christian king of England.

AILILL   page II-38
One of the husbands of Queen MAEVE (Medb), of
Connacht. While in bed, they jokingly compared
their individual riches, (women held their property
separate from their husbands). Maeve discovered
that Ailill possessed a bull superior to any in her
herd. A prideful woman, she insisted on having
equal property. The only other bull of equal
quality was a brown one owned by a farmer in
Ulster. The farmer refused to sell. An attempt to
take it from the farmer caused the armies of
Connacht and Ulster to engage in a battle recounted
in the famous epic, "The Cattle Raid of Cooley."

ALEXANDER   page II-113
King of Scotland.

AMAZONS   page II-2
A race of female warriors living near the Black
sea.

AODH DUBH   page II-15
Ancestor of the O'Sullivans

AONGHUS TIREACH   page II-18

ART AONFHIR 185 A.D.   page II-43
Called "The Lonely One." A son of Conn of the 100
battles. Art was the father of CORMAC ULFHADA. He
traveled widely and came into contact with
Christianity in Europe before the time of St.
Patrick.

ASSYRIANS 1650 B.C.   page II-1
Expert astronomers who early developed an accurate
calendar. They also kept a genealogy of their
kings.

AURI MARSON 983 A.D.   page II-111
Sailing from Iceland, a storm forced his ship to a
landfall on the North American Continent. There he
discovered white men, dressed in robes and waving
banners as they marched. Most likely they were
Irish monks.

BABALONIANS   page II-2

BALDAR   page II-106
An ancestor god of the Angles and Saxons.

BADHBHACHADH   page II-40
Had the shortest reign of any Irish king. He was
king for one day.

BALOR   page II-7
Called "The Evil Eye." He was a noted Fomorian
chief and "a thorn in the side," of early Irish.

BASQUES   page II-2
Noted for their unique language unlike any other in
Europe. The tribe has long resided in the Western
Pyrenees mountains on the border between Spain and
France.

BEOTHACH   page II-6
Ancestor of the old race on the Isle of Man.   A
branch of this clan went to Scotland.

BRIAN BORU (Brian Boroimhe) 1001 A.D.
                               page II-19-20
One of Ireland's most brilliant kings.   It was he,
who on April 23, 1014, defeated the North-Men at
the battle of Clontarf, outside Dublin.   He was
murdered in his tent after the battle, by a
maurading Dane who recognized him.   Nevertheless,
he freed Ireland of foreign rulers until 1169.   In
that year the Normans (men of North-Man ancestry)
arrived.

BRIAN LEITHDHEARG   page II-78

BRIAN MAGUIRE   page II-51
Commissioned O'Lunin, his historian and the
O'Clery's, who were O'Donnell's historians, to
write the "Leabhar Gabhala," "the book of the
talkings." A recording of oral traditions and a
history of Ireland.

BRIOTAN MAOL   page II-6
Said to be the ancestor of SAINT PATRICK and some
of the Gaelic clans in Wales.

BRITONS   The Old Race.   7000 B.C.
They were a straight-haired, dark-skinned tribe who
migrated to the isle which took their name.

CAS   page II-13-17

CAETHANN CASOUFF   page II-45
The Saxon wife of EOCHAIDH MOIDHMEODHAIN.

CAIBRE CINN CAIT 125 B.C.   page II-4
A slave and member of the old race, who deposed the
Gaels and became a rebel High-King.

CAIBRE LIFFECHAR   page II-45

CAIBRE RIADA 490 A.D.   page II-44
Led a migration of his clan from what is now County
Kerry to Antrim. Later, part of the clan crossed
from Ireland to Scotland, a distance of about 13
miles at the closest point.

CAIRBRE CLUITHEACHAIR   page II-102

CANAANITES   page II-2
A people of mixed heritage who lived on the coast
between the Mediterranian and the Dead Sea. The
oldest inhabitants were primarily Semetic in
origin. Notable among others who came into the
land were the Hyksos and the Hebrews.   The
Phoenicians were either these same people under a
new name, or later invaders who lived in Tyre and
Sidon.

CATHAL og O'CONNOR 1362 A.D.
The last king of Connacht. page II-91

CATHOIR MOR 170 A.D.   page II-94

CIANN   page II-12

CINNEIGH (Kennedy)   page II-9
Ancestor of the great BRIAN BROIME (Brian Boru) and
many other famous families including the Kennedys
and the Reagans.

CONGAL CONGALRCH (Conal Claingheach) 120 B.C.
                          page II-19
This king, while attending a banquet, was almost
killed by his enemies. His chief poet, sensing the
danger, bade him sit among the poets rather than in
his usual place. His enemies, fearing the poets
more than the king, did him no harm.

CONAL CLARINACH   page II-127

CONALL CEARNACH   page II-30
Foster father of Cu-Chulainn (one of ancient
Ireland's great military heroes).

CONALL GULBAN   page II-53-68

CONN BACHACH 1550 A.D.   page II-60
"The O'Neill" who gave up his Irish title to become
the Earl of Tyrone under the English.

CONN CEADCHADHACH 180 A.D.   page II-42,43,44
The famous Conn of the 100 Battles.

CONOR MAC NESSA 1 A.D.   page II-29
Also called Conchobar, who was the son of Nessa and
said to have been born about the time of Christ.

COLLAS 315 A.D.   page II-46,48,49,52
Colla Uais, Colla Meann and Colla de Chrioch were
the sons of EOCHAIDH DUBHLEIN. Descendants of
Colla Uais married into Viking and Pictish
families, spawning numerous clans in both Ireland
and Scotland.

CORMAC CONNLONGES 30 A.D. page II-29
As High-King he was given hostages by the
provincial kings as evidence of their good
behavior. Some of the hostages under his authority
were killed without his consent. This was a breach
of the High-King's honor. He went into exile in
Connacht for failure to protect them.

CORMAC CAS 250 A.D.   page II-12
Son of the wise OILILL OLOM. He became the head of
the collective families called the DAL CAIS, the
tribe of Cas or "Dalcassians."

CORMAC GAILEANG   page II-25,27

CORMAC ULFHADA 253 A.D.   page II-45
Said to have built the hall at Tara, big enough to
hold 1,000 people. It was the largest building in
the western Europe in its time. He revised the
Brehon Laws. The unwritten legal code of the
Gaels. Some say that he had the laws written down
at this time in the Psalter of Tara.

COSMOS LOPEZ   page II-115
A descendant of the Vikings who founded a colony in
Italy. This clan migrated to Normandie, Wales and
finally to Ireland.

CREODA 625 A.D.   page II-106
King of Merca, a kingdom on the big island.

CRIOMTHANN (Griffin)   page II-14
His sister, MONG FIONN, took poison in order to induce Criomthann to do the same.

CU-CHULAINN (Setanta)   page II-29,40
Called "The Hound of Culann," he was one of old Ireland's great military heroes. His mother was Irish but his father was said to have been a foreigner. He was educated by a female warrior in Scotland and became a militiaman in King Cormac's army at the age of seven. He was one of the heroes of "The Cattle Raid of Cooley." He died in battle at age 27.

CUNEDDA   page II-114
An early Welsh king and an ancestor of Nesta I.

DAIRE BARRACH   page II-95,98

DAIRE CEARB   page II-13

DATHY   398 A.D.   page II-72,73
One of Ireland's most aggressive kings. He was killed at the foot of the Alps on one of his numerous raids across the Continent. His body was returned to Rath Croghan where his red stone marker may still be seen. He was Ireland's last pagan monarch.

DEAGHA DUIRNN   page II-50

DEARBFURGAIL (Dervulia) O'Roairc   1170 A.D.
                         page II-84
Abducted by Dermott Mac Murrough (page II-96), setting the stage for the Norman invasion.

DERVORGALL   page II-59,88
Wife of Turlough Mor O'Connor

DECTAIRE   page II-29
Mother of Cu-Chulann. She was the sister of Conchobar (page II-29) the king of Ulster about 1 A.D.

DELBHRAOICH   500 A.D.   page II-50
Mother of TIGHERNACH of Clones.

DELA   page II-4
First king of the Fir Bolg.

DIARMUID Mac MORROUGH   1160 A.D.
                         page II-96,97,118

Father of Eva, who was pledged to the Norman, Earl Strongbow in return for his help in gaining the return of Mac Murrough's kingdom. Under Irish law, the marriage was just a match. However, the Normans under English law could inherit property coming to the wife from her father. Mac Murrough made this possible by submitting to the English King.

DOMHNALL O'Neill   page II-59

DONALD Mac LOUGHLIN   1140 A.D.
                                 page II-59

DULACH GALACH   425 A.D.   page II-45,82
Ancestor of the O'Connors of Connacht. He was said to have been the first of this clan to consider reducing the genealogies to writing.

DUNWARTH HEN   page II-6
The first king of North Wales.

EANDA AIGHNACH   page II-41
Called "The Hospitable."

EARC   503 A.D.   page II-46
Father of FERGUS, who went to Scotland as chief of the Irish in the newly established colony of DAL RIADA.

EARL STRONGBOW (Richard de Clare) 1140 A.D.
                               page II-125
He was Earl of Pembrokeshire in Wales. Invaded Ireland on behalf of Mac Murrough. His marriage to Eva, daughter of Mac Murrough, set the stage for the occupation of Ireland by the English.

EGAN AIDHNE   page II-75
First chief of the clan called, "The Hy-Fiachrach Aidhne."

ENDA DEARG
The first Irish king to mint silver coins.

EOGAN BEL   547 A.D.   page II-73
A fierce warrior. Ordered that on his death he should be buried standing up, facing the enemy, spear in hand.

EOCHAIDH   page II-4
The last king of the Fir Bolg.

EOCHAIDH AIREAMH   75 B.C.   page II-42
Replaced cremation with burial in graves. Perhaps
an indication of change in religious practices.

EOCHAIDH BAILLDEARG   470 A.D.
                              page II-18
Called "The Red Mole." He was baptized by St.
Patrick and was the ancestor of King Brian Boroimhe
(Brian Boru).

EOCHAIDH CHOBNA   page II-31
The last High-King in the race of IR.

EOCHAIDH DUBHLEIN   page II-45,46
Ancestor of the clans of the Oirghialla.

EOCHAIDH EADGHADHACH
Originated the use of colors one to seven in
number, to indicate the social and governmental
position from kings to commoners.

EOCHAIDH FIEDLIOC   75 B.C.   page II-42
He built the first kings palace upon Rath Crogan
(an ancient burial mound). He was the father of
Queen Maeve and the three Fineniana. From him
descended the O'Connors of Connacht.

EOCHAIDH MOIDHMEODHAIN (Eochie Movie)   358 A.D.
                              page II-45

EOCHAIDH MOR   page II-13,127

EOCHAIDH OLLATHAR   1400 B.C.
                              page II-5
Called "The Daga Mor." An ancestor god of the
Tuatha de Danaan.

EOCHAIDH OLLAMH FODHLA   924 B.C.
                              page II-28
He was first to hold a genealogical and political
convention.   He is also credited with building the
great hall at Tara. He was first to delegate local
authority to local chiefs.

EOGHAN   page II-53
From him came the clan called "Cineal Eoghain."

EOGAN MOR (Mogh Nuadt)   220 A.D.
                              page II-12
Some of the slaves brought to Ireland from the
Continent were said to have been Christians. Eogan
heard their testimony but preferred the old god

Nuadu who had been introduced to the island by the Tuatha de Danaan.

ERIC THE RED   page II-11
A viking who lived in Iceland and Greenland.

ERIE - BANBHA - FODHLA   page II-5,7
Three Queens, whose husbands ruled in turn. They were of the Tuatha de Danaan and from them Ireland got her names.

ETHIOPIANS   page II-2

EVA 1170 A.D.   page II-97,118
Daughter of Diarmuid Mac Murrough. Her father pledged her in marriage to the Norman-Welsh, Earl Strongbow, in exchange for his help in returning Mac Murrough to his throne. Marriage to Eva would, according to Norman law, give Strongbow rights to Mac Murrough's kingdom. Under Irish law, however, the kingdom did not belong . to Mac Murrough, but to the people.

FEARGHUS Mac RIOCH   page II-34
Tricked into resigning the kingship of Ulster by the beautiful NESSA.

FEARBISEACH   page II-73
Beginning of Clan Mac FIRBISIGH.

FEARGUS DUBHEADH 525 A.D.   page II-98
Called "The Black Tooth."

FEARGUS MOR   503 A.D.
Extended his kingdom to Argyllshire in Scotland.

FEINUS FARSAIDH 1700 B.D.   page II-8
A king of Scythia from whom the Gaels of Ireland are said to be descended.

FIACAD FIONOUD
"Owner of the White Cows." Ancestor of the clan called "The DAL FIATACH."

FIACH ARUIDHE   page II-31
Ancestor of clan DIAL nARUIDHE.

FIARACHA EALGACH   page II-73

Ancestor of clan "Hy-FIACHRACH MUAIDE."

FIACHA TORT   page II-46,47

FINN Mac COOL (Fionn Mac Cumail) 250 A.D.
                              page II-18,45,93
Considered a military hero in both Ireland and
Scotland. He was leader of the king's standing
army called, "The Finna." He was the husband of
ALBE, daughter of Cormac Ulfhada. The Finna
enforced the king's commands but also spent a lot
of time having fun.

FIRBOLG 1560 B.C.   page II-4
Called "The Old Race," they were farming folk.
Their ancestors left Ireland because of Fomorian
oppression and returned to their original homeland
North of Greece. Forced to live on the poorest
land, later generations rebelled and returned to
Ireland.

FOMORIANS   page II-5,106
Sea-going pirates who preferred to live on islands
rather than the mainland. They were assumed to have
been Phoenicians from colonies of that race in North
Africa. They ranged as far north as Scandanavia
from an Irish base of Tory Island, off the coast of
Donegal.

FORNJOT   page II-112
An early king of Finland. Said to have been the
ancestor of one branch of the Vikings, who became
Normans and Kings of England.

FOUR MASTERS   page II-77
The men who wrote THE ANNALS OF THE KINGDOM OF
IRELAND. During the 1600's they traveled across
Ireland collecting data from old records and living
persons. The Annals are Irelands record of
herself.

FURBAIDE FERBENN   page II-29
Son of Conor Mac Nessa. He was suspected of having
killed Queen Maeve (Medb).

GERALDUS CAMBRENSIS 1150 A.D.
                              page II-115
The Latin name of a Welsh cleric who took part in
the invasion of Ireland. He wrote a rather slanted
history of the events of his time.

GOMER   2250 B.C.   page II-2
Brother of Magog and son of the Biblical JAPHETH.
Gomer is considered to be the ancestor of the
Northern European tribes.

GORM ESKE   900 A.D.   page II-80
A king of Denmark. He was called, "The
Englishman," having been born there.

GRACE O'MALLEY   1600 A.D.   page II-80
She was a pirate sea captain with ships and castles
held in her own right. While one of her husbands
was away on a religious pilgrimage, she moved her
own soldiers into his castle. On his return she
shouted from the ramparts, "I divorce you!" It's
said that Queen Elizabeth secretly admired her
bravery and independance.

GRAINNE and DIARMUID   250 A.D.
                       page II-45
True lovers in the Irish tradition. They eloped.
The king wanting Grainne for himself had them
hunted down. One of the great love stories of
ancient Irish literature.

GREEKS   page II-2
They believed in clannish independance, probab
inherited from the Nomads. They lived in self-
contained city states which were often at war with
each other.

GUIRE   page II-75
Called, "The Hospitable," because of the generosity
to the poets. One tradition blames him for the
death of Saint Cellach. Probably untrue, since
there was almost 100 years difference in their
ages.

HAROLD BLUE TOOTH   930 A.D. page II-108
The first Christian king of Denmark.

HAROLD FINEHAIR   850 A.D.   page II-107
King of Norway.

HARTHACNUT   1040 A.D.   page II-108
King of Denmark and England.

HEBER FIONN (Eber Finn)   1045 B.C.
                       page II-8,12
Heber Fionn and Heremon divided the Green Island
between them. Heber's wife insisted on building a
house in Heremon's half. This caused conflict
between the brothers.

HENRY I   1130 A.D.   page II-113
King of England. He ravished the famous Welsh

maiden, Nesta I. He is considered to be the first English king to use and grant "Coats of Arms."

HENRY II   1154-1189 A.D.   page II-113
King of England. Tradition says that the Pope (he was an Englishman named Nicholas Breakspear) gave Henry permission to invade Ireland as a kind of punishment for that country's deviation from customs prescribed by the Roman Church.

HEREMON (Eremon) 1034 B.C. page II-8,40
Ancestor of one of the four branches of the Gaels in Ireland. The Picts came during his reign as High-King. He gave them wives with the understanding that the line of ruling monarchs would always pass throught the female line.

HITTITES   1800 B.C.   page II-2
Indo-Europeans originating in Asia Minor, who later moved to Syria.

HUGH SLANE   590 A.D.   page II-65,67

HYKSOS   page II-2
Central European nomads who, in their wanderings, mixed with the Semites of Canaan. They conquered Egypt using the horse-drawn chariot and the short bow. They probably introduced iron weapons to Egypt.

IARBHOINEOL FAIDH   1700 B.C.
                            page II-4
A king of the Scythians.

IR   1005 B.C.   page II-8,28
One of the three surviving sons of Mile. Head of one of the four original Gaelic clans in Ireland.

IRIALFAIDH   page II-40
"The Prophet."

ITH 1000 B.C.   page II-8,9
Uncle of Ir. Head of one of the four original Gaelic clans.

IVAR VIDFADMI 700 A.D.   page II-107
An Early King of Denmark.

JAPHETH   page II-1,2
The Biblical son of Noah. Considered to be the ancestor of the people who developed the Scythian

language. thus he was also the legendary ancestor of the Celts and Gaels.

KENNETH II   page II-10
King of Scotland.

KENNITH Mac ALPIN   page II-59
King of the Gaels in Scotland.

LAEGHAIRE   468 A.D.
Saint Patrick arrived while he was High-King. He organized the first prize fight in Ireland. It was held at Rath Croghan. He died of sun stroke.

LAOGHAIRE LORC   page II-40
Called "The Fierce One."

LEIF ERICKSON II   870 A.D. page II-111
Leif was born in Vineland (Greenland).

LUIGHAIDH LAMBHFADH   1420 B.C.
                             page II-7
Called "The Long Armed One." He was the foster son of TAILLTE. He was the first to hold a fair in honor of a foster parent. The event became the annual olympics of Ireland. Parents also used the annual gathering for "match making."

Mac CEARBHALL
The last king to reign at Tara.

MACHA MONGRUATH   377 B.C. page II-28
"The Golden Head." She was the 76th Monarch of Ireland.
She was bright and aggressive. She personally supervised the construction of her palace, called Emain Macha.

Mac FIRBIS   1650 A.D.   page II-73
A family of historians. DUALD Mac FIRBIS (Firbishigh) lived in the mid 1600's. He compiled "The Great Book of Genealogies." Much of his work was done during the Cromwillian wars.

MAIN LEAMNA   page II-13
Ancestor of the STEWART family of Scotland.

MAINE MAIL   page II-94
Ancestor of the Clan called the UI-MAIL.

MANGUS BARELEGS 1130 A.D. page II-107
King of Norway. Adopted the Irish custom of wearing trousers of knee length.

MANNIN Mac LIR   page II-7
King of the Isle of Man and one of the Tuatha de
Danann.

MANGHUS O'DONNELL 1537 A.D. page II-70
Wrote "The Life of Saint Collumcill (Columbo)."

MAOIN 50 B.C.   page II-4
"Of the Golden Collar." The son of Caibre Cinn
Cait (the rebel king). The first king to wear the
gold collar when sitting in judgment. If his
judgment tended to be false, the collar tightened
about his neck. He made many laws in favor of the
people. He renounced the kingship because he was
not of the royal Milesian line.

MILE 1060 B.C.   page II-8
A renowned Scythian military leader and founder
along with his brother of the Gaelic families who
migrated to Ireland.

MONG FIONN   page II-14,45
"The blonde head."

MORTOUGH MOR Mac EARCA 495 A.D.
                                  page II-55,56

MUIRCHEARTACH 443 A.D.   page II-59,110
"Of the Leather Cloakes." Invented a furlined
sleeping bag for his army. This made it possible
for him to do battle in winter. He was the
ancestor of the O'Neills of Ulster.

MUIREADHACH MUILLEATHAN 700 A.D.
                                  page II-82,86
Ancestor of the SOIL MUIREDHAIGH, a collective name
for several Connacht clans including the O'Connors.

NAISI   page II-29
Son of USNEACH, one of three brothers who kidnapped
DEIRDRE from the court of King CONCHOBAR (Conor).

NATFRAOICH   page II-13,15

NEMEDIUS 1740 B.C.   page II-4
Ancestor of the FIRBOLG. Had two wives: MACHA "Of
the Red and Gold Hair," and REILBHO.

NESSA   25 B.C.   page II-29
A warrior queen. Women went to war with their men
until it was forbidden by the Church in later
times.

NESTA I   1135 A.D.   page II-113,114,115,116
Considered one of the most beautiful women in
Wales. She has been called, "The Mother of the
Norman invasion of Ireland." She was either
sister, mother or relative of many Norman leaders.

NIALL   page II-8
Son of FEINUS FARSAIDH. He was sent by his father
to the African coast at the request of the
Egyptians. He was to found a language school for
their mariners. He became the ancestor of the
Gaels who eventually found their way to Ireland.

NIALL CAILLE   833 A.D.   page II-58,59

NIALL MOR O'DUIRNIN   page II-51
One of the officers in MAGUIRES army. The Chief,
Connacht Maguire, was slain in battle. O'Duirnin
severed the Chief's head and carried it all the way
back to the Maguire burial ground on Devenish
Island, Co. Fermanagh. This was considered a very
valiant deed.

NAILL NAOIGHIALLACH   400 A.D.
                               page II-45,53
"Of the Nine Hostages." He was the foster son of
the renowned chief poet, Ollama TORNA. The poets
influence on his childhood made him one of
Ireland's greatest kings.

NIMROD   page II-2
An old testament character. He was a great hunter
and one of the first to build a great city. It was
called Nineveh (Genesis 10:11,12).

NOS   page II-24
Gave the land for the famous monestary which bore
his name, CLONMACNOIS. It was also a school. At
its zenith, 5,000 students studied there.

NUADH AIRIOTHLAMH   page II-5
A king of the Tuatha de Danann. He lost an arm in
battle which disqualified his kingship. He had a
skillful silver smith forge a fully functional arm
of silver. He was thus able to regain the throne.

ODIN (WODEN) 1150 B.C.   page II-106
A folk hero of the northern peoples. He migrated
with his Clan from near Troy, all the way across
Europe. The tribe settled in present day Denmark.
Tradition turned him into a god of the Norse and
German peoples.

OGHMA GRIAINEIGIS   page II-5
A king who worshiped the sun. Worship as used here
means that the functions of the kingdom were
regulated by the position of the sun rather than
the phases of the moon.

OILILL MOLT 470 A.D.   page II-73
Ancestor of the warrior chief EOGAN BEL and the
historian SAINT CELLACH.

OILILL OLOM 200 A.D.   page II-12
A political genius. He reduced conflict between the
tribes by uniting members of opposing families in
marriage.

PALLADIUS 431 A.D.
The Irish, in their raids on the Continent,
occasionally brought back Christians as slaves.
Irish slaves had a great deal of freedom. They
sent a messenger to Pope CELESTINE I requesting a
pastor. Palladus was sent on this mission. He was
a product of the stiff, unbending Roman culture and
his mission failed. SAINT PATRICK came later as a
slave, learned Irish ways and his mission
succeeded.

PERSIANS   page II-1
Indo-Europeans who settled in Iran.

PHOENICIANS   page II-2
Great traders and seamen. An early branch of these
people are probably the folks the Irish called
Fomorians.

PICTS (The Cruithne)   page II-2
They were big, with round heads, heavy-set, light
brown skin and black hair. Their original homeland
was Thrace, a region now called Bulgaria.

RAIGAN   page II-19
Ancestor of the O'Raigans of Clare.

RAYMOND le GROS 1170 A.D. page II-116
"The Fat One." A grandson of GERALD of WINDSOR and
the famous NESTA I. He was an aggressive leader
among the Norman invaders.

RENAR LODBROG 810 A.D.   page II-107
A mysterious figure in Viking history. He may be
the same person as the fearsome TURGESUS of Irish
history.

RICHARD I of Normandie   page II-108

ROBERT BRUCE   page II-124
King of Scotland.

RODERIC O'CONNOR   1198 A.D. page II-88,89,124
The High-King of Ireland when the Normans arrived.
His father was a military genius while Roderic was
a scholar. He lacked the ability to foresee the
national tragedy which would result from the entry
of a few Norman mercenary soldiers. More
aggressiveness on his part would have delayed but
probably not prevented the occupation of Ireland by
the English. History has not granted him a
favorable position, although in many other respects
he was an outstanding monarch. He was the last
Gaelic king of Ireland.

RODERIC the GREAT   page II-28,29

ROITHEACHTAIGH
First to use four horses to pull a chariot.

ROLLO (Hrolf) 890 A.D.   page II-112
A famous Viking who founded the kingdom of
Normandie in France. He was an ancestor of WILLIAM
the CONQUEROR.

ROUSSA RUADH   page II-29,34

ROMANS   page II-2

RUADIHRI na SOIGHE BUIDHE   1118 A.D.
                                page II-88
Ancestor of the O'Connors of Connacht.

SAINT AILBE (Ailbhe, Albeus) 530 A.D.
                                page II-36
Son of a chieftan and a servant girl. Rejected by
his father. Left in the woods to die, as was the
custom. Said to have been mothered by a she-wolf
until found by a hunter. He proclaimed the Gospel,
demanding a repentant and sacrificial life of
converts.

SAINT ATRACHTA   page II-31

SAINT BRENDAN of Clonfert   585 A.D.
                                page II-45
Born near Tralee. Noted for his voyages into the
Atlantic. Tradition says he reached the New World.

SAINT BRIGHID (Bride)   475 A.D.
page II-42
Abbess of a religious house in Kildare. She dearly
loved animals and was known all over Ireland for
her generosity. She kept a sacred fire burning
representing women as the source of life. Another
Brigid of pre-Christian times was a poetess and
perhaps a goddess (page II-7).

SAINT CAILLEN of Fenagh   page II-38
in County Leitrim.

SAINT CARROLL   page II-31

SAINT CELLACH   570 A.D.   page II-73
Son of Egan BEL, he could have been king, but
preferred to study at Clonmacnois. Said to have
been murdered by his classmates who were bribed by
a rival wanting to be king.

SAINT CIARAN   page II-37
The founder of Clonmacnois.

SAINT CIRAN (Kieran)   page II-82
A missionary to the South of England. Said to have
authored "The Book of Cin" (Dromsneacht).

SAINT COLEMAN of Dromore   520 A.D.
page II-36
He was the educator of St. Finnian of Moville.
Later he was a missionary to Austria.

SAINT COLLUMCILL (St. Columbo - Columbia) 563 A.D.
page II-68
Copied a book belonging to another saint. This and
other deeds caused him to exile himself to the
Island of Iona, off the coast of Scotland. His act
of self-privation changed him into one of Ireland's
great missionaries. He was educated both as a
priest and a poet.

SAINT COMAN   page II-31,100
Two saints of different lineage are said to have
this name.

SAINT COMHGALL   520 A.D.   page II-31
He founded the monestary at Bangor in Co. Down. An
austere individual, he practiced self-denial in the
extreme. He taught Saint Columban who in turn
founded monestaries in France and Italy. At its
height, 3,000 monks studied at Bangor.

SAINT LAWRENCE O'TOOLE   1170 A.D.
He was ambassador for High-King Roderic O'Connor.

SAINT MOHIA   608 A.D.   page II-82
Studied under St. Comgall at Bangor. Visited Pope
Gregory in Rome. Loved life and it's said that he
never killed even the smallest insect.

SAINT MALACHY   1100 A.D.

Up to his time most Irish buildings were
constructed of wood. He built a stone church at
Bangor. He was archbishop of Armagh. He traveled
frequently to the continent spreading the Gospel.
His full name was, Mael Maedoc ua Morgair - Malachy
O'More.

SAINT PATRICK   390 A.D.   page II-6
The apostle who did the most to convert the Irish
from heathenism to Christianity. His exact
birthplace is uncertain. It may have been Wales or
on the border between Scotland and England. His was
a Christian family whose members had been for
several generations. His grandfather was a priest
and his father a deacon. He was born about 370
A.D. and was taken to Ireland as a slave about 386
A.D. Escaping after seven years, he worked his way
to the Continent where he continued his education
in the Church. In a dream, he received a special
call to return to Ireland as a missionary. The
continuing success of his mission is evidence of
the tremendous influence for change which can be
brought about by a single dedicated individual.

SAINT SENAICH   page II-36
The student cow herder who became a missionary.

SCOTA   page II-8
Scota, wife of Niall, an Egyptian princess. Some
generations later, Mile visited Egypt and was given
a wife of the same name.

SEDNA INNARRAIGH
He is said to have been the first king to maintain
a standing army.

SEVEN MAINES   page II-38

O'SGINGIN   page II-77
Historian and genealogist for the O'Donnell Clan.

SIGARD of Denmark   page II-107
Called "The Serpent Eye."

SIGGE   page II-106
Ancestor of the Franks.

SITRICK SILK BEARD 900 A.D. page II-109
King or Earl of the Danes in Dublin. Becomes a
Christian. Builds a priory in Dublin, 980 A.D. In
1014 he leads the Danes in battle against King
Brian at Clontarf. Eleven thousand of his men died
on the battle field. He was defeated by the Irish.

SKOGOLOR   page II-106
The Scandanavians call him the ancestor of the
Tuatha de Danann.

SNORI   900 A.D.   page II-107
Born in North America. He was of Icelandic-Viking
descent. He collected the oral traditions of the
Vikings in Iceland and America.

TEA   page II-10
Wife of Heremon.

THRACIANS   page II-2
A people who lived north of the Agean Sea. Their
land is now the nation of Bulgaria. They were
Indo-Europeans.

THREE FINENIANS   page II-42

TIGHEARNMHAS   900 B.C.   page II-40
He was the first Irish king to smelt gold. He
imported the colors blue, green and saffron. He
allowed foreigners (probably Phoenicians) to
introduce idols into Ireland.

TIGERNAN O'RUAIRC   1170 A.D.
                            page II-84
His wife, Dearbforgail, was spirited away by rival
king, Mac Murrough. This was a personal insult
which resulted in the banishment of Mac Murrough,
who returned with the Normans. Traditionally, this
was the beginning of the conflict between England
and Ireland.

TOIRDHEALBHACH an FHIONA   1380 A.D.
                          page II-69
"Turlough of the Wine." His son, Donnchadh na
Coilled, married a daughter of Tadig O'Dhuirnin.

TOIRDHEALBHACH MOR O'CONNOR   1151 A.D.
From him branched the numerous O'Connor families.

TRYTILA   page II-106
King of the East Angles.

TUATHIL MAOLGARBH   528 A.D. page II-65
Slain by Maelmor, the tutor of a son of DIARMIUD
Mac CEARBHALL.

TUATHAL TEACHTMAR   95 A.D.   page II-42
Imposed a unilateral tax on the province of
Linster.

VIKINGS   page II-2,106

WILLIAM THE CONQUEROR   1025 A.D.
                        page II-113

WILLIAM PENN   page II-128

ZEUS   page II-3

IRISH COATS OF ARMS

Colors, marks and symbols were used to identify persons and property long before the dawn of history. Of these choices our oldest ancestors preferred the use of color. Clansmen were divided into seven social ranks. The ordinary freeman, performing menial tasks, was permitted a single color, usually saffron, for his garments. Moving up the social scale tradesmen, skilled workers and government officials were granted additional colors. The chief druid, when acting as judge, wore six colors. The king, during official events, wore seven.

From a very early date African potentates used symbols as a means of identification. The Crusaders fighting in Africa observed this custom and added markings to their tunics and shields as a means of distinquishing friend from foe. The marks chosen were simple and individual. Returning home many transferred their battle markings to personal property. "Coats of Arms" came to Ireland with the Normans but an Irish (Ulster) King of Arms was not appointed until 1482.

The Rank of Baron has an aristocratic ring but it was the lowest order of royalty until the 1600's. On October 14, 1620, King James authorized the new order of BARONET. The new rank was created to raise money and to seduce the remaining Irish chiefs into submission to the English Crown. Commoners were eligable for this new rank. It could be purchased or granted on the kings order. Along with the granting of "Arms" the recipient was entitled to precede his name with the title "Sir." The first person in Ireland to receive this honor was Sir Francis Blundel (John Durning held the political rank of Baron of the Exchequer for Ireland in 1575). The office of Ulster King of Arms was transferred to the Republic in 1943 and is now a function of the Genealogical Office in Dublin Castle.

From the beginning, conflict existed between Irish and English Law. One such problem was the title to land. Under the Fuedal system brought to England by the Normans, the King held title to land which he could in turn grant to others as he saw fit. Under Irish Law, the chief was a caretaker and the land belonged to the clan. Irish chiefs surrendered tribal lands. The king there-up-on regranted the land to the chief along with a title and "Coat of Arms." This can be taken to mean that all members of a clan may display the arms of their chief. For those who have the same surname as their chief this is fine but for the remainder of us a disappointment. Some years ago Dublin Castle decided that on proof of one's Irishness and payment of a substantial sum anyone of Irish descent could have issued a properly registered "Coat of Arms" in their current surname.

A full discussion of English, Scotch and Irish Heraldry is a subject outside the scope of this book but can be investigated in your own local library. For some examples of Irelands oldest "Coats of Arms" turn to page III-48.

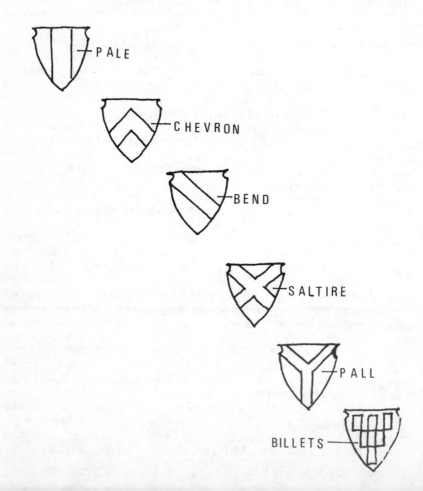

HOW TO DISCOVER YOUR PERSONAL ROOTS

Seeking evidence of your family roots may be a lengthy and expensive process. Two avenues of research are open to you. You can do your own research or obtain the services of a qualified genealogist. The most rewarding method is to do the work yourself. Should you later desire professional help, the experience gained will aid in giving instructions to the researcher and probably help to reduce costs.

Assuming you choose to do your own research, the following steps can serve as a guide.

STEP I

WRITE OR VISIT YOUR RELATIVES

If you have a maiden aunt, she may be the best source of information. Next would be the oldest female relative. Men in the family have a good memory for events but usually are not fully reliable when questioned about birth dates. Finally, contact anyone else who might have some knowledge of the family history. If you make a personal visit, take along a tape recorder. When writing, be sure to explain your reason for the collection of information. On the first contact, it is wise to limit your request to one or two easily answered questions. Be sure to mention that you would like to know of others to whom you should write. The correspondent will usually volunteer additional information if it's known.

STEP II

JOIN A LOCAL GENEALOGICAL SOCIETY

Your local library is a good place to ask about genealogical and historical societies in your community. By joining with others, you can profit by their experience. Genealogical societies in larger communities frequently have their own specialized libraries. If your home is in a rural area, ask your librarian if a list is available of societies in cities nearby. Ask if there is a country wide list of genealogical societies. If one exists in other communities where your ancestors have lived, try writing to them.

STEP III

USING THE TELEPHONE BOOK

Until recently, the local telephone companies had a collection of country wide directories for cities most frequently called. With the advent of the computer, a directory library was no longer needed. Perhaps a call to your local phone company might turn up an old directory for an ancestrial community. Some libraries and many colleges also have a collection of telephone books. Their value to you, of course, is the list of persons of the surname you're searching. The phone book provides names and addresses and the zip code can be looked up at your local Post Office.

If you would like a new phone directory from another city, it may be possible to arrange the purchase through your local phone company.

AT&T now makes directories from other countries available to U.S. citizens. Write to: AT&T Communications, Room 1R05, Directory Dept., 202 Johnson St., Morris Plains, NJ 07950. Ask for a copy of, "The International Telephone Directory Price List." The cost of a directory is near the price of a 600 page best selling novel.

STEP IV

THE QUERY LETTER

When writing to non-relatives, explain your reason for the letter. Rather than asking for specific birth and death dates of "John Jones," explain that you are writing a history of the Jones family specifically of John, who once lived in that community. Also ask whether some one else in the community might be able to help.

Response to unsolicited mail is often no more than 4%. When doing this type of mailing, it's usually too costly to include a postpaid envelope. If a reply is received and another contact is warranted, then send an addressed envelope and two stamps.

The telephone book may also contain business people who have been in the community a long time. On occasion, particularly in small communities, business people can be helpful.

STEP V

THE CITY DIRECTORY

Most of the larger cities have city
directories. Often persons without telephones can
be found within their pages. Most libraries as
well as chambers of commerce will have a copy.
Older directories will usually be found in the city
library. Businesses are listed as well as
individuals. The friendly local undertaker, found
in its pages, should not be overlooked. He may be
a source of death records of a family member.

STEP VI

THE COLLEGE OR UNIVERSITY LIBRARY

When your search extends backward for four or
more generations, your search will become one of
family origins. The institutional library then
becomes your best source. All public and many
private libraries will welcome your visit.
Beginning with the card or computer index, look
under "Author" for the surnames you're searching.
Some one may have done your work for you. Under
"Title" look for state, county, city and other
information which might be helpful. If your family
lived in a large city, the library might have
copies of the community newspaper on film. In the
1880's, histories were written for many of the
counties in the nation. Most contained
genealogical information. Domestic and foreign
phone books are almost always available. Census
records and other government documents are
generally available along with historical and war
records.

If you happen to live near one of the regional
branches of the National Archives, you will find
the 1900 and perhaps the 1910 census records.
These are just now being released for public use.
Ask your librarian for the address of the nearest
archive branch. You will also find information
regarding holdings in the National Archives in
Washington.

STEP VII

VISIT THE HOME STATE AND COMMUNITY OF YOUR
ANCESTORS

Americans are constantly on the move. Many of us no longer live in the community where we were born. As a nation, we have lost the close ties which make possible the direct transfer of family history from generation to generation. Personal research should include a return to the ancestrial community. In addition to the county histories of the 1880's, others were compiled by the WPA during the 1930's depression. Since that time, interested persons all over the country have been collecting and recording the doings of our families. Recently, new county histories have been appearing. The authors were delighted to find, when visiting the ancestrial community of Renzi, Mississippi, that a recently completed county history contained much useful family information.

The local community is the most likely place to find family acquaintances, old local newspapers, vital records and burial sites of family members.

When a search of local and county records is complete, visit the state archives at the state capitol. The archives often contain historical data which may no longer be available in the local community.

STEP VIII

VISIT THE GREAT RESEARCH LIBRARIES

Now is the time to plan a vacation which will take you to one of the great research libraries. These include: The National Library of Canada, Ottawa, Ontario, The Sutro Library, San Francisco, CA, Yale University Library, New Haven CT, The Newberry Library, Chicago, IL, Massachusetts State Library, Boston, Mass., New York City Public Library, New York, The Library of Congress, The D.A.R. and The National Genealogical Society, all in Washington, D.C.

The largest collection of genealogical material in the U.S. will be found in the library of the Genealogical Society which is maintained by the Church of Jesus Christ of Latter Day Saints, located in Salt Lake City, Utah. There can be found a vast collection of personal genealogies and filmed vital records from all over the world. In this one location, it's possible to do world wide research. At least three days should be devoted to this visit - a week would be better. The extensive card index contains thousands of surnames. Here is the most likely place to discover research into your family which has been done by others. The Church also has more than 150 local libraries both in America and over seas. A list can be obtained by sending a stamped, addressed envelope to: The LDS Genealogical Society, Salt Lake City, Utah.

STEP IX

PLAN A VISIT TO THE HOMELAND

Your research isn't complete until you have paid a visit to the homeland of your ancestors. There is no substitute for walking on the same soil your ancestors trod. Include in your plans the collection of information from the tourist agency of the countries you plan to visit. Your friendly travel agent can furnish names and addresses. Ask for a map of the country and any other items the travel agent might suggest. Some countries provide special pamphlets for genealogists.

When planning a visit to Ireland, do your home work. Read Irish ancient and modern history. Decide whether to rent a car (they drive on the left-hand side). Try staying in a bed and breakfast home in the community of your ancestors. You may even find yourself among distant relatives. With careful planning, a visit to Ireland can be the most rewarding part of your family research.

HOW TO USE THE CHARTS

Genealogical charts are much more than a collection of names. They demonstrate many characteristics of the life and times of our ancestors. The charts reveal the naming process used by the various ethnic groups who peopled Europe. Some systems take into consideration the characteristics of the individual. Others stress father-son relationships. Materialism is evident in those names which were chosen from occupations or tools of the trade. The characteristics of the natural world are present in some names taken from fish, animals, trees, physical characteristics and the forces of nature. The influence of the Church is evident in the choice of Biblical names. Language style shows up in the changes in spelling.

Ireland's oldest names are usually Gaelic in

origin. The charts employ Gaelic spelling of surnames as given to us by our informants. It should be noted that one Gaelic name may be translated or transliterated into more than one English name. These variations are included when known.

It's only in recent times that dates have assumed the importance we attach to them today. The ancients kept track of time on a lunar rather than a daily basis. With the coming of Christianity, an attempt was made to establish an exact dating system. Unfortunately, the calendar was changed during this period. As a result, the same event may have differing dates when comparing ancient manuscripts. For this reason, the dates in the following charts represent a period during the life of an individual rather than a specific date of birth or death.

The charts were collected from various sources, primarily folk memory. Thus, they will parallel but may not specifically agree with a particular historical text. They are, however, an excellent guide to the discovery of the origins of the family lines they represent.

The charts are arranged in consecutive order. Once the position of a surname has been discovered, one can follow the connecting lines from that point back toward the front of the book. This will be the traditional lineage of the family. The lines will frequently pass through names which are in capitals. These are names of important personages. Their stories can usually be found in ancient Irish history books. Since the clan system was a collection of families, a newer family line is often derived from an older one. For example, the O'Dhuirnin (now Durning) family branches from the O'Connors of Connacht.

The key to the charts is THE SURNAME INDEX (Part III). Most old surnames in Ireland are Gaelic. A few Danish-Norse can be recognized from the Viking days. Norman-English names came to Ireland beginning in the late 1100's. Scotch and French Heuguenot names date mostly from the plantations of the 1600's, as do some German.

As might be expected, the most complete charts are those of the oldest ruling families. In ancient times, the knowledge of one's genealogy served to verify one's identity much as a Social Security number does today. Many lines are incomplete due in large part to the shifting of population which took place between the 16 and 1700's. Some Scotch, English and Heuguenot names are indexed. Their charting is limited because their origins lie outside Ireland and are beyond the scope of this book. Finally, some well known Irish names are missing because we haven't yet determined their place in the charts.

The index lists surnames in English first. This name is then followed by its Gaelic form. Next come variations of the Gaelic name in English.

The prefixes "O'" and "Mac" are shown following the surname. Many families in recent times dropped the prefixes for various reasons. We have placed the prefix after the surname to eliminate double listing of many surnames. The "O'" is probably the more ancient prefix. It means "Descendant Of" and refers to a grandfather or someone older than that in the family line. "Mac" means "Son Of." It was derived from the letter "M" used by the old chroniclers to show a father-son relationship.

An easy way to follow a family relationship from generation to generation is to trace over the connecting black line with a transparent yellow marking pen. Occasionally the connecting line will be broken by this symbol = . This indicates one or more generations missing. Not every person, nor written source for that matter, has the complete lineage from the current family name back to ancient times. The blanks are an indication of the task still ahead of the Society in filling in the missing gaps.

The charts don't necessarily rank children in order of birth. Unlike the European medieval system, the transfer of an Irish Kingship didn't automatically go to the oldest son. Rather, the heir was chosen from within the ruling family. Among the qualifications he had to meet were physical perfection and military prowess. While the Irish system probably did a better job of qualifying a successor, it gave rise to considerable competition among potential heirs with resulting bloodshed and unrest. Thus, the charts show main lines and sublines without necessarily indicating birth order. Further, the Ancient Irish

families were large and very probably there were
children in every generation who aren't shown in
the charts.

The missing items mentioned above points out
the continuing research of the Society. Our
current objective is collection, while information
can still be obtained from older people who retain
a knowledge of family relationships. Later it is
hoped that the blanks can be filled in.

HOW TO USE THE INDEX

The index lists more than 2,000 surnames in
English and a near equal number of variations.
Following the English surname is the Gaelic form of
that name as given us by those from whom
information was collected. Since information was
collected in Ireland, England, Scandanavia, Canada
and the U.S., both English and Irish names may be
translated, transliterated, interpreted or
misspelled by admitting agents. Never the less, in
most cases the names are easily recognizable.
since the respondents felt the spelling given was
the correct one, we have honored their form.

To simplify indexing the prefixes, (0') and
(Mac - Mc) have been placed after the English
surname. By doing so we have avoided two problems.
The first, double listing of some surnames and
second, the confusion which may occur when prefixes
are dropped or added as some families have done.

Since this book deals with origins only, those
surnames have been included which could be attached
to the tables. More than 1,500 well-known Irish
surnames have yet to be traced.

In the time period covered by this book, the
Gaelic language has passed through at least three
changes in its written form. In most cases, the
respondent was asked for the oldest known form of
the name since in most cases this form could be
most easily recognized in historical works.

It should be noted that most Gaelic surnames
are descriptive and were usually derived from
personal names. The study of names is a science in
its own right.

Following the English form of a surname will
be two or three groups of numbers. The first

number notes the page number of the Part II charts where the surname is first found in English. From this point a transparent marker can be used to follow the connecting lines backward all the way to the front of the book. In doing so, you will pass through three stages of Irish history. Your starting point will be the Irish under the influence of the English. Backward past the year 1100 you will be in the Gaelic period. As you approach 400 A.D. you will have entered Irelands romantic period.

When the Irish kings became Christian and acquainted with the genealogies of the Old Testament, which were so similar to their own, they naturally wanted to know how their lines fitted to those found in the Bible. The earliest part of the charts show this traditional relationship.

Your traditional lineage will pass through some names which have been capitalized. These are usually individuals of importance who may be found in an ancient Irish history book, O'Curry's lectures and numerous sources. If you should desire more details than the brief history in this book, consult the bibliography and then pay a visit to a near-by university library.

Following the first group of numbers will be another enclosed in ( ). This number is the Irish County where your ancestors were believed to have lived for an extended period. Because many records important to the genealogist do not exist in Ireland, one usually needs to know the county in order to begin a search. Location is of prime importance if yours is a name used by more than one family group.

Some names have numbers in brackets [ ]. These usually follow a Scotch name and indicate where that family was originally located in Scotland.

If your surname is not among the first English listings, scan the secondary names following every surname in the Index. These secondary surnames may not be cross indexed.

The search for the origin of our names is a continuing process. This volume is the basic tool, later discoveries will be issued as an appendix. When research is as complete as possible - which will take some years, our work will be revised as a literary form, rather than a research tool.

Our names are more than just an epitaph commemorating our time on Earth. Name giving is a form of reasoning. The bearer in turn is a creator of some degree of history as well as the genetic link between the past and the future. In this respect, our time on Earth is important. We are each one, creating a genetic future for the human race which is currently unknown to us. Just as each of us wish to know the part that our ancestors played in bringing us to this time and place, so will our children of the future want to know - who we were - and how we spent our time on Earth. You are to be congratulated for having an interest in preserving your past history for future generations.

The Authors

GRANNAGH, AGLISH - COUNTY KILKENNY

a guide to
IRISH ROOTS
Including Celts, Vikings,
Normans, Kings, Queens
and Commoners.

by William and Mary Durning

A BIBLIOGRAPHY OF IRISH TRADITION AND HISTORY

The following is a list of books useful in gaining full understanding of our ancestral origins. Many of these volumes can be found in larger public libraries, the remainder in college and university libraries.

AMERICA B.C.
Barry Fell
Quandrangle-New York Times
Book Company   1976

ANCIENT LEGENDS OF IRELAND
Lady Wilde
Ward and Downey
London   1888

ANNALS OF CLONMACNOISE
Translation, C. Mageoghagan
Editor, Rev. Denis Murphy S.J.
The University Press
Dublin   1896

ANNALS OF CONNACHT (THE)
Editor, A. Martin Freeman
Dublin Institute of Advanced
Studies
Dublin   1944

ANNALS OF LOUGH CE'
Editor, W.M. Hennessy
and B. Mac Carthy
Dublin   1887

ANNALA RIOGHACTA EIREANN
(The Annals of the Kingdom
of Ireland)
By the Four Masters
Translation, John O'Donovan
Hodges, Smith and Company
Dublin   1854

BOOK OF BALLYMOTE   1380
In the Royal Irish Academy
Dublin

BOOK OF LECAN (THE)
Gilla-Isa Mac Firbis   1416
In the Royal Irish Academy
Dublin

CELTIC   MYTH AND
LEGEND
Charles Squire
Newcastle Publishing
Co. Hollywood, CA
1970

CELTIC MYTHOLOGY
Proinsias Mac Cana
The Hamlyn Publishing
 Group London 1970

CELTS (THE)
Georges Dutton
Translation, David
Mac Rae, Minerva,
S.A., Geneva   1977

CENSUS OF IRELAND
 1659
Editor, Seamus Pender
Dublin   1939

CONOR CRUISE O'BRIEN
INTRODUCES IRELAND
Editor Owen D.
Edwards
McGraw-Hill Book Co.
New York   1968

DEAR DARK HEAD
Helen Landreth
Whittlesey House
McGraw-Hill Book Co.
New York   1968

DRUIDS (THE)
Stuart Piggott
Penguin Books
Harmondsworth and
London   1974

ENCYCLOPEDIA OF IRELAND
Allen Figgis & Co. Ltd.
Dublin   1968

ENGLISH IN IRELAND (THE)
James Anthony Froude
AMS Press NY   10003

EUROPAS FYRSTESLAEGTER
En Genealogisk Nogle
Robert W. Harvest and
Helga Tulinius
Politikens Forlag   1977

FORAS FEASA ar EIRINN
(The History of Ireland)
Geoffrey Keating
London 1902

GENEALOGICAL TRACTS I
T. O'Raithbheartaigh M.A.
The Stationary Office
Dublin   1932

GERALDINES (THE)
Brian Fitzgerald
Devin-Adair Company
New York   1952

GUIDE TO NATIONAL MONUMENTS
OF IRELAND
Peter Harbison
Gill & MacMillan
Dublin   1970

HANDBOOK OF IRISH GENEALOGY
Heraldic Artists Ltd.
Dublin   1970

HERALDRY OF THE ROYAL
FAMILIES OF EUROPE
Jiri Louda and Michael
MacLagan
Clark N. Potter Inc.
Dist. by Crown NY

HERE'S IRELAND
Harold Speakman
Robert M. Mc Bride Co.
New York   1925

HISTORY OF IRELAND
(A)
Mac Geoghan

HISTORY   OF   THE
NATIONS, IRELAND
Patrick W. Joyce LLD
P.F. Collier & Son
New York   1928

HISTORY OF ULSTER
(THE)
Ramsay Colles LLD
The Gresam Pub. Co.
Convent Garden -
            London
Reprint - Barnes &
Noble NY   1971

HISTORICAL WORKS OF
GERALDUS CAMBRENSIS
(THE)
Thomas Wright Esq.
H.G. Bohn York Street
London   1863
Reprint AMS Press NY

ILLUSTRATED ROAD BOOK
OF IRELAND
The Automobile Assoc.
Dublin   1970

IRELAND AND THE
FOUNDATIONS OF EUROPE
Benedict Fitzpatrick
Funk & Wagnalls Co.
New York   1927

IRISH - ENGLISH DICT-
IONARY
Rev.   Patrick S.
Dinneen MA
The Educational Co.
of Ireland   Dublin
1927 Reprint 1970

IRISH FAMILIES
Edward MacLysaght
D. Litt
Crown Publishers
New York 1972

IRISH FOLK WAYS
E. Estyn Evans
Routledge & Kegan Paul Ltd.
London   1957

IRISH MYTOLOGICAL CYCLE (THE)
D'Arbois de Jubainville
Hodges and Figgis
Dublin   1903

IRISH PEDIGREES, THE
ORIGINAND STEM OF THE
IRISH NATION
John O'Hart
1892 - 1976
The Genealogical Publishing
Company, Baltimore

JACOBITE NARRATIVE (THE)
1688 - 1691
John T. Gilbert
Joseph Dollard
Dublin   1892

LITERARY HISTORY OF
IRELAND FROM EARLIEST
TIMES TO THE PRESENT DAY
(A)
Doublas Hyde, LLD

MANUSCRIPT MATERIALS OF
IRISH HISTORY
Eugene O'Curry

MYTHS AND FOLKLORE OF
IRELAND
Jeremiah Curtin   1890
Republished, Weathervane
Books, New York

NEW HISTORY OF IRELAND (A)
T.W. Moody, F.X. Martin
The Clarendon Press
Oxford, Eng. 1982

NORMAN INVASION OF IRELAND
(THE)
Richard Roche
Anvil Books Ltd.
Tralee, Ireland 1970

PADDY THE COPE
Patrick Gallagher
Devin-Adair Co.
Old Greenwich, CN
   1942

PEADAR O'DOIRIN
(Durning)
Sean de Ris
Oifig an tSolathair
Dublin   1969

POEMS OF BILLY
   DURNING
Manuscript in the
Royal Irish Academy

PHASES OF IRISH
HISTORY
Eoin Macneill
Gill and Son
Dublin   1968

ROYAL HORDES (THE)
E.D. Phillips
Thames and Hudson
London   1965

SCOTTISH MIGRATION TO
ULSTER IN THE REIGN
OF JAMES I (THE)
M. Perceval - Maxwell
Routledge & Kegan
Paul   London
Humanities Press, NY

SEARCH OF SCOTTISH
ANCESTRY (IN) 1972
Hamilton - Edwards
Gen. Publishing Co.
Baltimore

SLOINNTE GAEDHEAL IS
GALL
(Irish Names and
Surnames) Wolfe
Reprint
Genealogical Pub. Co.
Baltimore

SOCIAL HISTORY OF ANCIENT IRELAND
P.W. Joyce

STORY OF THE IRISH RACE (THE)
Seumas Mac Manus
Devin-Adair Company
New York and Old Greenwich CT

SURNAMES OF IRELAND
Edward MacLysaght
Irish University Press
Dublin 1973

O Neill
Mag Uidir
O'Domhnaill,
O Conchobair

T'AIN BO' CUAILNGE
Cecile O'Rahilly
Dublin Institute for
Advanced Studies
Dublin 1967

TREASURY OF IRISH FOLKLORE (A)
Padraic Colum
Crown Publishing Company
New York 1967

VIEW OF THE IRISH LANGUAGE (A)
Brian O'Cuiv
The Stationary Office
Dublin 1969

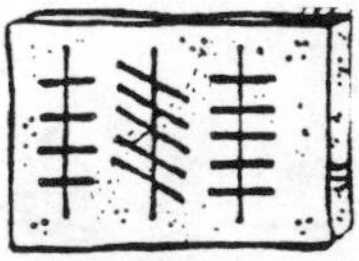

VIKING SETTLEMENTS OF NORTH AMERICA (THE)
Frederick J. Pohl
Clarkson N. Potter, Inc.
New York 1972

VIKINGS (THE)
Johannes Brondsted
Penquin Books 1970
Harmondsworth and London

WHAT'S IN A NAME?
La Reina Rule and
Wm. K. Hammond
Pyramid Books
New York 1973

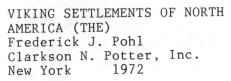

O Ruairc .i. Lochlainn dhec.
O'Ruairc, i.e. Lochlainn, died.

OOLA CASTLE - COUNTY LIMERICK

LEA CASTLE - COUNTY LAOIS

TARA HILL, HOME OF HI-KINGS, COUNTY MEATH

IRISH ROOTS

part

two

a guide to
IRISH ROOTS
Including Arts & Things
Plonagres, Rings, Stones
and Clonowders

by William and Mary Flanery

II-1

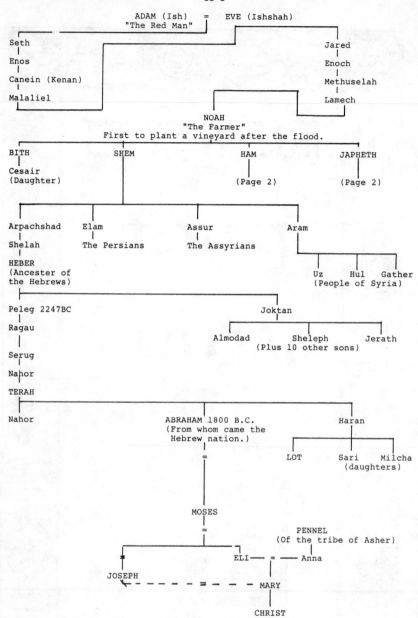

For a complete history of the Hebrews, see the Bible and the historian
Josephus Flavius.

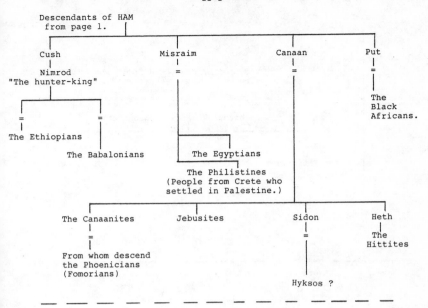

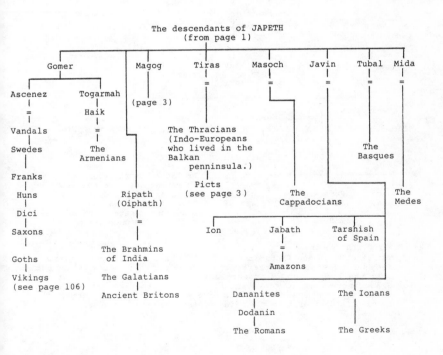

Descendants of MAGOG
from page 2

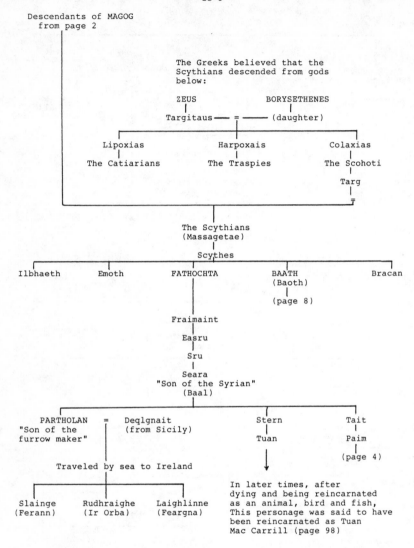

The Greeks believed that the
Scythians descended from gods
below:

ZEUS   BORYSETHENES

Targitaus —— = —— (daughter)

Lipoxias   Harpoxais   Colaxias

The Catiarians   The Traspies   The Scohoti

Targ

The Scythians
(Massagetae)

Scythes

Ilbhaeth   Emoth   FATHOCHTA   BAATH   Bracan
                                     (Baoth)
                                     (page 8)

Fraimaint

Easru

Sru

Seara
"Son of the Syrian"
(Baal)

PARTHOLAN = Deqlgnait   Stern   Tait
"Son of the (from Sicily)
furrow maker"   Tuan   Paim
                                                 (page 4)

Traveled by sea to Ireland

Slainge   Rudhraighe   Laighlinne
(Ferann)   (Ir Orba)   (Feargna)

In later times, after
dying and being reincarnated
as an animal, bird and fish,
This personage was said to have
been reincarnated as Tuan
Mac Carrill (page 98)

(PICTS from page 2)
Tradition says the Picts arrived in Ireland seeking a new homeland.
They were advised that there was no place for them on the Island but
that the land which is present day Scotland was then unoccupied.
Since there were no women in this group as they were given Irish
wives, upon agreement that their kingly lines would pass through the
female line rather than the male. This agreement was adhered to.

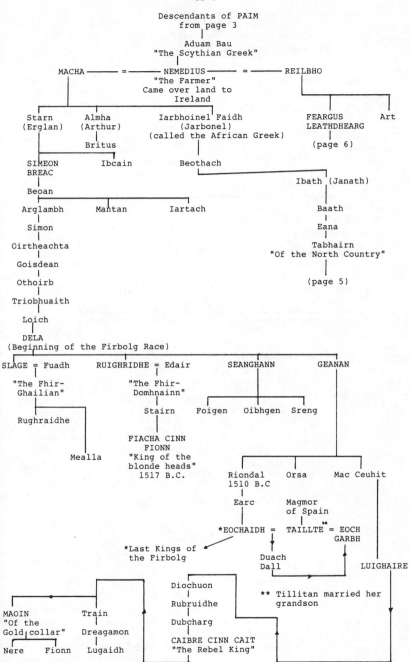

Descendants of PAIM
from page 3

Aduam Bau
"The Scythian Greek"

MACHA ——— = ——— NEMEDIUS ——— = ——— REILBHO
"The Farmer"
Came over land to
Ireland

Starn   Almha   Iarbhoinel Faidh   FEARGUS   Art
(Erglan)   (Arthur)   (Jarbonel)   LEATHDHEARG
                          (called the African Greek)
             | (page 6)
             Britus

SIMEON   Ibcain   Beothach
BREAC
                                              Ibath (Janath)
Beoan
                                              Baath
Arglambh   Mantan   Iartach
                                              Eana
Simon
                                              Tabhairn
Oirtheachta   "Of the North Country"

Goisdean
                                              (page 5)
Othoirb

Triobhuaith

Loich

DELA
(Beginning of the Firbolg Race)

SLAGE = Fuadh   RUIGHRIDHE = Edair   SEANGHANN   GEANAN
"The Fhir-   "The Fhir-
Ghailian"   Domhnainn"
                    Stairn   Foigen   Oibhgen   Sreng
Rughraidhe
                    FIACHA CINN
                    FIONN
                    "King of the
          Mealla   blonde heads"
                    1517 B.C.
                                    Riondal   Orsa   Mac Ceuhit
                                    1510 B.C

                                    Earc   Magmor
                                               of Spain

                               *EOCHAIDH = TAILLTE = EOCH
                                                       GARBH
                    *Last Kings of ←
                     the Firbolg   Duach
                                              Dall   LUIGHAIRE

                          Diochuon
                                         ** Tillitan married her
                          Rubruidhe   grandson

MAOIN   Train   Dubcharg
"Of the
Gold collar" Dreagamon   CAIBRE CINN CAIT
                          "The Rebel King"
Nere   Fionn Lugaidh

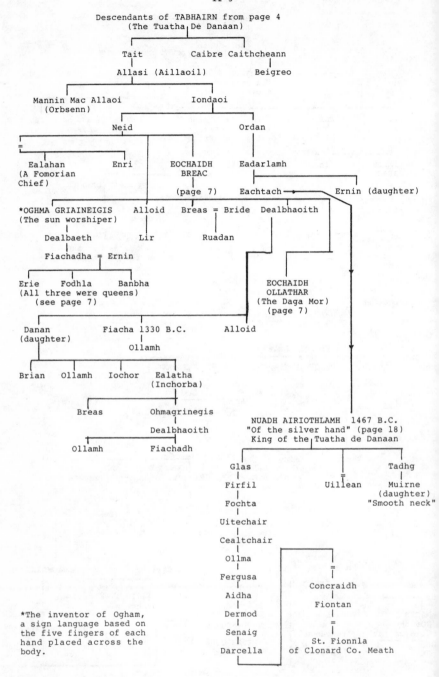

Descendants of TABHAIRN from page 4
(The Tuatha De Danaan)

Tait   Caibre Caithcheann

Allasi (Aillaoil)   Beigreo

Mannin Mac Allaoi   Iondaoi
(Orbsenn)

Neid   Ordan

Ealahan   Enri   EOCHAIDH   Eadarlamh
(A Fomorian   BREAC
Chief)   (page 7)   Eachtach ➞   Ernin (daughter)

*OGHMA GRIAINEIGIS   Alloid   Breas = Bride   Dealbhaoith
(The sun worshiper)

Dealbaeth   Lir   Ruadan

Fiachadha = Ernin

Erie   Fodhla   Banbha   EOCHAIDH
(All three were queens)   OLLATHAR
(see page 7)   (The Daga Mor)
    (page 7)

Danan   Fiacha 1330 B.C.   Alloid
(daughter)

Ollamh

Brian   Ollamh   Iochor   Ealatha
(Inchorba)

Breas   Ohmagrinegis

Dealbhaoith   NUADH AIRIOTHLAMH 1467 B.C.
"Of the silver hand" (page 18)
Ollamh   Fiachadh   King of the Tuatha de Danaan

Glas   Tadhg

Firfil   Uillean   Muirne
    (daughter)
Fochta   "Smooth neck"

Uitechair

Cealtchair

Ollma

Fergusa   Concraidh

Aidha   Fiontan

Dermod

Senaig   St. Fionnla

Darcella   of Clonard Co. Meath

*The inventor of Ogham,
a sign language based on
the five fingers of each
hand placed across the
body.

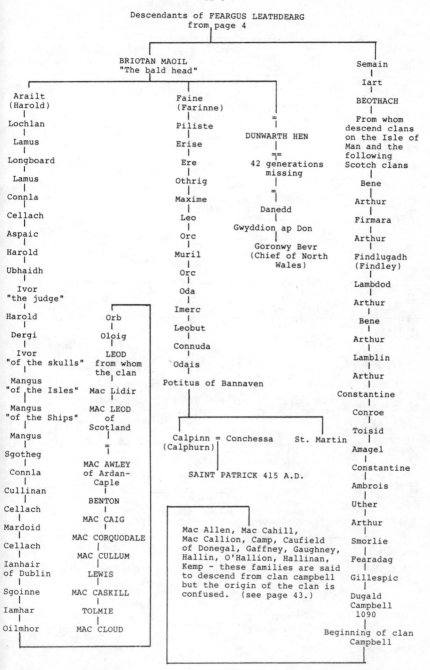

Descendants of FEARGUS LEATHDEARG
from page 4

BRIOTAN MAOIL
"The bald head"

Semain
Iart
BEOTHACH

Arailt
(Harold)

Lochlan

Lamus

Longboard

Lamus

Connla

Cellach

Aspaic

Harold

Ubhaidh

Ivor
"the judge"

Harold

Dergi

Ivor
"of the skulls"

Mangus
"of the Isles"

Mangus
"of the Ships"

Mangus

Sgotheg

Connla

Cullinan

Cellach

Mardoid

Cellach

Ianhair
of Dublin

Sgoinne

Iamhar

Oilmhor

Faine
(Farinne)

Piliste

Erise

Ere

Othrig

Maxime

Leo

Orc

Muril

Orc

Oda

Imerc

Leobut

Connuda

Odais

Potitus of Bannaven

Orb

Oloig

LEOD
from whom
the clan

Mac Lidir

MAC LEOD
of
Scotland
=
MAC AWLEY
of Ardan-
Caple

BENTON

MAC CAIG

MAC CORQUODALE

MAC CULLUM

LEWIS

MAC CASKILL

TOLMIE

MAC CLOUD

=
DUNWARTH HEN
==
42 generations
missing
=
Danedd
Gwyddion ap Don
Goronwy Bevr
(Chief of North
Wales)

Calpinn = Conchessa   St. Martin
(Calphurn)

SAINT PATRICK 415 A.D.

Mac Allen, Mac Cahill,
Mac Callion, Camp, Caufield
of Donegal, Gaffney, Gaughney,
Hallin, O'Hallion, Hallinan,
Kemp - these families are said
to descend from clan campbell
but the origin of the clan is
confused. (see page 43.)

From whom
descend clans
on the Isle of
Man and the
following
Scotch clans

Bene

Arthur

Firmara

Arthur

Findlugadh
(Findley)

Lambdod

Arthur

Bene

Arthur

Lamblin

Arthur

Constantine

Conroe

Toisid

Amagel

Constantine

Ambrois

Uther

Arthur

Smorlie

Fearadag

Gillespic

Dugald
Campbell
1090

Beginning of clan
Campbell

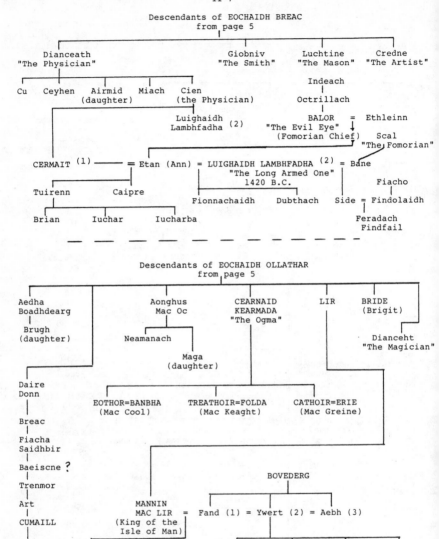

Descendants of EOCHAIDH BREAC
from page 5

Dianceath "The Physician"   Giobniv "The Smith"   Luchtine "The Mason"   Credne "The Artist"

Cu   Ceyhen   Airmid (daughter)   Miach   Cien (the Physician)

Indeach
Octrillach
BALOR = Ethleinn
"The Evil Eye"
(Fomorian Chief)

Luighaidh Lambhfadha (2)

Scal "The Fomorian"

CERMAIT (1) ——— = Etan (Ann) = LUIGHAIDH LAMBHFADHA (2) = Bane
"The Long Armed One"
1420 B.C.

Tuirenn   Caipre   Fionnachaidh   Dubthach   Side = Findolaidh   Fiacho

Brian   Iuchar   Iucharba

Feradach
Findfail

Descendants of EOCHAIDH OLLATHAR
from page 5

Aedha Boadhdearg   Aonghus Mac Oc   CEARNAID KEARMADA "The Ogma"   LIR   BRIDE (Brigit)

Brugh (daughter)   Neamanach   Dianceht "The Magician"

Maga (daughter)

Daire Donn

Breac

Fiacha Saidhbir

Baeiscne ?

Trenmor

Art

CUMAILL

FINN MAC COOL ?
(Page 18)

EOTHOR=BANBHA (Mac Cool)   TREATHOIR=FOLDA (Mac Keaght)   CATHOIR=ERIE (Mac Greine)

BOVEDERG

MANNIN MAC LIR = Fand (1) = Ywert (2) = Aebh (3)
(King of the Isle of Man)

Lug   Aife (Eva) (daughter)   Finola (Flora, Penny)   Aedh   Fiacha   CONN

Eithni

Descendants of BAATH
from page 3

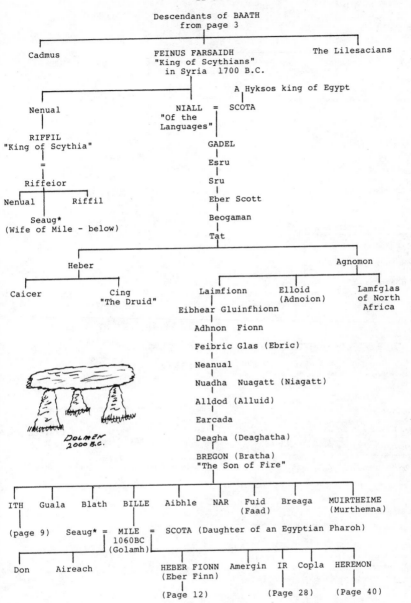

Cadmus   FEINUS FARSAIDH   The Lilesacians
"King of Scythians"
in Syria 1700 B.C.

A Hyksos king of Egypt

Nenual   NIALL = SCOTA
"Of the
Languages"

RIFFIL
"King of Scythia"   GADEL
=
      Esru

Riffeior   Sru

Nenual   Riffil   Eber Scott

Seaug*   Beogaman
(Wife of Mile - below)

Tat

Heber   Agnomon

Caicer   Cing   Laimfionn   Elloid   Lamfglas
"The Druid"   (Adnoion)   of North
Eibhear Gluinfhionn   Africa

Adhnon Fionn

Feibric Glas (Ebric)

Neanual

Nuadha Nuagatt (Niagatt)

Alldod (Alluid)

Earcada

Deagha (Deaghatha)

BREGON (Bratha)
"The Son of Fire"

DOLMEN
2000 B.C.

ITH Guala Blath BILLE Aibhle NAR Fuid Breaga MUIRTHEIME
                            (Faad)   (Murthemna)

(page 9)   Seaug* = MILE = SCOTA (Daughter of an Egyptian Pharoh)
             1060BC
             (Golamh)

Don   Aireach   HEBER FIONN Amergin IR Copla HEREMON
                    (Eber Finn)

(Page 12)   (Page 28)   (Page 40)

Descendants of ITH
from page 8
|
Luighaioh

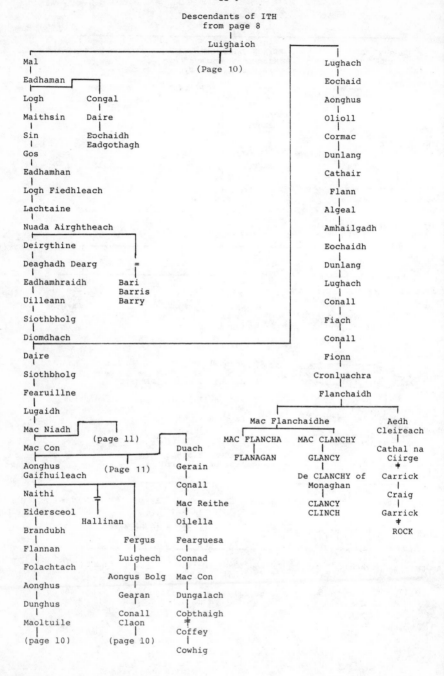

(Page 10)

Mal

Eadhaman ——— Congal

Logh | Daire
Maithsin | Eochaidh
Sin Eadgothagh
Gos

Eadhamhan

Logh Fiedhleach

Lachtaine

Nuada Airghtheach

Deirgthine

Deaghadh Dearg =

Eadhamhraidh   Bari
Barris
Uilleann   Barry

Siothbholg

Diomdhach

Daire

Siothbholg

Fearuillne

Lugaidh

Mac Niadh ——— (page 11)

Mac Con

Aonghus   (Page 11)
Gaifhuileach

Naithi

Eidersceol   Hallinan

Brandubh

Flannan   Fergus

Folachtach   Luighech

Aonghus   Aongus Bolg

Dunghus   Gearan

Maoltuile   Conall
    Claon
(page 10)   (page 10)

Duach

Gerain

Conall

Mac Reithe

Oilella

Fearguesa

Connad

Mac Con

Dungalach

Cobthaigh
╪
Coffey

Cowhig

Lughach

Eochaid

Aonghus

Olioll

Cormac

Dunlang

Cathair

Flann

Algeal

Amhailgadh

Eochaidh

Dunlang

Lughach

Conall

Fiach

Conall

Fionn

Cronluachra

Flanchaidh

Mac Flanchaidhe

MAC FLANCHA   MAC CLANCHY

FLANAGAN   GLANCY

De CLANCHY of
Monaghan

CLANCY
CLINCH

Aedh
Cleireach

Cathal na
Ciirge
╪
Carrick

Craig

Garrick
╪
ROCK

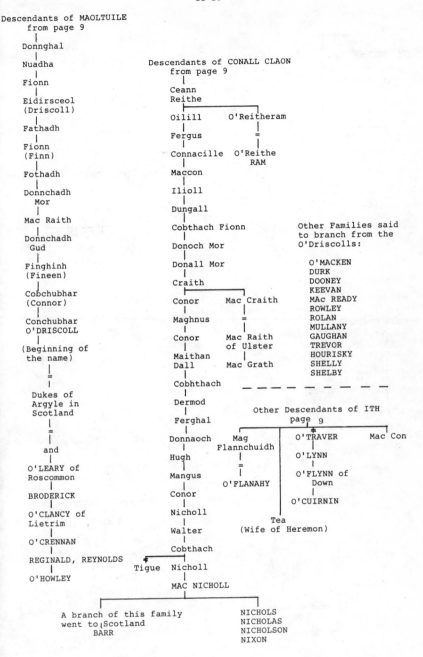

Descendants of MAOLTUILE
from page 9

Donnghal

Nuadha

Fionn

Eidirsceol
(Driscoll)

Fathadh

Fionn
(Finn)

Fothadh

Donnchadh
Mor

Mac Raith

Donnchadh
Gud

Finghinh
(Fineen)

Cobchubhar
(Connor)

Conchubhar
O'DRISCOLL

(Beginning of
the name)

Dukes of
Argyle in
Scotland

=

and

O'LEARY of
Roscommon

BRODERICK

O'CLANCY of
Lietrim

O'CRENNAN

REGINALD, REYNOLDS

O'HOWLEY

Descendants of CONALL CLAON
from page 9

Ceann
Reithe

Oilill   O'Reitheram

Fergus   =

Connacille   O'Reithe
                  RAM

Maccon

Ilioll

Dungall

Cobthach Fionn

Donoch Mor

Donall Mor

Craith

Conor   Mac Craith

Maghnus   =

Conor   Mac Raith
               of Ulster

Maithan
Dall   Mac Grath

Cobhthach

Dermod

Ferghal

Donnaoch   Mag
            Flannchuidh

Hugh   =

Mangus   O'FLANAHY

Conor

Nicholl

Walter   Tea
            (Wife of Heremon)

Cobthach

Tigue Nicholl

MAC NICHOLL

Other Families said
to branch from the
O'Driscolls:

O'MACKEN
DURK
DOONEY
KEEVAN
MAc READY
ROWLEY
ROLAN
MULLANY
GAUGHAN
TREVOR
HOURISKY
SHELLY
SHELBY

Other Descendants of ITH
page 9

O'TRAVER   Mac Con

O'LYNN

O'FLYNN of
Down

O'CUIRNIN

A branch of this family   NICHOLS
went to Scotland   NICHOLAS
        BARR   NICHOLSON
                                 NIXON

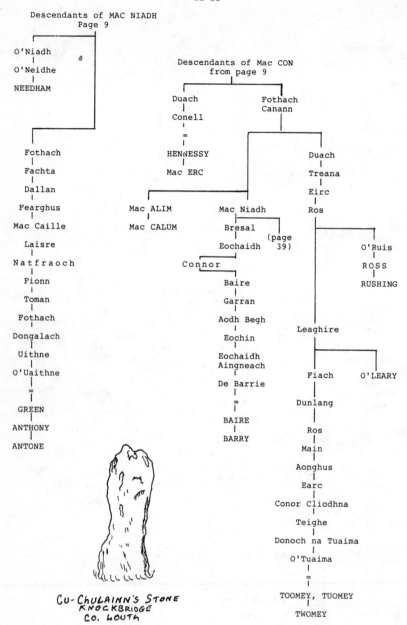

Descendants of MAC NIADH
Page 9

O'Niadh
|
O'Neidhe
|
NEEDHAM

Descendants of Mac CON
from page 9

Duach   Fothach
| Canann
Conell
|
=
|
HENNESSY
|
Mac ERC

Fothach
|
Fachta
|
Dallan
|
Fearghus
|
Mac Caille
|
Laisre
|
Natfraoch
|
Fionn
|
Toman
|
Fothach
|
Dongalach
|
Uithne
|
O'Uaithne
|
=
|
GREEN
|
ANTHONY
|
ANTONE

Mac ALIM   Mac Niadh
| |
Mac CALUM   Bresal   (page
                  | 39)
                  Eochaidh
       Connor
       |
       Baire
       |
       Garran
       |
       Aodh Begh
       |
       Eochin
       |
       Eochaidh
       Aingneach
       |
       De Barrie
       |
       =
       |
       BAIRE
       |
       BARRY

Duach
|
Treana
|
Eirc
|
Ros

                    O'Ruis
                    |
                    ROSS
                    |
                    RUSHING

Leaghire
|
Fiach   O'LEARY
|
Dunlang
|
Ros
|
Main
|
Aonghus
|
Earc
|
Conor Cliodhna
|
Teighe
|
Donoch na Tuaima
|
O'Tuaima
|
=
|
TOOMEY, TUOMEY
|
TWOMEY

CU-CHULAINN'S STONE
KNOCKBRIDGE
CO. LOUTH

Descendants of HEBER FIONN
From page 8

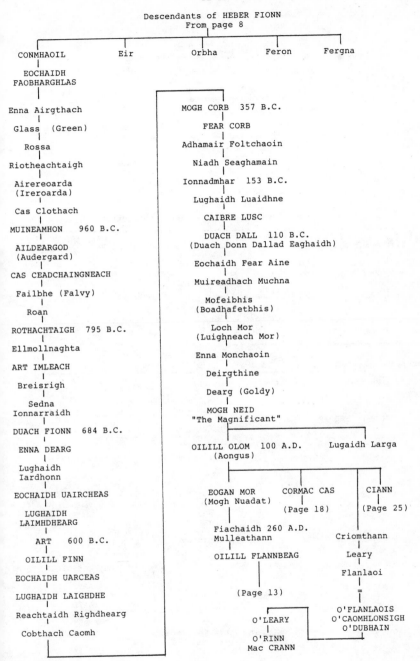

CONMHAOIL   Eir   Orbha   Feron   Fergna

EOCHAIDH
FAOBHARGHLAS

Enna Airgthach

Glass (Green)

Rossa

Riotheachtaigh

Airereoarda
(Ireroarda)

Cas Clothach

MUINEAMHON   960 B.C.

AILDEARGOD
(Audergard)

CAS CEADCHAINGNEACH

Failbhe (Falvy)

Roan

ROTHACHTAIGH 795 B.C.

Ellmollnaghta

ART IMLEACH

Breisrigh

Sedna
Ionnarraidh

DUACH FIONN 684 B.C.

ENNA DEARG

Lughaidh
Iardhonn

EOCHAIDH UAIRCHEAS

LUGHAIDH
LAIMHDHEARG

ART 600 B.C.

OILILL FINN

EOCHAIDH UARCEAS

LUGHAIDH LAIGHDHE

Reachtaidh Righdhearg

Cobthach Caomh

MOGH CORB 357 B.C.

FEAR CORB

Adhamair Foltchaoin

Niadh Seaghamain

Ionnadmhar 153 B.C.

Lughaidh Luaidhne

CAIBRE LUSC

DUACH DALL 110 B.C.
(Duach Donn Dallad Eaghaidh)

Eochaidh Fear Aine

Muireadhach Muchna

Mofeibhis
(Boadhafetbhis)

Loch Mor
(Luighneach Mor)

Enna Monchaoin

Deirgthine

Dearg (Goldy)

MOGH NEID
"The Magnificant"

OILILL OLOM 100 A.D.   Lugaidh Larga
(Aongus)

EOGAN MOR   CORMAC CAS   CIANN
(Mogh Nuadat)
            (Page 18)   (Page 25)

Fiachaidh 260 A.D.   Criomthann
Mulleathann

OILILL FLANNBEAG   Leary

                   Flanlaoi

(Page 13)   =

                  O'FLANLAOIS
O'LEARY   O'CAOMHLONSIGH
                  O'DUBHAIN
O'RINN
Mac CRANN

Descendants of OILILL FLANNBEAG
From page 12

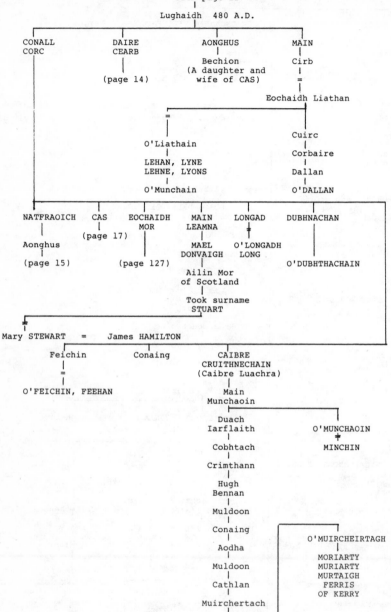

Lughaidh   480 A.D.

CONALL CORC | DAIRE CEARB (page 14) | AONGHUS — Bechion (A daughter and wife of CAS) | MAIN Cirb = Eochaidh Liathan

O'Liathain
LEHAN, LYNE
LEHNE, LYONS
O'Munchain

Cuirc
Corbaire
Dallan
O'DALLAN

NATFRAOICH — Aonghus (page 15) | CAS (page 17) | EOCHAIDH MOR (page 127) | MAIN LEAMNA — MAEL DONVAIGH — Ailin Mor of Scotland — Took surname STUART | LONGAD — O'LONGADH LONG | DUBHNACHAN — O'DUBHTHACHAIN

Mary STEWART = James HAMILTON

Feichin = O'FEICHIN, FEEHAN | Conaing | CAIBRE CRUITHNECHAIN (Caibre Luachra)

Main Munchaoin
Duach Iarflaith
O'MUNCHAOIN
MINCHIN
Cobhtach
Crimthann
Hugh Bennan
Muldoon
Conaing
Aodha
O'MUIRCHEIRTAGH
MORIARTY
MURIARTY
MURTAIGH
FERRIS
OF KERRY
Muldoon
Cathlan
Muirchertach

Descendants of DAIRE CEARB
From page 13

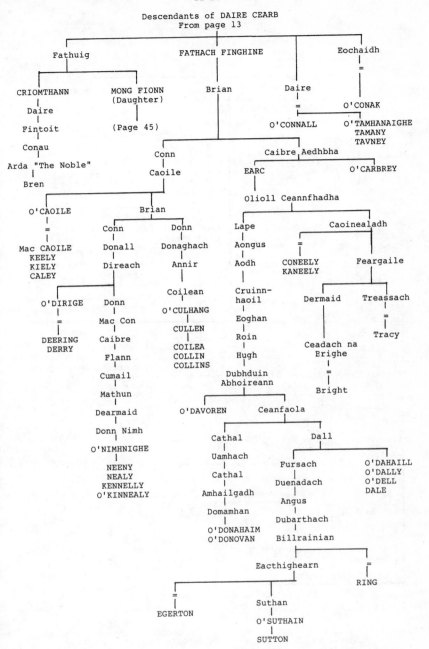

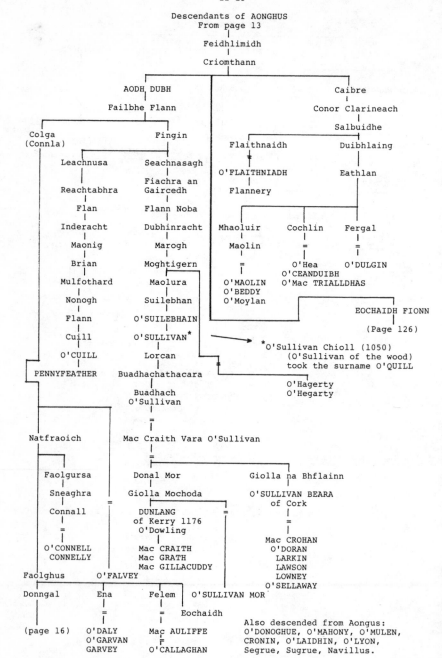

Descendants of AONGHUS
From page 13

Feidhlimidh

Criomthann

AODH DUBH

Failbhe Flann

Caibre

Conor Clarineach

Salbuidhe

Colga
(Connla)

Fingin

Leachnusa

Reachtabhra

Flan

Inderacht

Maonig

Brian

Mulfothard

Nonogh

Flann

Cuill

O'CUILL

PENNYFEATHER

Seachnasagh

Fiachra an
Gaircedh

Flann Noba

Dubhinracht

Marogh

Moghtigern

Maolura

Suilebhan

O'SUILEBHAIN

O'SULLIVAN*

Lorcan

Buadhachathacara

Buadhach
O'Sullivan

Flaithnaidh
‡
O'FLAITHNIADH

Flannery

Duibhlaing

Eathlan

Mhaoluir

Maolin

=

O'MAOLIN
O'BEDDY
O'Moylan

Cochlin

=

O'Hea
O'CEANDUIBH
O'Mac TRIALLDHAS

Fergal

=

O'DULGIN

EOCHAIDH FIONN

(Page 126)

*O'Sullivan Chioll (1050)
(O'Sullivan of the wood)
took the surname O'QUILL

‡
O'Hagerty
O'Hegarty

Mac Craith Vara O'Sullivan

Natfraoich

Faolgursa

Sneaghra

Connall

=

O'CONNELL
CONNELLY

Donal Mor

Giolla Mochoda

=

DUNLANG
of Kerry 1176
O'Dowling

Mac CRAITH
Mac GRATH
Mac GILLACUDDY

Giolla na Bhflainn

O'SULLIVAN BEARA
of Cork

=

Mac CROHAN
O'DORAN
LARKIN
LAWSON
LOWNEY
O'SELLAWAY

Faolghus

Donngal

(page 16)

O'FALVEY

Ena

=

O'DALY
O'GARVAN
GARVEY

Felem

=

Mac AULIFFE
=
O'CALLAGHAN

O'SULLIVAN MOR

Eochaidh

Also descended from Aongus:
O'DONOGHUE, O'MAHONY, O'MULEN,
CRONIN, O'LAIDHIN, O'LYON,
Segrue, Sugrue, Navillus.

Descendants of DONNGAL
From page 15

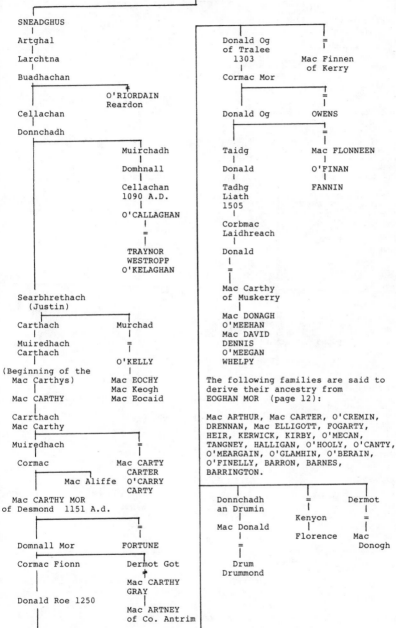

SNEADGHUS
|
Artghal
|
Larchtna
|
Buadhachan
|
       O'RIORDAIN
       Reardon
|
Cellachan
|
Donnchadh

Muirchadh
|
Domhnall
|
Cellachan
1090 A.D.
|
O'CALLAGHAN
|
=
|
TRAYNOR
WESTROPP
O'KELAGHAN

Searbhrethach
(Justin)

Carthach   Murchad
|
Muiredhach   =
Carthach
| O'KELLY
(Beginning of the
Mac Carthys)   Mac EOCHY
| Mac Keogh
Mac CARTHY   Mac Eocaid
|
Carrthach
Mac Carthy
|
Muiredhach   =
|
Cormac   Mac CARTY
| CARTER
Mac Aliffe O'CARRY
| CARTY
Mac CARTHY MOR
of Desmond 1151 A.d.

Domnall Mor   FORTUNE
|
Cormac Fionn Dermot Got
|
| Mac CARTHY
| GRAY
Donald Roe 1250 Mac ARTNEY
          of Co. Antrim

Donald Og
of Tralee   =
1303   Mac Finnen
| of Kerry
Cormac Mor

Donald Og   OWENS

Taidg   Mac FLONNEEN
|
Donald   O'FINAN
|
Tadhg   FANNIN
Liath
1505
|
Corbmac
Laidhreach
|
Donald
|
=
|
Mac Carthy
of Muskerry
|
Mac DONAGH
O'MEEHAN
Mac DAVID
DENNIS
O'MEEGAN
WHELPY

The following families are said to
derive their ancestry from
EOGHAN MOR (page 12):

Mac ARTHUR, Mac CARTER, O'CREMIN,
DRENNAN, Mac ELLIGOTT, FOGARTY,
HEIR, KERWICK, KIRBY, O'MECAN,
TANGNEY, HALLIGAN, O'HOOLY, O'CANTY,
O'MEARGAIN, O'GLAMHIN, O'BERAIN,
O'FINELLY, BARRON, BARNES,
BARRINGTON.

Donnchadh   =   Dermot
an Drumin
| Kenyon |
Mac Donald | =
| Florence Mac
=   Donogh
|
Drum
Drummond

Descendants of CAS brother of Natfraoich
From page 13

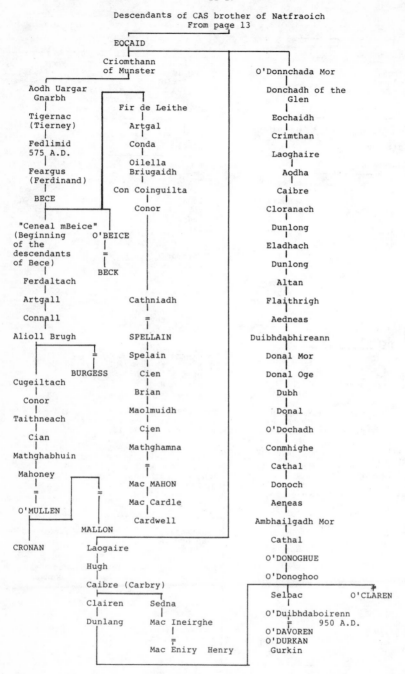

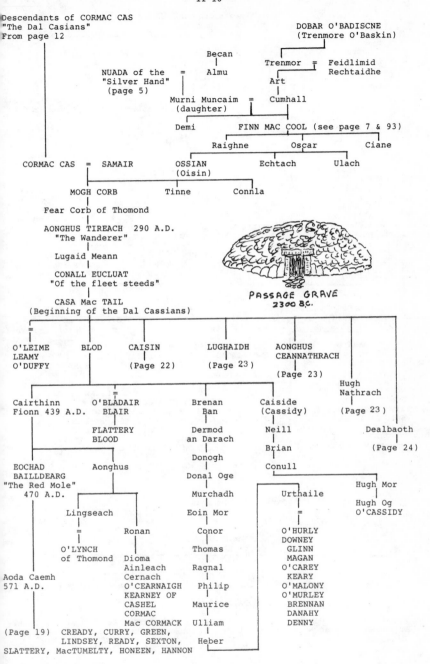

Descendants of CORMAC CAS
"The Dal Casians"
From page 12

DOBAR O'BADISCNE
(Trenmore O'Baskin)

Becan

NUADA of the
"Silver Hand"
(page 5)

Almu

Trenmor = Feidlimid
Rechtaidhe

Art

Murni Muncaim = Cumhall
(daughter)

Demi   FINN MAC COOL (see page 7 & 93)

Raighne   Oscar   Ciane

CORMAC CAS = SAMAIR   OSSIAN   Echtach   Ulach
                              (Oisin)

MOGH CORB   Tinne   Connla

Fear Corb of Thomond

AONGHUS TIREACH   290 A.D.
"The Wanderer"

Lugaid Meann

CONALL EUCLUAT
"Of the fleet steeds"

CASA Mac TAIL
(Beginning of the Dal Cassians)

PASSAGE GRAVE
2300 B.C.

O'LEIME   BLOD   CAISIN   LUGHAIDH   AONGHUS
LEAMY   CEANNATHRACH
O'DUFFY   (Page 22)   (Page 23)
                                                                 (Page 23)
                                                                              Hugh
                                                                              Nathrach

Cairthinn   O'BLADAIR   Brenan   Caiside   (Page 23)
Fionn 439 A.D.   BLAIR   Ban   (Cassidy)
                                                                              Dealbaoth
                 FLATTERY   Dermod   Neill
                 BLOOD   an Darach   (Page 24)
                                                   Brian
                                   Donogh
EOCHAD   Aonghus   Conull
BAILLDEARG   Donal Oge
"The Red Mole"   Hugh Mor
470 A.D.   Murchadh   Urthaile
                                                                             Hugh Og
          Lingseach   Eoin Mor   O'CASSIDY

              =   Ronan   Conor   O'HURLY
                                                     DOWNEY
          O'LYNCH   Thomas   GLINN
          of Thomond Dioma   MAGAN
                      Ainleach   Ragnal   O'CAREY
Aoda Caemh   Cernach   KEARY
571 A.D.   O'CEARNAIGH   Philip   O'MALONY
                      KEARNEY OF   O'MURLEY
                      CASHEL   BRENNAN
                      CORMAC   Maurice   DANAHY
                      Mac CORMACK Ulliam   DENNY
(Page 19) CREADY, CURRY, GREEN,
          LINDSEY, READY, SEXTON, Heber
SLATTERY, MacTUMELTY, HONEEN, HANNON

Descendants of AODHA CAEMH
From page 18

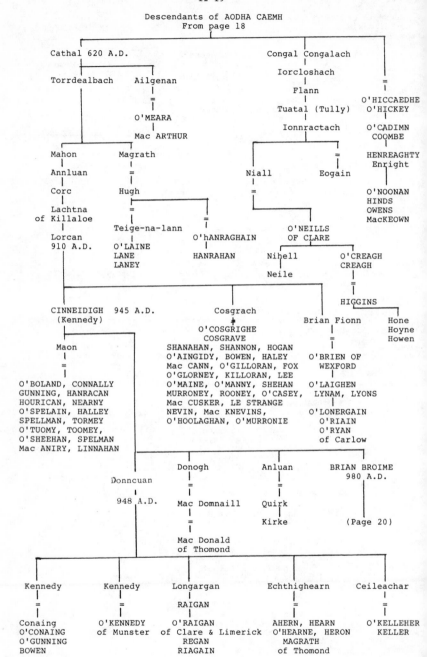

Cathal 620 A.D.

Torrdealbach   Ailgenan
                    =
                O'MEARA
                Mac ARTHUR

Mahon   Magrath
  |
Annluan   =
  |
Corc   Hugh
  |
Lachtna
of Killaloe
  |
Lorcan   Teige-na-lann   O'hANRAGHAIN
910 A.D.   O'LAINE |
             LANE   HANRAHAN
             LANEY

CINNEIDIGH   945 A.D.   Cosgrach
(Kennedy)   O'COSGRIGHE
                               COSGRAVE
Maon   SHANAHAN, SHANNON, HOGAN
  | O'AINGIDY, BOWEN, HALEY
  =   Mac CANN, O'GILLORAN, FOX
                               O'GLORNEY, KILLORAN, LEE
O'BOLAND, CONNALLY   O'MAINE, O'MANNY, SHEHAN
GUNNING, HANRACAN   MURRONEY, ROONEY, O'CASEY,
HOURICAN, NEARNY   Mac CUSKER, LE STRANGE
O'SPELAIN, HALLEY   NEVIN, Mac KNEVINS,
SPELLMAN, TORMEY   O'HOOLAGHAN, O'MURRONIE
O'TUOMY, TOOMEY,
O'SHEEHAN, SPELMAN
Mac ANIRY, LINNAHAN

Congal Congalach
     |
Iorcloshach
     |
  Flann
     |
Tuatal (Tully)   O'HICCAEDHE
     | O'HICKEY
Ionnractach   O'CADIMN
     | COOMBE
     =
Niall   Eogain   HENREAGHTY
  | Enright
  =
O'NEILLS   O'NOONAN
OF CLARE   HINDS
                  OWENS
Nihell   O'CREAGH MacKEOWN
  | CREAGH
Neile   =
         HIGGINS

         Brian Fionn   Hone
            | Hoyne
            =   Howen
         O'BRIEN OF
         WEXFORD
         O'LAIGHEN
         LYNAM, LYONS
         O'LONERGAIN
         O'RIAIN
         O'RYAN
         of Carlow

Donncuan   Donogh   Anluan   BRIAN BROIME
   | =   =   980 A.D.
948 A.D.   Mac Domnaill Quirk
                =   Kirke
             Mac Donald   (Page 20)
             of Thomond

Kennedy   Kennedy   Longargan   Echthighearn   Ceileachar
   =   =   RAIGAN   =   =
Conaing   O'KENNEDY   O'RAIGAN   AHERN, HEARN   O'KELLEHER
O'CONAING   of Munster   of Clare & Limerick O'HEARNE, HERON KELLER
O'GUNNING   REGAN   MAGRATH
BOWEN   RIAGAIN   of Thomond

Descendants of BRIAN BROIME
From page 19

Mac FLANN was the father of Maelmora and GORMFLATH, a dauther,
who was married successively to Olaf "The Dane," King Malachy
and lastly to BRIAN BROIME.

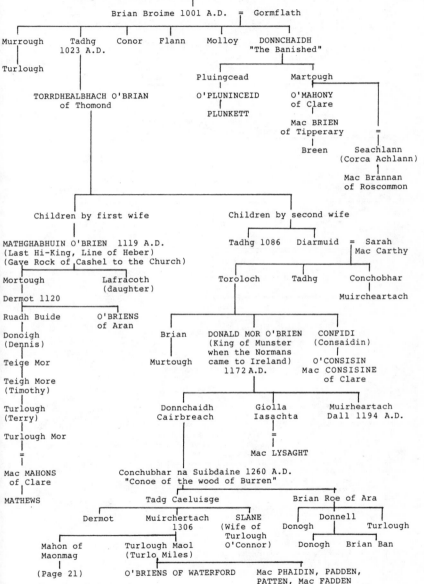

Brian Broime 1001 A.D. = Gormflath

Murrough   Tadhg   Conor   Flann   Molloy   DONNCHAIDH
           1023 A.D.   "The Banished"

Turlough

                                   Pluingcead   Martough
           TORRDHEALBHACH O'BRIAN O'PLUNINCEID   O'MAHONY
                of Thomond   of Clare
                                   PLUNKETT
                                                     Mac BRIEN
                                                   of Tipperary   =

                                                       Breen   Seachlann
                                                              (Corca Achlann)

                                                              Mac Brannan
                                                             of Roscommon

Children by first wife   Children by second wife

MATHGHABHUIN O'BRIEN 1119 A.D.   Tadhg 1086   Diarmuid = Sarah
(Last Hi-King, Line of Heber)   Mac Carthy
(Gave Rock of Cashel to the Church)

Mortough   Lafracoth   Toroloch   Tadhg   Conchobhar
                  (daughter)
Dermot 1120   Muircheartach

Ruadh Buide   O'BRIENS
                  of Aran   Brian   DONALD MOR O'BRIEN   CONFIDI
Donoigh   (King of Munster   (Consaidin)
(Dennis)   when the Normans
                                Murtough came to Ireland)   O'CONSISIN
Teige Mor   1172 A.D.   Mac CONSISINE
                                                              of Clare
Teigh More
(Timothy)   Donnchaidh   Giolla   Muirheartach
                                Cairbreach   Iasachta   Dall 1194 A.D.
Turlough
(Terry)   =

Turlough Mor   Mac LYSAGHT

    =   Conchubhar na Suibdaine 1260 A.D.
                       "Conoe of the wood of Burren"
Mac MAHONS
of Clare   Tadg Caeluisge   Brian Roe of Ara

MATHEWS   Dermot   Muirchertach   SLANE   Donnell
                        1306   (Wife of   Donogh   Turlough
                                       Turlough
Mahon of   Turlough Maol   O'Connor)   Donogh   Brian Ban
Maonmag   (Turlo Miles)

(Page 21)   O'BRIENS OF WATERFORD   Mac PHAIDIN, PADDEN,
                                       PATTEN, Mac FADDEN

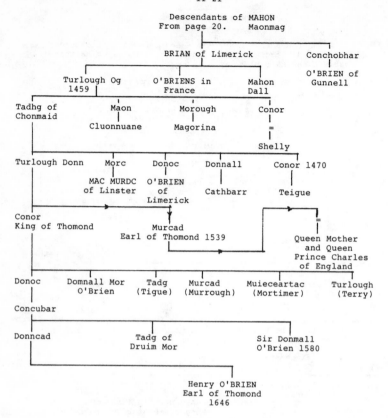

Descendants of MAHON
From page 20.   Maonmag

BRIAN of Limerick   Conchobhar

                                     O'BRIEN of
                                     Gunnell

Turlough Og   O'BRIENS in   Mahon
   1459   France   Dall

Tadhg of   Maon   Morough   Conor
Chonmaid
           Cluonnuane   Magorina
                                          =

                                        Shelly

Turlough Donn   Morc   Donoc   Donnall   Conor 1470

              MAC MURDC O'BRIEN   Teigue
              of Linster of   Cathbarr
                         Limerick

Conor   Murcad
King of Thomond   Earl of Thomond 1539
                                            Queen Mother
                                            and Queen
                                            Prince Charles
                                            of England

Donoc   Domnall Mor   Tadg   Murcad   Muieceartac   Turlough
          O'Brien   (Tigue) (Murrough) (Mortimer)   (Terry)

Concubar

Donncad   Tadg of   Sir Donmall
                   Druim Mor   O'Brien 1580

                   Henry O'BRIEN
                   Earl of Thomond
                   1646

The following families are said to descend from
CORMAC CASS
(page 18)

The branching from the descendants of this personage have not yet been
discovered. Early family names are usually derived from the personal
name of an ancestor. In later times, these Irish names were translated
and transliterated into English usually as a concession to retaining
family property or rights. In some cases, Irish families assumed English
or Norman names. Added to these changes were mispelling of surnames or
more correctly, the spelling of them as the English clerks learned to
spell in their individual schools. Uniform spelling in English did not
come into being until a rather late date. Further problems occured when
O' or Mac was dropped by a family, later to be assumed in reverse order.
Finally, distruction of records have left some families with no
documentation of their past, only the remnants of a memory of their
heritage.

Mac BRIDE, BRODIE, BROLLY, BRYANT, CANNING, O'COLLOPY, O'CONCANNON,
CONING, CURNEEN, Mac CURTIN, O'DIFF, O'DUHIG, O'FINNELLAN, O'HALLORAN,
HINNIGAN, KENNYON, KILBRIDE, Mac BRIDE, O'NOLAN, O'NUNAN, RIDER, RYDER,
O'DUFFY, DARRICK, CUDAHY.

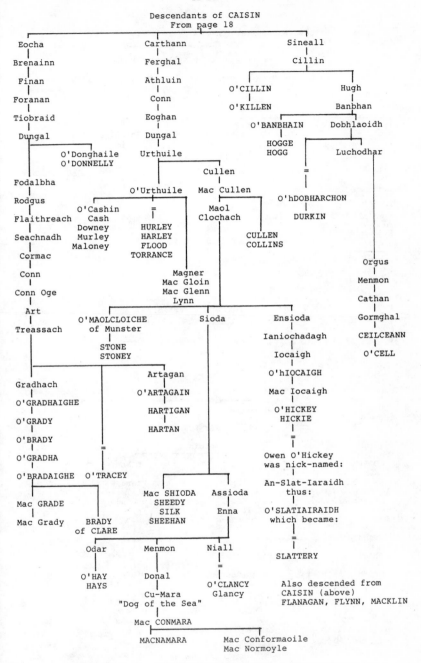

SEE PAGE II-23 for DESCENDANTS OF LUGHAIDH & HUGH NATHRACH

Descendants of LUGHAIDH (page 18)

DOBHARCAN = O'Durkan, DURKIN. LIOHDA = O'LIDDY of Clare
O'Davoran, O'Duhig

Descendants of HUGH NATHRACH (Page 18)

Mac COUGHLIN, DAY, O'HEA, HAY, O'HEADY, and HUGHES

Descendants of AONGHUS CEANNATHRACH
from page 18

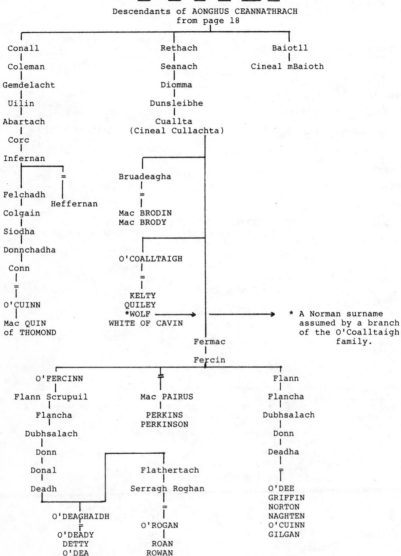

Conall	Rethach	Baiotll
Coleman	Seanach	Cineal mBaioth
Gemdelacht	Diomma	
Uilin	Dunsleibhe	
Abartach	Cuallta	
Corc	(Cineal Cullachta)	
Infernan		

```
Felchadh        =
Colgain      Heffernan
Siodha
Donnchadha
Conn

O'CUINN
Mac QUIN
of THOMOND
```

```
Bruadeagha
    =
Mac BRODIN
Mac BRODY

O'COALLTAIGH
    =
KELTY
QUILEY
*WOLF ————→
WHITE OF CAVIN
```

→ * A Norman surname
assumed by a branch
of the O'Coalltaigh
family.

Fermac
Fercin

O'FERCINN	Mac PAIRUS	Flann
Flann Scrupuil	PERKINS	Flancha
Flancha	PERKINSON	Dubhsalach
Dubhsalach		Donn
Donn		Deadha
Donal	Flathertach	
Deadh	Serragh Roghan	O'DEE
	=	GRIFFIN
O'DEAGHAIDH	O'ROGAN	NORTON
O'DEADY		NAGHTEN
DETTY	ROAN	O'CUINN
O'DEA	ROWAN	GILGAN
DAY		

Descendants of DEALBAOTH
From page 18

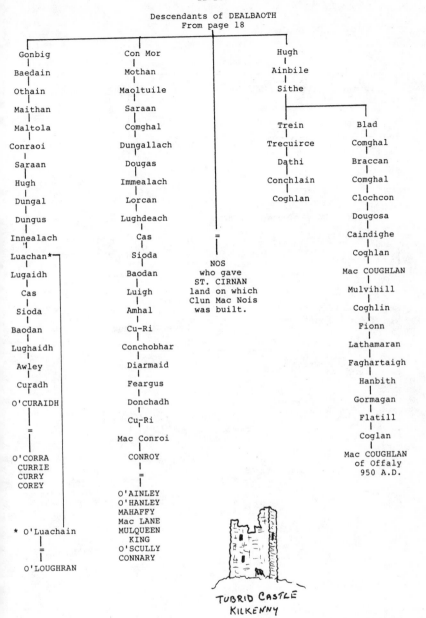

Gonbig	Con Mor	Hugh	
Baedain	Mothan	Ainbile	
Othain	Maoltuile	Sithe	
Maithan	Saraan		
Maltola	Comghal	Trein	Blad
Conraoi	Dungallach	Trecuirce	Comghal
Saraan	Dougas	Dathi	Braccan
Hugh	Immealach	Conchlain	Comghal
Dungal	Lorcan	Coghlan	Clochcon
Dungus	Lughdeach		Dougosa
Innealach	Cas		Caindighe
Luachan*	Sioda	=	Coghlan
Lugaidh	Baodan	NOS	Mac COUGHLAN
Cas	Luigh	who gave	Mulvihill
Sioda	Amhal	ST. CIRNAN	Coghlin
Baodan	Cu-Ri	land on which	Fionn
Lughaidh	Conchobhar	Clun Mac Nois	Lathamaran
Awley	Diarmaid	was built.	Faghartaigh
Curadh	Feargus		Hanbith
O'CURAIDH	Donchadh		Gormagan
	Cu-Ri		Flatill
=	Mac Conroi		Coglan
O'CORRA	CONROY		Mac COUGHLAN
CURRIE			of Offaly
CURRY	=		950 A.D.
COREY	O'AINLEY		
	O'HANLEY		
	MAHAFFY		
	Mac LANE		
	MULQUEEN		
* O'Luachain	KING		
=	O'SCULLY		
O'LOUGHRAN	CONNARY		

TUBRID CASTLE
KILKENNY

Descendants of CIANN
From page 12.

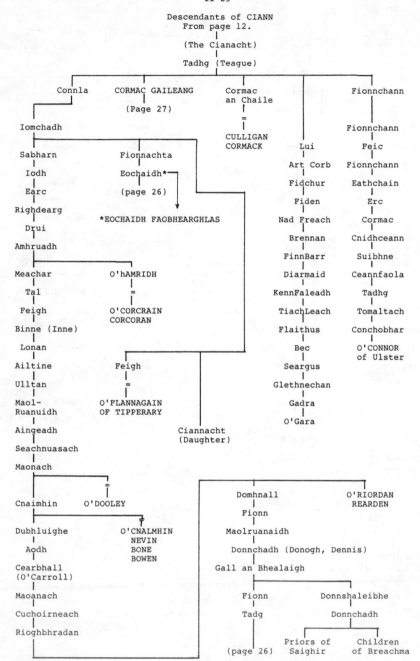

(The Cianacht)

Tadhg (Teague)

Connla	CORMAC GAILEANG	Cormac an Chaile	Fionnchann
	(Page 27)	=	
		CULLIGAN CORMACK	

Iomchadh

Sabharn — Fionnachta

Iodh

Earc

Righdearg

Drui

Amhruadh

Meachar — O'hAMRIDH
| | =
Tal | O'CORCRAIN CORCORAN
Feigh

Binne (Inne)

Lonan

Ailtine — Feigh
| | =
Ulltan | O'FLANNAGAIN OF TIPPERARY

Maol-Ruanuidh

Aingeadh

Seachnuasach

Maonach

Eochaidh*
(page 26)

*EOCHAIDH FAOBHEARGHLAS

Ciannacht
(Daughter)

Lui

Art Corb — Fionnchann

Fidchur — Feic

Fiden — Fionnchann

Nad Freach — Eathchain

Brennan — Erc

FinnBarr — Cormac

Diarmaid — Cnidhceann

KennFaleadh — Suibhne

TiachLeach — Ceannfaola

Flaithus — Tadhg

Bec — Tomaltach

Seargus — Conchobhar

Glethnechan — O'CONNOR of Ulster

Gadra

O'Gara

Cnaimhin — O'DOOLEY
| =
Dubhluighe | O'CNALMHIN NEVIN BONE BOWEN
Aodh

Cearbhall (O'Carroll)

Maoanach

Cuchoirneach

Rioghbhradan

Domhnall — O'RIORDAN REARDEN

Fionn

Maolruanaidh

Donnchadh (Donogh, Dennis)

Gall an Bhealaigh

| |
Fionn — Donnshaleibhe

Tadg — Donnchadh

(page 26)

Priors of Saighir — Children of Breachma

Descendants of TADG
From page 25.

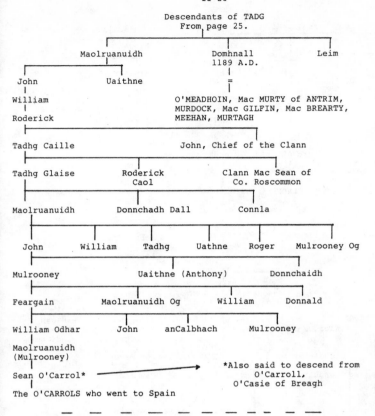

```
                    Maolruanuidh          Domhnall              Leim
                                          1189 A.D.
    John              Uaithne                 =
                                    O'MEADHOIN, Mac MURTY of ANTRIM,
  William                           MURDOCK, Mac GILFIN, Mac BREARTY,
                                    MEEHAN, MURTAGH
  Roderick

  Tadhg Caille                        John, Chief of the Clann

  Tadhg Glaise        Roderick          Clann Mac Sean of
                        Caol               Co. Roscommon

  Maolruanuidh        Donnchadh Dall       Connla

    John      William     Tadhg     Uathne     Roger    Mulrooney Og

  Mulrooney         Uaithne (Anthony)         Donnchaidh

  Feargain      Maolruanuidh Og      William      Donnald

  William Odhar     John     anCalbhach     Mulrooney

  Maolruanuidh
  (Mulrooney)
                                    *Also said to descend from
  Sean O'Carrol*                              O'Carroll,
                                          O'Casie of Breagh
  The O'CARROLS who went to Spain
```

— — — — — — — — — —

Descendants of EOCHAIDH
From page 25

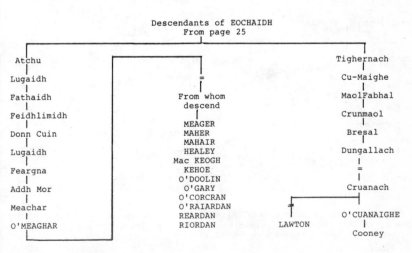

```
  Atchu                                          Tighernach

  Lugaidh                                         Cu-Maighe

  Fathaidh              =                         MaolFabhal

  Feidhlimidh      From whom                      Crunmaol
                   descend
  Donn Cuin                                        Bresal
                   MEAGER
  Lugaidh          MAHER                          Dungallach
                   MAHAIR
  Feargna          HEALEY                             =
                   Mac KEOGH
  Addh Mor          KEHOE                         Cruanach
                   O'DOOLIN
  Meachar           O'GARY
                   O'CORCRAN
  O'MEAGHAR         O'RAIARDAN
                   REARDAN          LAWTON      O'CUANAIGHE
                   RIORDAN
                                                  Cooney
```

Descendants of CORMAC GAILEANG
From page 25

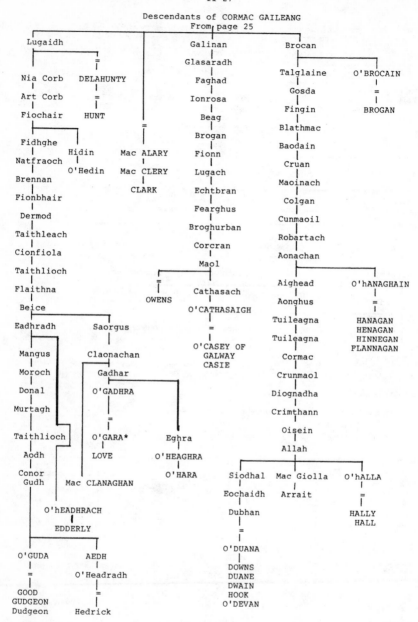

Lugaidh
=
Nia Corb   DELAHUNTY
Art Corb   =
Fiochair   HUNT

Fidhghe
Hidin   Mac ALARY
Natfraoch   O'Hedin   Mac CLERY
Brennan   CLARK
Fionbhair
Dermod
Taithleach
Cionfiola
Taithlioch
Flaithna
Beice

Eadhradh   Saorgus
Mangus
Moroch   Claonachan
Donal   Gadhar
Murtagh   O'GADHRA
Taithlioch   =
Aodh   O'GARA*
Conor   LOVE
Gudh   Mac CLANAGHAN

O'hEADHRACH
EDDERLY

O'GUDA   AEDH
=   O'Headradh
GOOD   =
GUDGEON   Hedrick
Dudgeon

Eghra
O'HEAGHRA
O'HARA

Galinan
Glasaradh
Faghad
Ionrosa
Beag
Brogan
Fionn
Lugach
Echtbran
Fearghus
Broghurban
Corcran
Maol
=
OWENS   Cathasach
O'CATHASAIGH
=
O'CASEY OF
GALWAY
CASIE

Brocan
Talglaine   O'BROCAIN
Gosda   =
Fingin   BROGAN
Blathmac
Baodain
Cruan
Maoinach
Colgan
Cunmaoil
Robartach
Aonachan
Aighead   O'hANAGHAIN
Aonghus   =
Tuileagna   HANAGAN
Tuileagna   HENAGAN
Cormac   HINNEGAN
Crunmaol   FLANNAGAN
Diognadha
Crimthann
Oisein
Allah

Siodhal   Mac Giolla   O'hALLA
Eochaidh   Arrait   =
Dubhan   HALLY
=   HALL
O'DUANA
DOWNS
DUANE
DWAIN
HOOK
O'DEVAN

* Sixteen generations after the beginning of the O'Gara surname, Fearghal
O'Gara, in Jan. 1632, commissiond the Four Masters to write a history of
Ireland which they completed in August 1636.

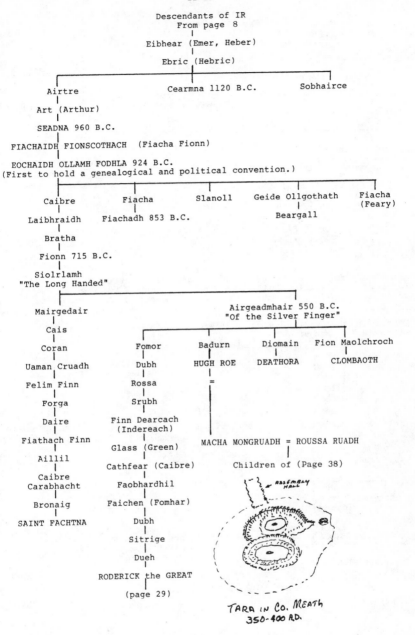

Descendants of IR
From page 8

Eibhear (Emer, Heber)

Ebric (Hebric)

Airtre   Cearmna 1120 B.C.   Sobhairce

Art (Arthur)

SEADNA 960 B.C.

FIACHAIDH FIONSCOTHACH (Fiacha Fionn)

EOCHAIDH OLLAMH FODHLA 924 B.C.
(First to hold a genealogical and political convention.)

Caibre   Fiacha   Slanoll   Geide Ollgothath   Fiacha (Feary)

Laibhraidh   Fiachadh 853 B.C.   Beargall

Bratha

Fionn 715 B.C.

Siolrlamh
"The Long Handed"

Mairgedair   Airgeadmhair 550 B.C.
             "Of the Silver Finger"

Cais

Coran   Fomor   Badurn   Diomain   Fion Maolchroch

Uaman Cruadh   Dubh   HUGH ROE   DEATHORA   CLOMBAOTH

Felim Finn   Rossa   =

Forga   Srubh

Daire   Finn Dearcach
           (Indereach)

Fiathach Finn   MACHA MONGRUADH = ROUSSA RUADH

Aillil   Glass (Green)

Caibre   Cathfear (Caibre)   Children of (Page 38)
Carabhacht

Bronaig   Faobhardhil

SAINT FACHTNA   Faichen (Fomhar)

Dubh

Sitrige

Dueh

RODERICK the GREAT

(page 29)

TARA IN Co. MEATH
350-400 A.D.

Descendants of RODERIC THE GREAT
Called "Clann Rory"
From page 28

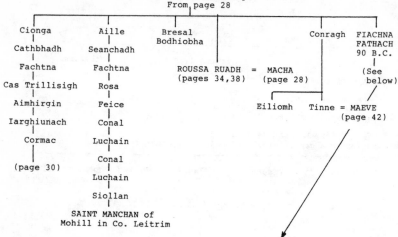

Cionga	Aille	Bresal Bodhiobha		Conragh	FIACHNA FATHACH 90 B.C.
Cathbhadh	Seanchadh				
Fachtna	Fachtna	ROUSSA RUADH (pages 34,38)	= MACHA (page 28)		(See below)
Cas Trillisigh	Rosa				
Aimhirgin	Feice		Eiliomh	Tinne = MAEVE (page 42)	
Iarghiunach	Conal				
Cormac	Luchain				
(page 30)	Conal				
	Luchain				
	Siollan				
	SAINT MANCHAN of Mohill in Co. Leitrim				

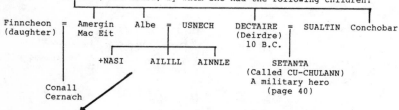

NESSA was a famous warrior queen of the late pre-Christian era.
Her father was EOCHAIDH SABUIDE. She had two husbands according to
tradition. CATHBAD, the druid, by whom she had the following children:

Finncheon (daughter)	=	Amergin Mac Eit	Albe = USNECH	DECTAIRE (Deirdre) 10 B.C.	= SUALTIN	Conchobar
			+NASI AILILL AINNLE	SETANTA (Called CU-CHULANN) A military hero (page 40)		
		Conall Cernach				

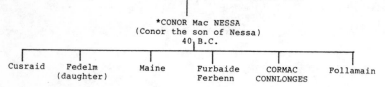

And FIACHA FATHACH (above). The child of this match was:

*CONOR Mac NESSA
(Conor the son of Nessa)
40 B.C.

Cusraid	Fedelm (daughter)	Maine	Furbaide Ferbenn	CORMAC CONNLONGES	Follamain

* Conor forbade the poets to use the old poetic language of their cast.
He ruled that education should be available to all in his kingdom.

Conor was also wedded to Maeve above.

Descendants of CORMAC
From page 29

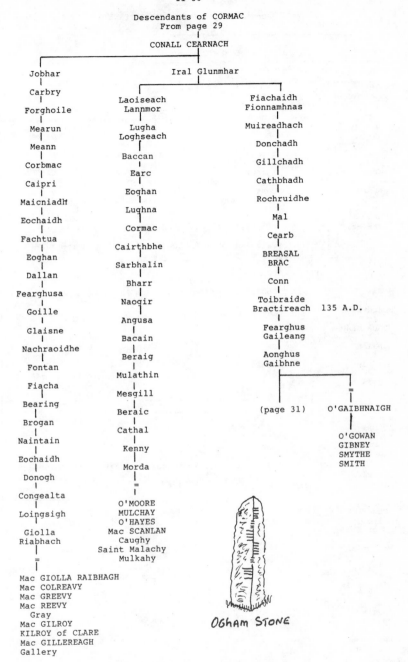

CONALL CEARNACH

Iral Glunmhar

Jobhar

Carbry

Forghoile

Mearun

Meann

Corbmac

Caipri

Maicniadh

Eochaidh

Fachtua

Eoghan

Dallan

Fearghusa

Goille

Glaisne

Nachraoidhe

Fontan

Fiacha

Bearing

Brogan

Naintain

Eochaidh

Donogh

Congealta

Loingsigh

Giolla
Riabhach
=

Mac GIOLLA RAIBHAGH
Mac COLREAVY
Mac GREEVY
Mac REEVY
 Gray
Mac GILROY
KILROY of CLARE
Mac GILLEREAGH
Gallery

Laoiseach
Lannmor

Lugha
Loghseach

Baccan

Earc

Eoghan

Lughna

Cormac

Cairthbhe

Sarbhalin

Bharr

Naogir

Angusa

Bacain

Beraig

Mulathin

Mesgill

Beraic

Cathal

Kenny

Morda
=

O'MOORE
MULCHAY
O'HAYES
Mac SCANLAN
Caughy
Saint Malachy
Mulkahy

Fiachaidh
Fionnamhnas

Muireadhach

Donchadh

Gillchadh

Cathbhadh

Rochruidhe

Mal

Cearb

BREASAL
BRAC

Conn

Toibraide
Bractireach   135 A.D.

Fearghus
Gaileang

Aonghus
Gaibhne

(page 31)   O'GAIBHNAIGH

O'GOWAN
GIBNEY
SMYTHE
SMITH

OGHAM STONE

Descendants of AONGHUS GAIBHNE
From page 30

FIACH ARUIDHE (Beginning of the Dial nAruidhe)

Sodhain   Cas

Iomchadh   Felim   Fiedilimidh

Degill   Fionchu   Iomchadh

Cas   Ros   Roussa 365 A.D.   Treana

Conall   Luchta   Lugaidh   Curnan

Flann Abrad   Amergin   EOCHAIDH CHOBNA   St. CARROLL

Maoinin   Ceneidh   Colman   (Last king,
      (Page   ST. LAIRIN   race of Ir)
    =   33)   Maoldubh

O'Madinein   Fionngal   Cronn   Creamthann
MANNING   Bhadhraoi

         Sealbhach   Caolbhadh   Eanine

Eocha   SELBY   Dunechar   Forga

Nar   Dobhalen   =   Brin

Reachtach   Gussan   O'Loingsidh   Eachach

NUADA DEARG   Labhras   O'LYNCH of   Sedna
                        Ulster   (page 32)
Ughaine   Sarcall   SAINT COMHGALL

Maighlen   Scoileach   (Of the monestary of
                          Bangor, Co. Down.)
Giolla De   O'Scoilaigh   550 A.D.
                         His school was
=   said to have
Mac Giollade   SCALLY   Madagan   numbered 3,000
GILDEA   SCELLY   students and staff.
KILDEA   SKELLY   =   =
           SCULLY   O'Madadhgain   O'Sheehan
Eachtigherna   SCALLAN   Finnagain
                  MADIGAN   of
Dermaid   Louth

=

Conor

Shane   Dubhthaig

Mac an Bhaird   Talain

=   ST. COMAN   ST. ATRACHTA

O'BAIRDAIN   of Ard Leathan
BRADE
BARDON
BARTEN
BURDON
VERDON
WARDEN
Mac WARD

Descendants of CAOLBHADH
From page 31

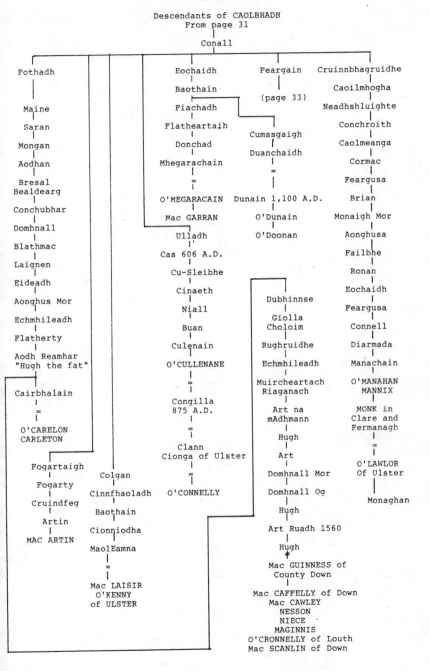

Conall

Fothadh
|
Maine
|
Saran
|
Mongan
|
Aodhan
|
Bresal
Bealdearg
|
Conchubhar
|
Domhnall
|
Blathmac
|
Laignen
|
Eideadh
|
Aonghus Mor
|
Echmhileadh
|
Flatherty
|
Aodh Reamhar
"Hugh the fat"
|
Cairbhalain
|
=
|
O'CARELON
CARLETON
|
Fogartaigh
|
Fogarty
|
Cruindfeg
|
Artin
|
MAC ARTIN

Colgan
|
Cinnfhaoladh
|
Baothain
|
Cionniodha
|
MaolEamna
|
=
|
Mac LAISIR
O'KENNY
of ULSTER

Eochaidh
|
Baothain
|
Fiachadh
|
Flatheartaih
|
Donchad
|
Mhegarachain
|
=
|
O'MEGARACAIN
|
Mac GARRAN
|
Ulladh
|
Cas 606 A.D.
|
Cu-Sleibhe
|
Cinaeth
|
Niall
|
Buan
|
Culenain
|
O'CULLENANE
|
=
|
Congilla
875 A.D.
|
=
|
Clann
Cionga of Ulster
|
=
|
O'CONNELLY

Feargain
|
(page 33)
|
Cumssgaigh
|
Duanchaidh
|
=
|
Dunain 1,100 A.D.
|
O'Dunain
|
O'Doonan

Dubhinnse
|
Giolla
Choloim
|
Rughruidhe
|
Echmhileadh
|
Muircheartach
Riaganach
|
Art na
mAdhmann
|
Hugh
|
Art
|
Domhnall Mor
|
Domhnall Og
|
Hugh
|
Art Ruadh 1560
|
Hugh
+
Mac GUINNESS of
County Down

Mac CAFFELLY of Down
Mac CAWLEY
NESSON
NIECE
MAGINNIS
O'CRONNELLY of Louth
Mac SCANLIN of Down

Cruinnbhagruidhe
|
Caoilmhogha
|
Neadhshluighte
|
Conchroith
|
Caolmeanga
|
Cormac
|
Feargusa
|
Brian
|
Monaigh Mor
|
Aonghusa
|
Failbhe
|
Ronan
|
Eochaidh
|
Feargusa
|
Connell
|
Diarmada
|
Manachain
|
O'MANAHAN
MANNIX
|
MONK in
Clare and
Fermanagh
|
=
|
O'LAWLOR
Of Ulster
|
Monaghan

Descendants of FEARGAIN
From page 32
|
Mongan

Descendants of CAS   Fogartach
From page 31   Cruinneith
|
Feidlime   Artan
|
Iomchadha   Cudicon
|
Rosa
|
Lughdheach
|
Cobnthaigh   Mac CARTAN
| of Down
Eochaidh
|
Cruinnbhardari   Crum na cruach
|
Caoilbhidh
|
Conla   CROOKE
| CROKE
Eochaidh
|
Baoidhain
|
Fachina   Concruach
|
Eochaidh   Eochaidh
Erlaithe
|
Congla   Serran
|
Cinnfhaoilidh   Bugmaille
|
Baoidhain   Ciannait
|
Cumusgaigh   Gillcolum
|
Duanchaidh   Donoch
|
Sgannlain   Sean
|
Fiachra   Thomas
|
Cinnaodha   Mac THOMAS
| THOM
Mongain   TOMHAIS
| TOMKINS
Connla
|
Conchubhair
|
DUNAIN   Thomas oge
From whom the family
O'Doonan   Serran
|
Giollapadriac
|
Giollapadriac
|
=
|
KILLPATRICK
O'GILCOLUIM
GILCOM
COLUM

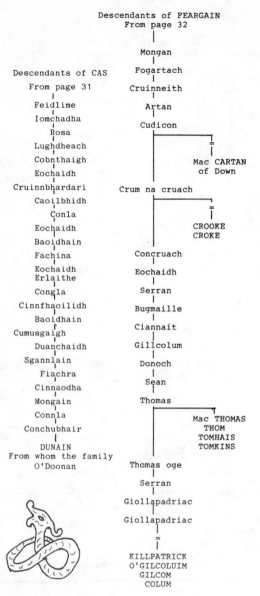

Descendants of ROUSSA RUADH
From page 29

The descendants of Roussa Ruadh occupy a very important place in Irish history and tradition. The most important were those of wives ROIGH AND MACHA "The Brown Head." The children of ROIGH are the first to be presented.

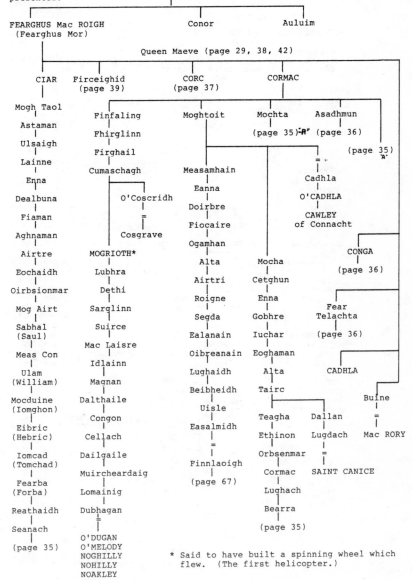

FEARGHUS Mac ROIGH   Conor   Auluim
(Fearghus Mor)

Queen Maeve (page 29, 38, 42)

CIAR   Firceighid   CORC   CORMAC
        (page 39)   (page 37)

Mogh Taol   Moghtoit   Mochta   Asadhmun
Astaman   Finfaling   (page 35):A" (page 36)
Ulsaigh   Fhirglinn   (page 35)
Lainne   Firghail   'A'
Enna   Cumaschagh   Measamhain
Dealbuna   O'Coscridh Eanna   Cadhla
Fiaman   =   Doirbre   O'CADHLA
Aghnaman   Cosgrave   Fiocaire   CAWLEY
Airtre   MOGRIOTH*   Ogamhan   of Connacht
Eochaidh Lubhra   Alta   Mocha   CONGA
Oirbsionmar Dethi   Airtri Cetghun   (page 36)
Mog Airt Sarqlinn   Roigne Enna
Sabhal   Suirce   Segda   Gobhre   Fear
(Saul)   Mac Laisre   Ealanain Iuchar   Telachta
Meas Con Idlainn   Oibreanain Eoghaman (page 36)
Ulam   Magnan   Lughaidh Alta
(William) Dalthaile   Beibheidh Tairc   CADHLA
Mocduine Congon   Uisle   Buine
(Iomghon) Cellach   Easalmidh Teagha Dallan   =
Eibric   Dailgaile   =   Ethinon Lugdach Mac RORY
(Hebric) Muircheardaig   Finnlaoigh Orbsenmar =
Iomcad   Lomainig   (page 67) Cormac   SAINT CANICE
(Tomchad) Dubhagan   Luqhach
Fearba   =   Bearra
(Forba)   O'DUGAN
Reathaidh O'MELODY   (page 35)
Seanach   NOGHILLY
          NOHILLY   * Said to have built a spinning wheel which
(page 35) NOAKLEY   flew. (The first helicopter.)

Descendants of SEANACH
From page 34
|
  Duarthacht
|
  Aodh
|
Maol Tuile
|
Reachtabhracht   O'MAOLTUILE
|
  Cobtach   TULLY
| FLOOD
  Coleman   Mac ATILLA of Cavin
|
Flanfeora
|
Maolseachlainn
Fionn
|
Conchubhar
|
Diarmaid
|
Cu-Luachra
|
Rugride
|
Tadg
|
Cathal   Ficheallach
|
Conchubhar   Narda   Marne
| O'DALY
Malbreathaigh   =   of
| Conamara
  Corc   TORMY   =
O'CONNOR   RUDDY
of Kerry   BARR   Duncan
         MERRYMAN Donegan
  =   GILMORE
         MOCHAN
O'LOUGHLIN MAUGHAN
of Clare   O'MORAN
| SAINT MOCHA
  =   O'CANAVAN
NESTOR   BIRNEY
|
Flaherty
of Munster
|
Arga

Descendants of BEARRA
From page 34
|
  Uisle   O'BEARR
| BERRY
  Eachdach   BURY
|
  Fornert
|
Meadhrua
|
  Dubh
|
Earcoll
|
  Earc
|
Eachdach
|
Cuscrach
|
Fionnfhear
|
Fionnlogh
|
  Onchu
|
  Neidhe

GILLIGAN   Finn
MacCUINN
O'CUINN   Fiodl
QUINN OF
LONGFORD   Mairdl
KERWIN
KERRIGAN   Croma.
SHERIDAN
O'BIRREN   Biobl
Mac BIRNEY saigl
O'BRANAGAN
BREDIN   Eolu.
MARTIN
O'KENNY (Muint
O'CIARROVAN Eoli
O'CIARAGAIN
           Maolmu
|
Muldo
|
Flan
|
Mulroo
|
Ivar-D
|
Muirch
Eardoi
|
RAGNAL
+
REYNOL
|
PRIOR

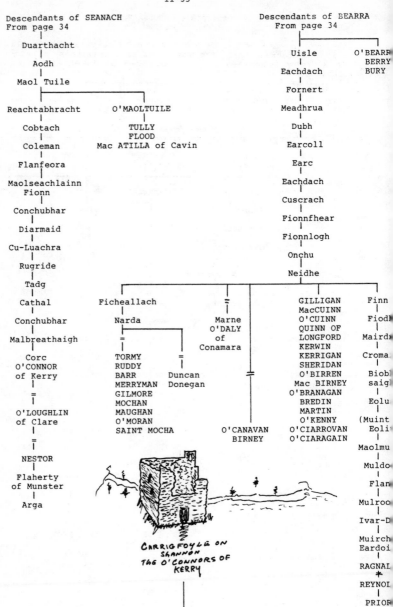

CARRIGFOYLE ON
SHANNON
THE O'CONNORS OF
KERRY

See following page for continued descendants from page 34.

Descendants of MOCHTA
From page 34
|
Calais
|
Iodanaich
|
Dailbhe
|
Fiachra
|
Oghamhain
|
Aillil
|
Cainth
|
Seadhna
|
Eitne
|
Nebsin
|
Lughaidh
|
Beadhbhda
|
Bheire
|
Uishle
|
Eachaidh
|
Finearta
|
Neatra
|
Mulrooney
|
Duabh
|
Erechthdal
|
Earc
|
Ceacht
|
Cumaschagh
|
Finbhir
|
Finnloga   Mac FINVAR
| |
Oucheon   =
| |
Neidhe   GAYNOR
|
Fionn
|
Fiodha
|
Mairdne
|
Cromain
|
Biobhsiagh
|
(page 36)

Other Descendants of CORMAC
From page 34
|
Cumasch   Carthaig
| =
Loga |
=   ST. CRUIMHTHEAR
|
SAINT IARLATH

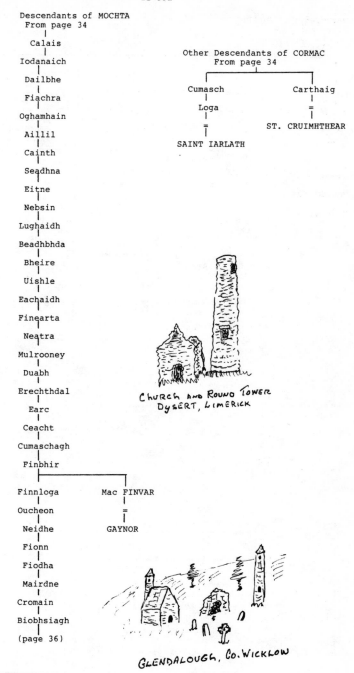

CHURCH AND ROUND TOWER
DYSERT, LIMERICK

GLENDALOUGH, CO. WICKLOW

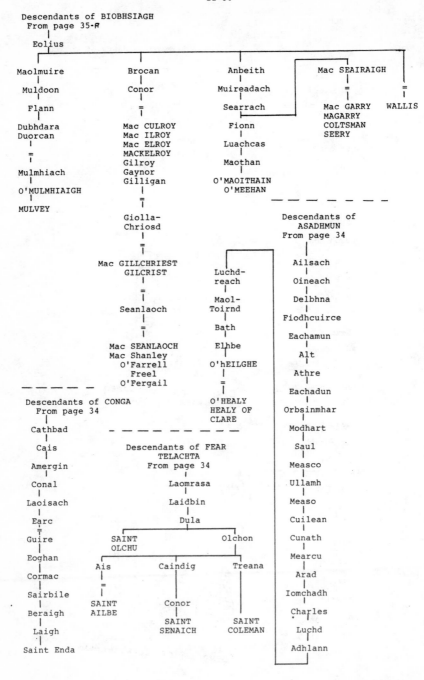

Descendants of BIOBHSIAGH
  From page 35-ₐ

Eolius

Maolmuire   Brocan   Anbeith   Mac SEAIRAIGH
   | | |
Muldoon   Conor   Muireadach   =
   | | |
Flann   =   Searrach   Mac GARRY   WALLIS
                                                   MAGARRY
Dubhdara   Mac CULROY   Fionn   COLTSMAN
Duorcan   Mac ILROY | SEERY
   | Mac ELROY   Luachcas
   =   MACKELROY |
                   Gilroy   Maothan
Mulmhiach   Gaynor |
   | Gilligan   O'MAOITHAIN
O'MULMHIAIGH | O'MEEHAN
                      |
MULVEY | Descendants of
                   Giolla-   ASADHMUN
                   Chriosd   From page 34
                      |
                      | Ailsach
                   Mac GILLCHRIEST |
                      GILCRIST   Luchd-   Oineach
                      | reach |
                      = | Delbhna
                      | Maol- |
                   Seanlaoch   Toirnd   Fiodhcuirce
                      | | |
                      =   Bath   Eachamun
                      | | |
                   Mac SEANLAOCH Elhbe   Alt
                   Mac Shanley | |
                   O'Farrell   O'hEILGHE   Athre
                   Freel | |
                   O'Fergail   =   Eachadun
                                                    |
Descendants of CONGA   O'HEALY   Orbsinmhar
  From page 34   HEALY |
                                 CLARE OF   Modhart
Cathbad   CLARE |
   | Saul
Cais   Descendants of FEAR |
   | TELACHTA   Measco
Amergin   From page 34 |
   | Laomrasa   Ullamh
Conal | |
   | Laidbin   Measo
Laoisach | |
   | Dula   Cuilean
Earc | |
   =   SAINT   Olchon   Cunath
Guire   OLCHU | |
   | | | Mearcu
Eoghan   Ais   Caindig Treana |
   | | | | Arad
Cormac   = | | |
   | | | Iomchadh
Sairbile   SAINT Conor | |
   | AILBE | | Charles
Beraigh   SAINT   SAINT |
   | SENAICH COLEMAN   Luchd
Laigh |
   | Adhlann
Saint Enda

Descendants of CORC
From page 34

```
Dathi                                          Sedna
  |                                              =
Ollaman                                       O'DRINAN
  |                                           OF CLARE
Moghruadh                                        =
  |                                           DRENNAN OF
Leathain            Aibhlt                     GALWAY
  |                   |                           =
Finanghi          Anbheith                   THORNTON OF
  |                   |                        GALWAY
Aedh Gnaoi        Aedh Agna
  |                   |
Athchuirb         Achorb      Scotch Clans
  |                   |        CONNOR OF
Nechain           Nechtain     SCOTLAND
                      |         FORBES
                  Mearchu       URQUART
Onchain    Mecon      |
  |          |      Oscar
Osgar      Earc       |                    Fraoch              
  |          |      Earc   Page          Carthann      QUIRK
Conbruil  Mesin-     |      39             |
  |       tulig    Enarc                 Lonan
Bric        |        |                     |
  |       Mesin-    Earc                  Seanan
Tail      sned       |                     |
  |         |      Meisinsalach          Labann
Amergin  Cosgrich    |
  |         |      Mesin Dunn        Brocan       O'LAPHAIN
Senaig   Nadfraoich  |                               =
  |         |      Oscar                          LAFFAN
Felene    Cas        |                            LEYDON
  |         |      Cubroc                         LIDDANE
Philim   Condeadh    |                            LIDDY
  |         |      Broc
Dubh     Deadh       |
  |         |      Tail            Cruitinfle
Maclach   Corc       |
  |         |      Amergin   MAC TAIL    Maolruana   O'CUARTH-
Reanh    Loindcoda   |          =           |         AIN
  |         |      Senach  O'AIMHEIR-    Feargus       |
Duibhruidh Bolgain   |       IGHIN          |       MAC CURTIN
  |         |      Fulen      =          Saorbreitheamh  CURTAIN
Flaherty  Baodan    |      BERGIN           =
  |         =      Dubh
Samhradain         |                     MACINTYRE
  |      SAINT    Beocall                CARPENTER
Ardga    CIARAN of  |                    FREEMAN
  =      Clonmacnois Cellach             JOINER
                     |                   JUDGE
O'ARGA            Maoldubh               MASON
O'CONNOR OF          |
CORK              Duba da
O'LOGHLEN OF      Chrioch
CLARE                =
O'ANNAIDH
HANNY, HANNA      O'FLAHERTY
O'LOUGHLEN
OF CO. CLARE
```

Children of ROUSSA RUADH *
and MACHA "The Brown Head"
From page 28

MATA MUIRISC

Eochaidh Feidlioch

| Cet | Anluan | Ferhus | Find | Cabre | Ailill | = | Maeve (page 42,29) |

Illaneinn

Nifer
Eru

(Oilill
Mor)

THE SEVEN MAINES   Sanb   Cet   Sadb = Eochu   *FINNABHAIR = FERDAID
Rond

* Finnabhair was promised as a wife
to Ferdaid should he defeat
CuChallain in combat.

Finloga

Onchon

Luachan

Finn

Mulquin

Ceagain

Dubhain

Mac DUBHAIN OF
CLARE
=
O'DUVAN
DUANE
OF CONNACHT
DOWNES
OF LIMERICK
DWANE
OF CORK
DIVANE
OF KERRY
DEVANE

Cuscridh

Fraoich

Dubhain

Machach
ⴕ
ST. CAILLEN
OF FENAGH
Co. Leitrim

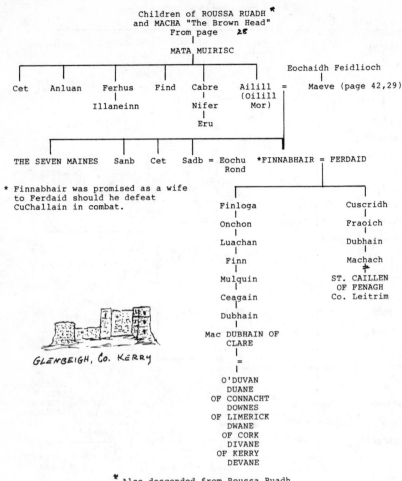

GLENBEIGH, Co. KERRY

* Also descended from Roussa Ruadh
O'Cahill of Kerry
O'Lalor
Kearn, Ward

Descendants of MAC NIADH
From page 11

```
Duach        Fatadh
  |          Canann
Gearan         |
  |            =
Connall        |
 Claen      The Scotch
  |          CANNONS
Macreithe─┐
          └─ Mac CREATH
Ailill
  |
Fergus
  |
Connad of
 Cillen
  |
Mac Con
  |
Ailill
  |
Dungalach
  |
Cobhthach
 Finn
  |
Donnchadh Mor
  |
Domhnall
  |
Mac Craith
  |
```

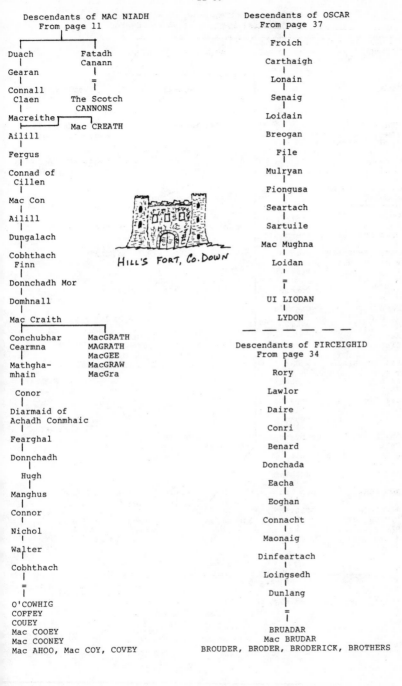

HILL'S FORT, Co. DOWN

```
Conchubhar    MacGRATH
Cearmna       MAGRATH
  |           MacGEE
Mathgha-      MacGRAW
mhain         MacGra
  |
 Conor
  |
Diarmaid of
Achadh Conmhaic
  |
Fearghal
  |
Donnchadh
  |
 Hugh
  |
Manghus
  |
Connor
  |
Nichol
  |
Walter
  |
Cobhthach
  |
  =
  |
O'COWHIG
COFFEY
COUEY
Mac COOEY
Mac COONEY
Mac AHOO, Mac COY, COVEY
```

Descendants of OSCAR
From page 37

```
Froich
  |
Carthaigh
  |
Lonain
  |
Senaig
  |
Loidain
  |
Breogan
  |
File
  |
Mulryan
  |
Fiongusa
  |
Seartach
  |
Sartuile
  |
Mac Mughna
  |
Loidan
  |
  =
  |
UI LIODAN
  |
LYDON
```

Descendants of FIRCEIGHID
From page 34

```
Rory
  |
Lawlor
  |
Daire
  |
Conri
  |
Benard
  |
Donchada
  |
Eacha
  |
Eoghan
  |
Connacht
  |
Maonaig
  |
Dinfeartach
  |
Loingsedh
  |
Dunlang
  |
  =
  |
BRUADAR
Mac BRUDAR
BROUDER, BRODER, BRODERICK, BROTHERS
```

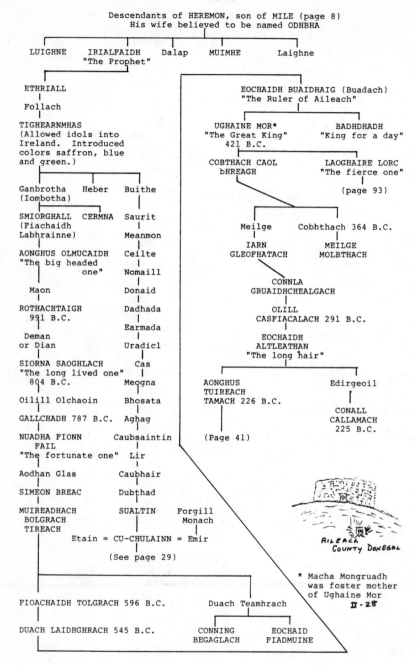

Descendants of HEREMON, son of MILE (page 8)
His wife believed to be named ODHBHA

LUIGHNE   IRIALFAIDH   Dalap   MUIMHE   Laighne
          "The Prophet"

ETHRIALL
|
Follach

TIGHEARNMHAS
(Allowed idols into
Ireland. Introduced
colors saffron, blue
and green.)

Ganbrotha   Heber   Buithe
(Iombotha)

SMIORGHALL CERMNA   Saurit
(Fiachaidh
Labhrainne)

AONGHUS OLMUCAIDH   Meanmon
"The big headed
         one"   Ceilte

Maon   Nomaill

ROTHACHTAIGH   Donaid
991 B.C.

Deman   Dadhada
or Dian

SIORNA SAOGHLACH   Earmada
"The long lived one"
804 B.C.   Uradicl

Oilill Olchaoin   Cas

GALLCHADH 787 B.C.   Meogna

NUADHA FIONN   Bhosata
    FAIL
"The fortunate one"   Aghag

Aodhan Glas   Caubsaintin

SIMEON BREAC   Lir

MUIREADHACH   Caubhair
 BOLGRACH
 TIREACH   Dubthad

SUALTIN   Forgill
          Monach

Etain = CU-CHULAINN = Emir

(See page 29)

EOCHAIDH BUAIDHAIG (Buadach)
"The Ruler of Aileach"

UGHAINE MOR*   BADHDHADH
"The Great King"   "King for a day"
 421 B.C.

COBHTHACH CAOL   LAOGHAIRE LORC
 bHREAGH   "The fierce one"

                (page 93)

Meilge   Cobhthach 364 B.C.

IARN   MEILGE
GLEOFHATACH   MOLBTHACH

CONNLA
GRUAIDHCHEALGACH

OLILL
CASFIACALACH 291 B.C.

EOCHAIDH
ALTLEATHAN
"The long hair"

AONGHUS   Edirgeoil
TUIREACH
TAMACH 226 B.C.   CONALL
                  CALLAMACH
(Page 41)   225 B.C.

AILEACA
COUNTY DONEGAL

* Macha Mongruadh
was foster mother
of Ughaine Mor
II-28

FIOACHAIDH TOLGRACH 596 B.C.   Duach Teamhrach

DUACH LAIDHGHRACH 545 B.C.   CONNING   EOCHAID
                             BEGAGLACH   FIADMUINE

Descendants of AONGHUS TUIREACH TAMACH
From page 40

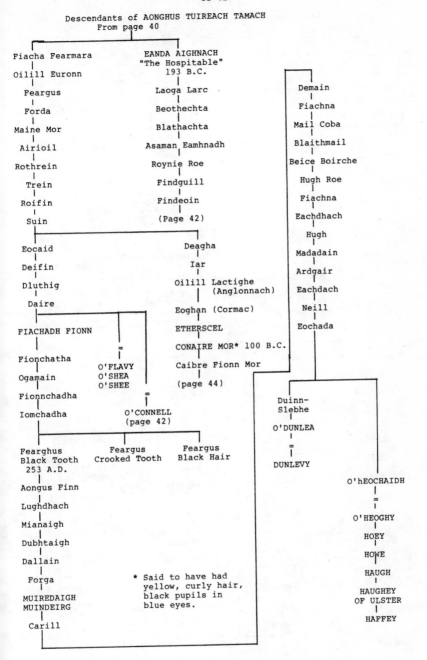

Fiacha Fearmara
|
Oilill Euronn
|
Feargus
|
Forda
|
Maine Mor
|
Airioil
|
Rothrein
|
Trein
|
Roifin
|
Suin

EANDA AIGHNACH
"The Hospitable"
193 B.C.
|
Laoga Larc
|
Beothechta
|
Blathachta
|
Asaman Eamhnadh
|
Roynie Roe
|
Findguill
|
Findeoin
(Page 42)

Demain
|
Fiachna
|
Mail Coba
|
Blaithmail
|
Beice Boirche
|
Hugh Roe
|
Fiachna
|
Eachdhach
|
Hugh
|
Madadain
|
Ardgair
|
Eachdach
|
Neill
|
Eochada

Eocaid
|
Deifin
|
Dluthig
|
Daire

Deagha
|
Iar
|
Oilill Lactighe
(Anglonnach)
|
Eoghan (Cormac)
|
ETHERSCEL
|
CONAIRE MOR* 100 B.C.
|
Caibre Fionn Mor
(page 44)

FIACHADH FIONN
|
Fionchatha
|
Ogamain
|
Fionnchadha
|
Iomchadha

=
O'FLAVY
O'SHEA
O'SHEE

=
O'CONNELL
(page 42)

Fearghus
Black Tooth
253 A.D.

Feargus
Crooked Tooth

Feargus
Black Hair

Aongus Finn
|
Lughdhach
|
Mianaigh
|
Dubhtaigh
|
Dallain
|
Forga
|
MUIREDAIGH
MUINDEIRG
|
Carill

Duinn-
Slebhe
|
O'DUNLEA
=
DUNLEVY

O'hEOCHAIDH
=
O'HEOGHY
|
HOEY
|
HOWE
|
HAUGH
|
HAUGHEY
OF ULSTER
|
HAFFEY

* Said to have had
yellow, curly hair,
black pupils in
blue eyes.

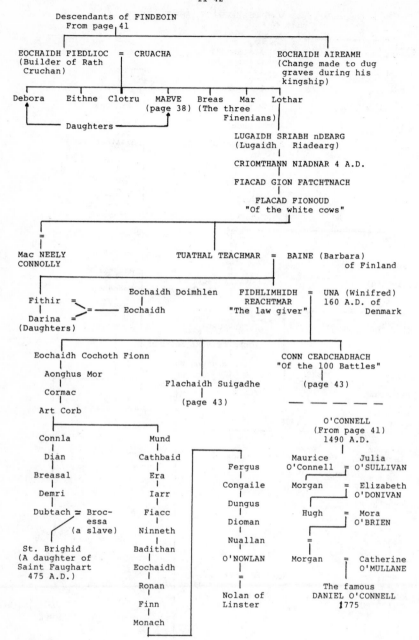

Descendants of FINDEOIN
From page 41

EOCHAIDH FIEDLIOC = CRUACHA
(Builder of Rath
Cruchan)

EOCHAIDH AIREAMH
(Change made to dug
graves during his
kingship)

Debora   Eithne   Clotru   MAEVE   Breas   Mar   Lothar
                              (page 38)   (The three
                                           Finenians)

————————— Daughters —————————

LUGAIDH SRIABH nDEARG
(Lugaidh Riadearg)

CRIOMTHANN NIADNAR 4 A.D.

FIACAD GION FATCHTNACH

FLACAD FIONOUD
"Of the white cows"

=

Mac NEELY
CONNOLLY

TUATHAL TEACHMAR = BAINE (Barbara)
                          of Finland

Fithir =
        >= ———— Eochaidh
Darina =
(Daughters)

Eochaidh Doimhlen
       |
    Eochaidh

FIDHLIMIDH = UNA (Winifred)
REACHTMAR   160 A.D. of
"The law giver"   Denmark

Eochaidh Cochoth Fionn
       |
   Aonghus Mor
       |
     Cormac
       |
    Art Corb

CONN CEADCHADHACH
"Of the 100 Battles"

(page 43)

Flachaidh Suigadhe

(page 43)

— — — — —

O'CONNELL
(From page 41)
1490 A.D.

Connla
  |
 Dian
  |
Breasal
  |
 Demri
  |
Dubtach = Broc-
          essa
        (a slave)

St. Brighid
(A daughter of
Saint Faughart
475 A.D.)

Mund
  |
Cathbaid
  |
  Era
  |
 Iarr
  |
 Fiacc
  |
Ninneth
  |
Badithan
  |
Eochaidh
  |
 Ronan
  |
  Finn
  |
 Monach

Fergus
  |
Congaile
  |
Dungus
  |
Dioman
  |
Nuallan
  |
O'NOWLAN
  |
  =
  |
Nolan of
Linster

Maurice   Julia
O'Connell = O'SULLIVAN

Morgan = Elizabeth
           O'DONIVAN

Hugh = Mora
         O'BRIEN

  =

Morgan = Catherine
           O'MULLANE

The famous
DANIEL O'CONNELL
1775

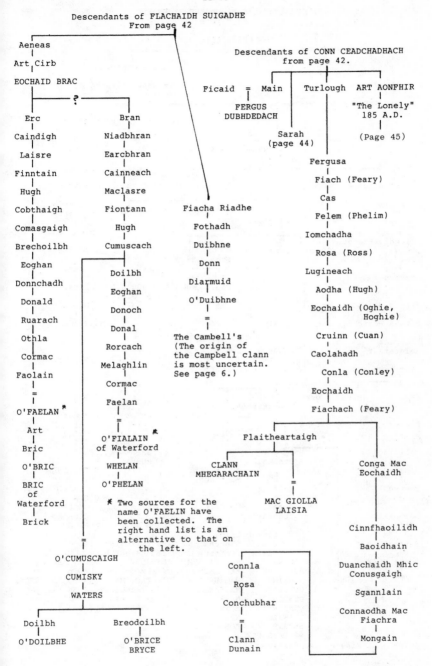

Descendants of FLACHAIDH SUIGADHE
From page 42

Aeneas
Art Cirb
EOCHAID BRAC

Erc
Caindigh
Laisre
Finntain
Hugh
Cobthaigh
Comasgaigh
Brechoilbh
Eoghan
Donnchadh
Donald
Ruarach
Othla
Cormac
Faolain
=
O'FAELAN *
Art
Bric
O'BRIC
BRIC
of
Waterford
Brick

Bran
Niadbhran
Earcbhran
Cainneach
Maclasre
Fiontann
Hugh
Cumuscach

Doilbh
Eoghan
Donoch
Donal
Rorcach
Melaghlin
Cormac
Faelan
=
O'FIALAIN *
of Waterford
WHELAN
O'PHELAN

* Two sources for the
name O'FAELIN have
been collected. The
right hand list is an
alternative to that on
the left.

O'CUMUSCAIGH
CUMISKY
WATERS

Doilbh
O'DOILBHE

Breodoilbh
O'BRICE
BRYCE

Descendants of CONN CEADCHADHACH
from page 42.

Ficaid = Main   Turlough   ART AONFHIR
FERGUS   "The Lonely"
DUBHDEDACH   185 A.D.

Sarah   (Page 45)
(page 44)

Fergusa
Fiach (Feary)
Cas
Felem (Phelim)
Iomchadha
Rosa (Ross)
Lugineach
Aodha (Hugh)
Eochaidh (Oghie, Hoghie)
Cruinn (Cuan)
Caolahadh
Conla (Conley)
Eochaidh
Fiachach (Feary)

Flaitheartaigh

CLANN
MHEGARACHAIN
=
MAC GIOLLA
LAISIA

Conga Mac
Eochaidh

Cinnfhaoilidh
Baoidhain
Duanchaidh Mhic
Conusgaigh
Sgannlain
Connaodha Mac
Fiachra
Mongain

Connla
Rosa
Conchubhar
=
Clann
Dunain

Fiacha Riadhe
Fothadh
Duibhne
Donn
Diarmuid
O'Duibhne
=
The Cambell's
(The origin of
the Campbell clann
is most uncertain.
See page 6.)

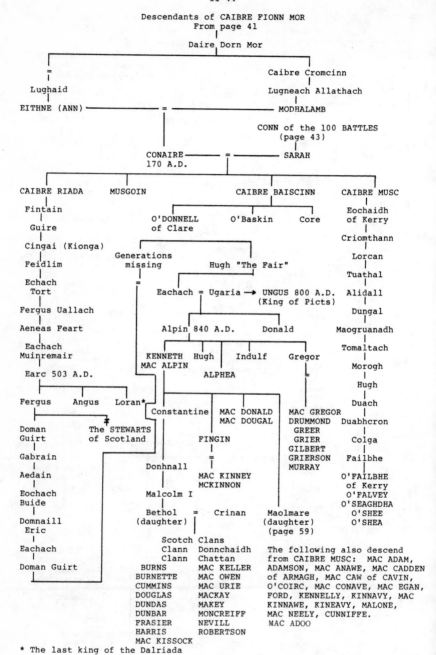

Descendants of CAIBRE FIONN MOR
From page 41

Daire Dorn Mor

Caibre Cromcinn

Lughaid

Lugneach Allathach

EITHNE (ANN) ──────── = ──────── MODHALAMB

CONN of the 100 BATTLES
(page 43)

CONAIRE ──── = ──── SARAH
170 A.D.

CAIBRE RIADA   MUSGOIN   CAIBRE BAISCINN   CAIBRE MUSC

Fintain   Eochaidh
                    O'DONNELL   O'Baskin   Core   of Kerry
Guire   of Clare
                                                     Criomthann
Cingai (Kionga)
                  Generations   Lorcan
Feidlim   missing   Hugh "The Fair"
                                                     Tuathal
Echach   =
Tort   Eachach = Ugaria → UNGUS 800 A.D.   Alidall
                              (King of Picts)
Fergus Uallach   Dungal

Aeneas Feart   Alpin 840 A.D.   Donald   Maogruanadh

Eachach   Tomaltach
Muinremair   KENNETH Hugh   Indulf   Gregor
                MAC ALPIN   Morogh
Earc 503 A.D.   ALPHEA   =
                                                      Hugh
Fergus Angus Loran* Constantine MAC DONALD MAC GREGOR Duach
                                     MAC DOUGAL DRUMMOND Duabhcron
Doman   The STEWARTS   GREER
Guirt   of Scotland   FINGIN   GRIER   Colga
                                                 GILBERT
Gabrain   =   GRIERSON   Failbhe
                     Donhnall   MAC KINNEY MURRAY
Aedain   MCKINNON   O'FAILBHE
                     Malcolm I   of Kerry
Eochach   O'FALVEY
Buide   Bethol = Crinan   Maolmare   O'SEAGHDHA
                     (daughter)   (daughter)   O'SHEE
Domnaill   (page 59)   O'SHEA
Eric   Scotch Clans
                     Clann Donnchaidh   The following also descend
Eachach   Clann Chattan   from CAIBRE MUSC: MAC ADAM,
                  BURNS   MAC KELLER   ADAMSON, MAC ANAWE, MAC CADDEN
Doman Guirt   BURNETTE MAC OWEN   of ARMAGH, MAC CAW of CAVIN,
                  CUMMINS MAC URIE   O'COIRC, MAC CONAVE, MAC EGAN,
                  DOUGLAS MACKAY   FORD, KENNELLY, KINNAVY, MAC
                  DUNDAS   MAKEY   KINNAWE, KINEAVY, MALONE,
                  DUNBAR   MONCREIFF   MAC NEELY, CUNNIFFE.
                  FRASIER NEVILL   MAC ADOO
                  HARRIS   ROBERTSON
                  MAC KISSOCK

* The last king of the Dalriada

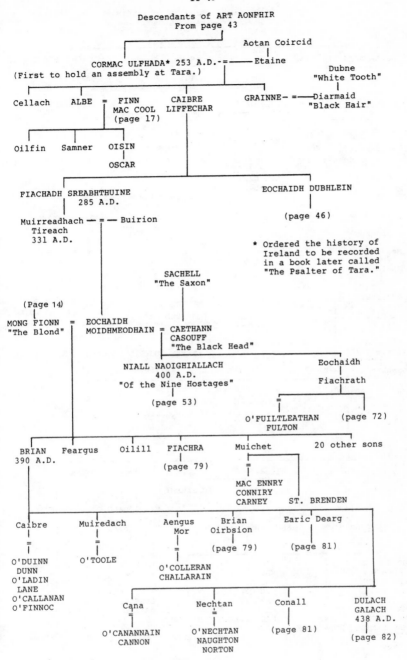

Descendants of ART AONFHIR
From page 43

Aotan Coircid

CORMAC ULFHADA* 253 A.D.-= Etaine
(First to hold an assembly at Tara.)

Dubne
"White Tooth"

Cellach   ALBE = FINN   CAIBRE   GRAINNE- =Diarmaid
MAC COOL   LIFFECHAR   "Black Hair"
(page 17)

Oilfin   Samner   OISIN

OSCAR

FIACHADH SREABHTHUINE
285 A.D.

EOCHAIDH DUBHLEIN

(page 46)

Muirreadhach — = — Buirion
Tireach
331 A.D.

* Ordered the history of
Ireland to be recorded
in a book later called
"The Psalter of Tara."

SACHELL
"The Saxon"

(Page 14)

MONG FIONN = EOCHAIDH   CAETHANN
"The Blond"   MOIDHMEODHAIN = CASOUFF
"The Black Head"

NIALL NAOIGHIALLACH
400 A.D.
"Of the Nine Hostages"

(page 53)

Eochaidh

Fiachrath

O'FUILTLEATHAN   (page 72)
FULTON

BRIAN   Feargus   Oilill   FIACHRA   Muichet   20 other sons
390 A.D.   (page 79)

=

MAC ENNRY
CONNIRY
CARNEY   ST. BRENDEN

Caibre   Muiredach   Aengus   Brian   Earic Dearg
Mor   Oirbsion

=   =   =   (page 79)   (page 81)

O'DUINN   O'TOOLE
DUNN
O'LADIN   O'COLLERAN
LANE   CHALLARAIN
O'CALLANAN
O'FINNOC

Cana   Nechtan   Conall   DULACH
GALACH
438 A.D.

=   =
(page 81)   (page 82)

O'CANANNAIN   O'NECHTAN
CANNON   NAUGHTON
NORTON

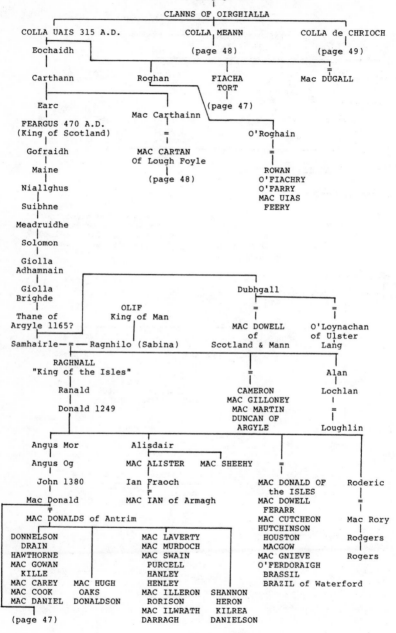

II-46

Descendants of EOCHAIDH DUBHLEIN
From page 45

CLANNS OF OIRGHIALLA

COLLA UAIS 315 A.D.   COLLA MEANN   COLLA de CHRIOCH

Eochaidh   (page 48)   (page 49)

Carthann   Roghan   FIACHA   Mac DUGALL
                               TORT

Earc   Mac Carthainn   (page 47)

FEARGUS 470 A.D.   O'Roghain
(King of Scotland)   MAC CARTAN
                          Of Lough Foyle
Gofraidh   ROWAN
                            (page 48)   O'FIACHRY
Maine   O'FARRY
                                                MAC UIAS
Niallghus   FEERY

Suibhne

Meadruidhe

Solomon

Giolla
Adhamnain
                                        Dubhgall
Giolla
Brighde   OLIF   MAC DOWELL   O'Loynachan
                  King of Man   of   of Ulster
Thane of   Scotland & Mann   Lang
Argyle 1165?

Samhairle——=——Ragnhilo (Sabina)

    RAGHNALL   Alan
"King of the Isles"   CAMERON   Lochlan
    Ranald   MAC GILLONEY
                                        MAC MARTIN   =
    Donald 1249   DUNCAN OF
                                        ARGYLE   Loughlin

Angus Mor   Alisdair

Angus Og   MAC ALISTER   MAC SHEEHY

John 1380   Ian Fraoch   MAC DONALD OF   Roderic
                    =   the ISLES
Mac Donald   MAC IAN of Armagh   MAC DOWELL   Mac Rory
    =   FERARR
MAC DONALDS of Antrim   MAC CUTCHEON   Rodgers
                                             HUTCHINSON
DONNELSON   MAC LAVERTY   HOUSTON   Rogers
DRAIN   MAC MURDOCH   MACGOW
HAWTHORNE   MAC SWAIN   MAC GNIEVE
MAC GOWAN   PURCELL   O'FERDORAIGH
  KILLE   HANLEY   BRASSIL
MAC CAREY   MAC HUGH   HENLEY   BRAZIL of Waterford
MAC COOK   OAKS   MAC ILLERON   SHANNON
MAC DANIEL   DONALDSON   RORISON   HERON
                          MAC ILWRATH   KILREA
(page 47)   DARRAGH   DANIELSON

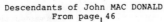

Descendants of John MAC DONALD
From page 46

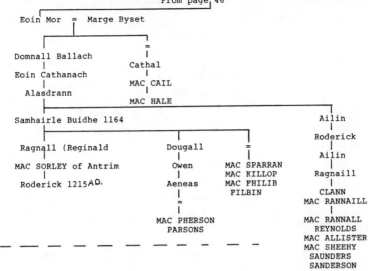

```
Eoin Mor  =  Marge Byset
   |
   |                      =
   |                      |
Domnall Ballach         Cathal
   |
Eoin Cathanach         MAC CAIL
   |
 Alasdrann             MAC HALE
```

```
Samhairle Buidhe 1164                                      Ailin
   |                                                         |
   |                                                      Roderick
   |                                                         |
Ragnall (Reginald       Dougall         =                 Ailin
   |                      |              |                   |
MAC SORLEY of Antrim     Owen        MAC SPARRAN          Ragnaill
   |                      |          MAC KILLOP              |
Roderick 1215 A.D.      Aeneas       MAC PHILIB           CLANN
                          |          FILBIN            MAC RANNAILL
                          =                               |
                          |                           MAC RANNALL
                      MAC PHERSON                      REYNOLDS
                      PARSONS                          MAC ALLISTER
                                                       MAC SHEEHY
                                                       SAUNDERS
                                                       SANDERSON
```

— — — — — — — — — — — — — —

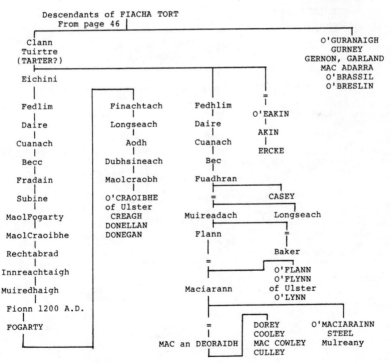

Descendants of FIACHA TORT
From page 46

```
Clann                                         O'GURANAIGH
Tuirtre                                        GURNEY
(TARTER?)                                      GERNON, GARLAND
                                               MAC ADARRA
Eichini                                        O'BRASSIL
   |                                           O'BRESLIN
   |
Fedlim          Finachtach      Fedlim
   |                |               |          =
Daire           Longseach       Daire          |
   |                |               |         O'EAKIN
Cuanach          Aodh          Cuanach          |
   |                |               |          AKIN
 Becc          Dubhsineach       Bec            |
   |                |               |          ERCKE
Fradain        Maolcraobh      Fuadhran
   |                |               |
Subine         O'CRAOIBHE          =          CASEY
   |           of Ulster            |
MaolFogarty    CREAGH          Muireadach    Longseach
   |           DONELLAN             |
MaolCraoibhe   DONEGAN           Flann           =
   |                                |            |
Rechtabrad                          |          Baker
   |                                =            |
Innreachtaigh                       |          O'FLANN
   |                                |          O'FLYNN
Muiredhaigh                    Maciarann      of Ulster
   |                                |          O'LYNN
Fionn 1200 A.D.                     |
   |                                |
FOGARTY                             =        DOREY      O'MACIARAINN
                                    |        COOLEY     STEEL
                          MAC an DEORAIDH   MAC COWLEY   Mulreany
                                             CULLEY
```

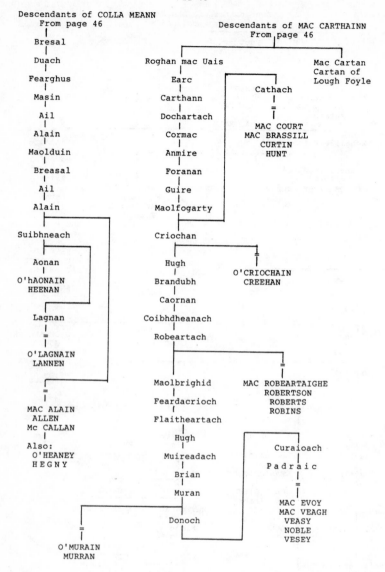

Descendants of COLLA MEANN
From page 46

Bresal

Duach

Fearghus

Masin

Ail

Alain

Maolduin

Breasal

Ail

Alain

Suibhneach

Aonan

O'hAONAIN
HEENAN

Lagnan
=
O'LAGNAIN
LANNEN

=

MAC ALAIN
ALLEN
Mc CALLAN

Also:
O'HEANEY
HEGNY

Descendants of MAC CARTHAINN
From page 46

Roghan mac Uais

Earc

Carthann

Dochartach

Cormac

Anmire

Foranan

Guire

Maolfogarty

Criochan

Hugh

Brandubh

Caornan

Coibhdheanach

Robeartach

Maolbrighid

Feardacrioch

Flaitheartach

Hugh

Muireadach

Brian

Muran

Donoch

O'MURAIN
MURRAN

Mac Cartan
Cartan of
Lough Foyle

Cathach
=
MAC COURT
MAC BRASSILL
CURTIN
HUNT

O'CRIOCHAIN
CREEHAN

MAC ROBEARTAIGHE
ROBERTSON
ROBERTS
ROBINS

Curaioach

Padraic
=
MAC EVOY
MAC VEAGH
VEASY
NOBLE
VESEY

Descendants of CIOLLA de CHRIOCH
From page 46

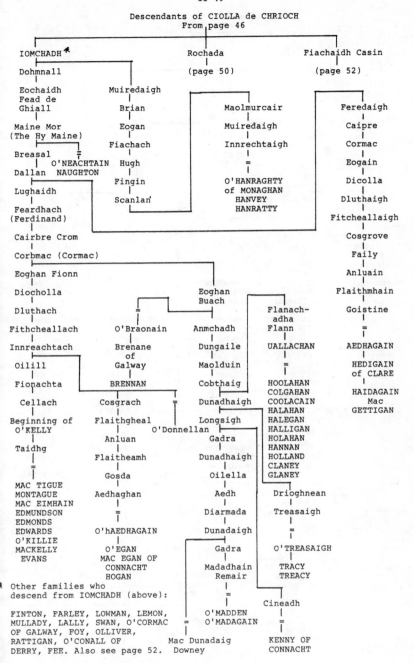

Descendants of ROCHADA
From page 49

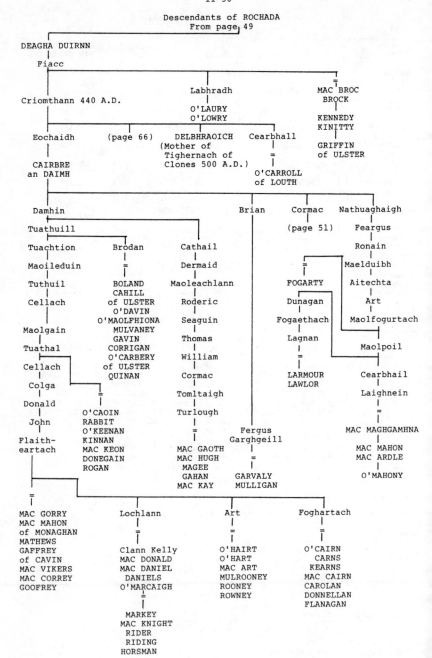

Descendants of CORMAC
From page 50

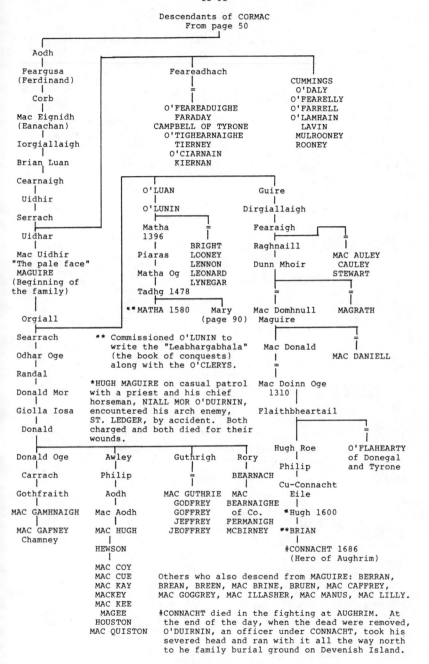

Aodh
|
Feargusa
(Ferdinand)
|
Corb
|
Mac Eignidh
(Eanachan)
|
Iorgiallaigh
|
Brian Luan
|
Cearnaigh
|
Uidhir
|
Serrach
|
Uidhar
|
Mac Uidhir
"The pale face"
MAGUIRE
(Beginning of
the family)
|
Orgiall
|
Searrach
|
Odhar Oge
|
Randal
|
Donald Mor
|
Giolla Iosa
|
Donald
|
Donald Oge
|
Carrach
|
Gothfraith
|
MAC GAMHNAIGH
|
MAC GAFNEY
Chamney

Feareadhach
=
O'FEAREADUIGHE
FARADAY
CAMPBELL OF TYRONE
O'TIGHEARNAIGHE
TIERNEY
O'CIARNAIN
KIERNAN

CUMMINGS
O'DALY
O'FEARELLY
O'FARRELL
O'LAMHAIN
LAVIN
MULROONEY
ROONEY

O'LUAN
|
O'LUNIN
|
Matha
1396
| =
Piaras   BRIGHT
| LOONEY
Matha Og   LENNON
| LEONARD
Tadhg 1478   LYNEGAR
|
**MATHA 1580   Mary
                (page 90)

** Commissioned O'LUNIN to
   write the "Leabhargabhala"
   (the book of conquests)
   along with the O'CLERYS.

*HUGH MAGUIRE on casual patrol
with a priest and his chief
horseman, NIALL MOR O'DUIRNIN,
encountered his arch enemy,
ST. LEDGER, by accident. Both
charged and both died for their
wounds.

Guire
|
Dirgiallaigh
|
Fearaigh
|
Raghnaill   MAC AULEY
| CAULEY
Dunn Mhoir   STEWART
|
=   =
Mac Domhnull   MAGRATH
Maguire
| =
Mac Donald   MAC DANIELL
|
=
Mac Doinn Oge
1310 |
|
Flaithbheartail
|
Hugh Roe   O'FLAHEARTY
| of Donegal
Philip   and Tyrone
|
Cu-Connacht
Eile
|
*Hugh 1600
|
**BRIAN
|
#CONNACHT 1686
(Hero of Aughrim)

Awley   Guthrigh   Rory
| | |
Philip   =   BEARNACH
|
Aodh   MAC GUTHRIE MAC
| GODFREY   BEARNAIGHE
Mac Aodh   GOFFREY   of Co.
| JEFFREY   FERMANIGH
MAC HUGH   JEOFFREY   MCBIRNEY
|
HEWSON
|
MAC COY
MAC CUE   Others who also descend from MAGUIRE: BERRAN,
MAC KAY   BREAN, BREEN, MAC BRINE, BRUEN, MAC CAFFREY,
MACKEY   MAC GOGGREY, MAC ILLASHER, MAC MANUS, MAC LILLY.
MAC KEE
MAGEE   #CONNACHT died in the fighting at AUGHRIM. At
HOUSTON   the end of the day, when the dead were removed,
MAC QUISTON   O'DUIRNIN, an officer under CONNACHT, took his
               severed head and ran with it all the way north
               to he family burial ground on Devenish Island.

Descendants of FIACHAIDH CASIN
From page 49

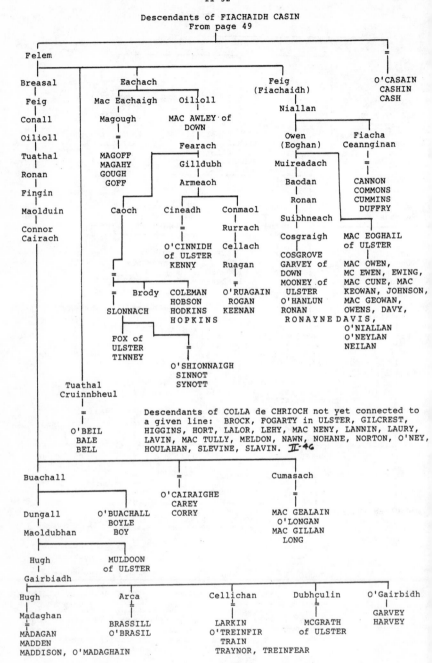

Descendants of COLLA de CHRIOCH not yet connected to a given line: BROCK, FOGARTY in ULSTER, GILCREST, HIGGINS, HORT, LALOR, LEHY, MAC NENY, LANNIN, LAURY, LAVIN, MAC TULLY, MELDON, NAWN, NOHANE, NORTON, O'NEY, HOULAHAN, SLEVINE, SLAVIN. II-46

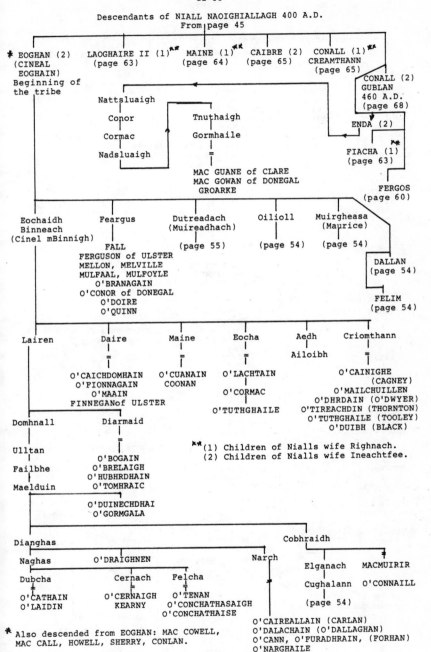

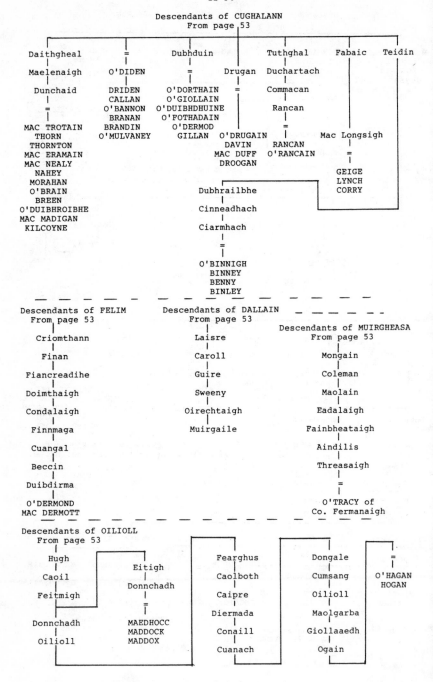

Descendants of CUGHALANN
From page 53

Daithgheal | = | Dubhduin | Drugan | Tuthghal | Fabaic | Teidin
Maelenaigh | O'DIDEN | = | | Duchartach
Dunchaid | DRIDEN | O'DORTHAIN | | Commacan
= | CALLAN | O'GIOLLAIN | | Rancan
MAC TROTAIN | O'BANNON | O'DUIBHDHUINE | | =
THORN | BRANAN | O'FOTHADAIN | | RANCAN
THORNTON | BRANDIN | O'DERMOD | O'DRUGAIN | O'RANCAIN
MAC ERAMAIN | O'MULVANEY | GILLAN | DAVIN | Mac Longsigh
MAC NEALY | | | MAC DUFF | =
NAHEY | | | DROOGAN | GEIGE
MORAHAN | | | | LYNCH
O'BRAIN | | | | CORRY
BREEN
O'DUIBHROIBHE
MAC MADIGAN
KILCOYNE

Dubhrailbhe
Cinneadhach
Ciarmhach
=
O'BINNIGH
BINNEY
BENNY
BINLEY

Descendants of FELIM
From page 53

Criomthann
Finan
Fiancreadihe
Doimthaigh
Condalaigh
Finnmaga
Cuangal
Beccin
Duibdirma
O'DERMOND
MAC DERMOTT

Descendants of DALLAIN
From page 53

Laisre
Caroll
Guire
Sweeny
Oirechtaigh
Muirgaile

Descendants of MUIRGHEASA
From page 53

Mongain
Coleman
Maolain
Eadalaigh
Fainbheataigh
Aindilis
Threasaigh
=
O'TRACY of
Co. Fermanaigh

Descendants of OILIOLL
From page 53

Hugh
Caoil
Feitmigh
Donnchadh
Oilioll

Eitigh
Donnchadh
=
MAEDHOCC
MADDOCK
MADDOX

Fearghus
Caolboth
Caipre
Diermada
Conaill
Cuanach

Dongale
Cumsang
Oilioll
Maolgarba
Giollaaedh
Ogain

=
O'HAGAN
HOGAN

Descendants of DUTREADACH (Muireadhach)
From page 53

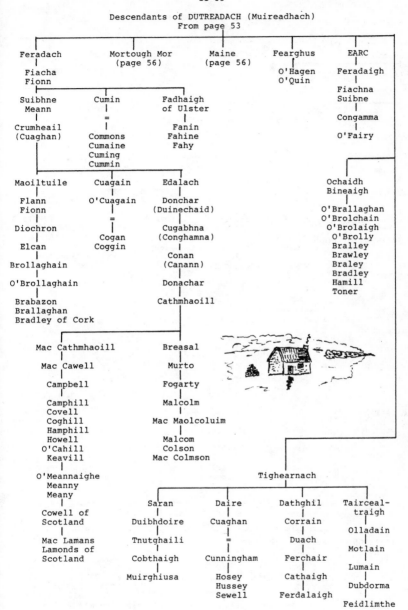

Feradach
|
Fiacha
Fionn
|
Suibhne
Meann
|
Crumheail
(Cuaghan)

Maoiltuile
|
Flann
Fionn
|
Diochron
|
Elcan
|
Brollaghain
|
O'Brollaghain
|
Brabazon
Brallaghan
Bradley of Cork

Mac Cathmhaoill
|
Mac Cawell
|
Campbell
|
Camphill
Covell
Coghill
Hamphill
Howell
O'Cahill
Keavill
|
O'Meannaighe
Meanny
Meany
|
Cowell of
Scotland
|
Mac Lamans
Lamonds of
Scotland

Mortough Mor
(page 56)

Cumin
|
=
|
Commons
Cumaine
Cuming
Cummin

Cuagain
|
O'Cuagain
|
=
|
Cogan
Coggin

Maine
(page 56)

Fadhaigh
of Ulster
|
Fanin
Fahine
Fahy

Edalach
|
Donchar
(Duinechaid)
|
Cugabhna
(Conghamna)
|
Conan
(Canann)
|
Donachar
|
Cathmhaoill

Breasal
|
Murto
|
Fogarty
|
Malcolm
|
Mac Maolcoluim
|
Malcom
Colson
Mac Colmson

Fearghus
|
O'Hagen
O'Quin

EARC
|
Feradaigh
|
Fiachna
Suibne
|
Congamma
|
O'Fairy

Ochaidh
Bineaigh
|
O'Brallaghan
O'Brolchain
O'Brolaigh
O'Brolly
Bralley
Brawley
Braley
Bradley
Hamill
Toner

Tighearnach

Saran
|
Duibhdoire
|
Tnutghaili
|
Cobthaigh
|
Muirghiusa

Daire
|
Cuaghan
|
=
|
Cunningham
|
Hosey
Hussey
Sewell

Dathghil
|
Corrain
|
Duach
|
Ferchair
|
Cathaigh
|
Ferdalaigh

Tairceal-
traigh
|
Olladain
|
Motlain
|
Lumain
|
Dubdorma
|
Feidlimthe

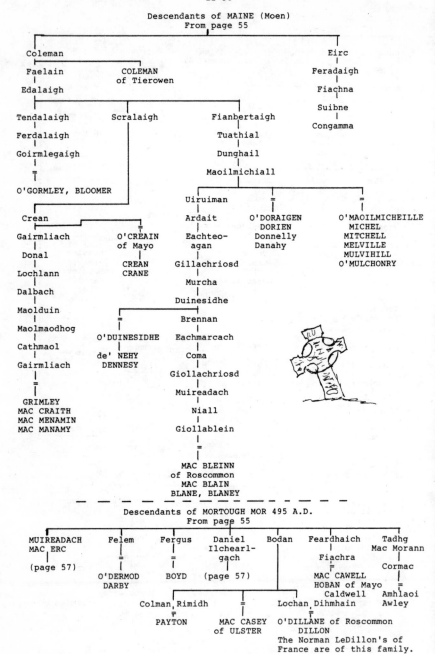

Descendants of MAINE (Moen)
From page 55

Coleman   Eirc

Faelain   COLEMAN   Feradaigh
                of Tierowen
Edalaigh   Fiachna

                                  Suibne

Tendalaigh   Scralaigh   Fianbertaigh   Congamma

Ferdalaigh   Tuathial

Goirmlegaigh   Dunghail
    =
                       Maoilmichiall
O'GORMLEY, BLOOMER

                       Uiruiman

Crean   Ardait   O'DORAIGEN   O'MAOILMICHEILLE
                            DORIEN   MICHEL
Gairmliach   O'CREAIN   Eachteo-   Donnelly   MITCHELL
           of Mayo   agan   Danahy   MELVILLE
Donal   MULVIHILL
           CREAN   Gillachriosd   O'MULCHONRY
Lochlann   CRANE

Dalbach   Murcha

Maolduin   Duinesidhe

Maolmaodhog   Brennan

Cathmaol   O'DUINESIDHE   Eachmarcach

Gairmliach   de' NEHY   Coma
 =   DENNESY
                     Giollachriosd
GRIMLEY
MAC CRAITH   Muireadach
MAC MENAMIN
MAC MANAMY   Niall

                     Giollablein
                       =
                  MAC BLEINN
                of Roscommon
                  MAC BLAIN
                BLANE, BLANEY

- -

Descendants of MORTOUGH MOR 495 A.D.
From page 55

MUIREADACH   Felem   Fergus   Daniel   Bodan   Feardhaich   Tadhg
MAC ERC   Ilchearl-   Mac Morann
                        gach   Fiachra
(page 57)   =   =   =   Cormac
           O'DERMOD   BOYD   (page 57)   MAC CAWELL |
           DARBY   HOBAN of Mayo
                                 Caldwell   Amhlaoi
                                             Awley
           Colman, Rimidh   Lochan, Dihmhain
           =   =   =
           PAYTON   MAC CASEY   O'DILLANE of Roscommon
                     of ULSTER   DILLON
                                 The Norman LeDillon's of
                                 France are of this family.

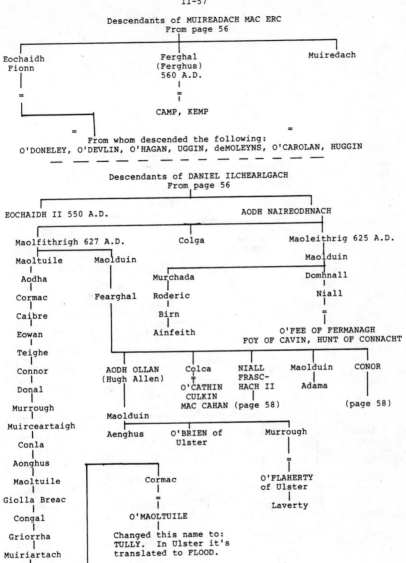

Descendants of MUIREADACH MAC ERC
From page 56

Eochaidh Fionn   Ferghal (Ferghus) 560 A.D.   Muiredach

=

=   CAMP, KEMP

From whom descended the following:
O'DONELEY, O'DEVLIN, O'HAGAN, UGGIN, deMOLEYNS, O'CAROLAN, HUGGIN

Descendants of DANIEL ILCHEARLGACH
From page 56

EOCHAIDH II 550 A.D.   AODH NAIREODHNACH

Maolfithrigh 627 A.D.   Colga   Maoleithrig 625 A.D.

Maoltuile   Maolduin   Maolduin

Aodha   Murchada   Domhnall

Cormac   Fearghal   Roderic   Niall

Caibre   Birn   =

Eowan   Ainfeith   O'FEE OF FERMANAGH

Teighe   FOY OF CAVIN, HUNT OF CONNACHT

Connor   AODH OLLAN   Colca   NIALL   Maolduin   CONOR

Donal   (Hugh Allen)   =   FRASC-   Adama

Murrough   O'CATHIN   HACH II   (page 58)

Muirceartaigh   CULKIN   (page 58)

Conla   Maolduin   MAC CAHAN

Aonghus   Aenghus   O'BRIEN of   Murrough

Maoltuile   Ulster

Giolla Breac   =

Congal   Cormac   O'FLAHERTY

Griorrha   =   of Ulster

Muiriartach   O'MAOLTUILE   Laverty

Cathal   Changed this name to:

Connor   TULLY. In Ulster it's
translated to FLOOD.

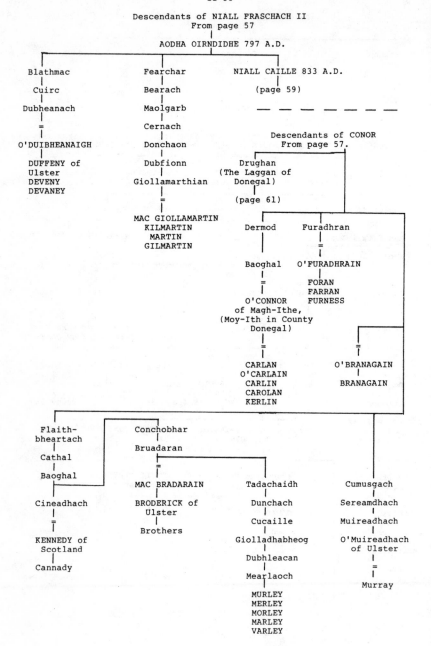

Descendants of NIALL FRASCHACH II
From page 57

AODHA OIRNDIDHE 797 A.D.

Blathmac
|
Cuirc
|
Dubheanach
|
=
|
O'DUIBHEANAIGH
|
DUFFENY of
Ulster
DEVENY
DEVANEY

Fearchar
|
Bearach
|
Maolgarb
|
Cernach
|
Donchaon
|
Dubfionn
|
Giollamarthian
|
=
|
MAC GIOLLAMARTIN
KILMARTIN
MARTIN
GILMARTIN

NIALL CAILLE 833 A.D.

(page 59)

Descendants of CONOR
From page 57.

Drughan
(The Laggan of
Donegal)

(page 61)

Dermod
|
Baoghal
|
=
|
O'CONNOR
of Magh-Ithe,
(Moy-Ith in County
Donegal)
|
=
|
CARLAN
O'CARLAIN
CARLIN
CAROLAN
KERLIN

Furadhran
|
=
|
O'FURADHRAIN
|
FORAN
FARRAN
FURNESS

O'BRANAGAIN
|
BRANAGAIN

Flaith-
bheartach
|
Cathal
|
Baoghal
|
Cineadhach
|
=
|
KENNEDY of
Scotland
|
Cannady

Conchobhar
|
Bruadaran
|
=
|
MAC BRADARAIN
|
BRODERICK of
Ulster
|
Brothers

Tadachaidh
|
Dunchach
|
Cucaille
|
Giolladhabheog
|
Dubhleacan
|
Mearlaoch
|
MURLEY
MERLEY
MORLEY
MARLEY
VARLEY

Cumusgach
|
Sereamdhach
|
Muireadhach
|
O'Muireadhach
of Ulster
|
=
|
Murray

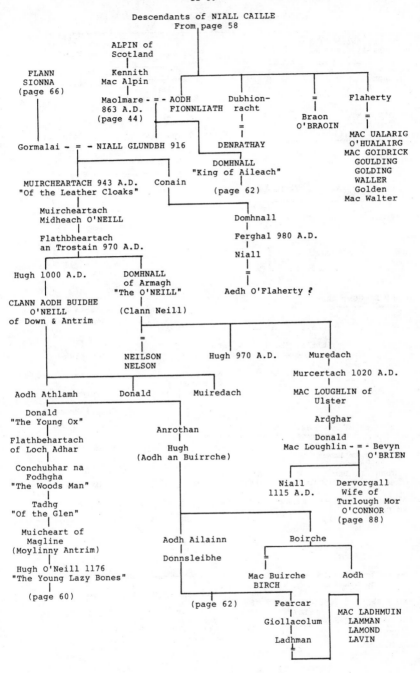

Descendants of NIALL CAILLE
From page 58

Descendants of HUGH "Lazy Bones" O'NEILL
From page 59

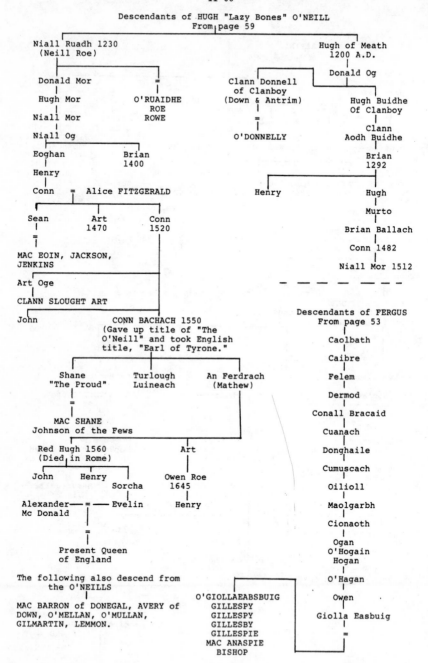

The following also descend from the O'NEILLS

MAC BARRON of DONEGAL, AVERY of DOWN, O'MELLAN, O'MULLAN, GILMARTIN, LEMMON.

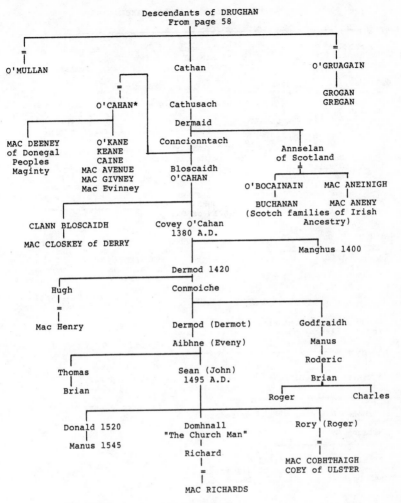

Descendants of DRUGHAN
From page 58

* Other families branching from O'Cahan:

O'Cahane, O'Cane, O'Caine, Gahan, Getthan, Keen, Kyan.

Descendants of DONNSLEIBHE
From page 59

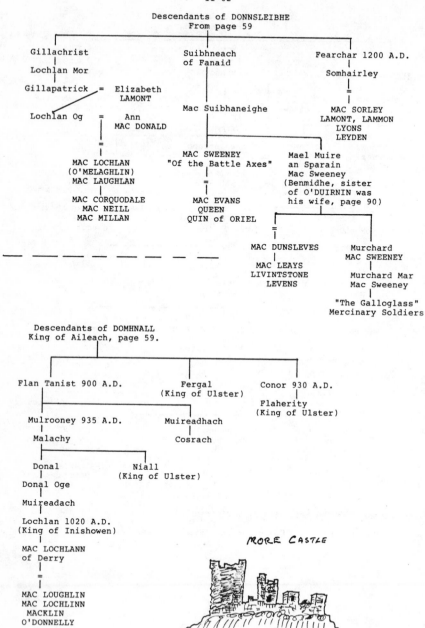

Gillachrist
|
Lochlan Mor
|
Gillapatrick = Elizabeth
| LAMONT
|
Lochlan Og = Ann
| MAC DONALD
|
=
|
MAC LOCHLAN
(O'MELAGHLIN)
MAC LAUGHLAN
|
MAC CORQUODALE
MAC NEILL
MAC MILLAN

Suibhneach
of Fanaid
|
Mac Suibhaneighe
|
MAC SWEENEY
"Of the Battle Axes"
=
|
MAC EVANS
QUEEN
QUIN of ORIEL

Fearchar 1200 A.D.
|
Somhairley
=
|
MAC SORLEY
LAMONT, LAMMON
LYONS
LEYDEN

Mael Muire
an Sparain
Mac Sweeney
(Benmidhe, sister
of O'DUIRNIN was
his wife, page 90)
=

MAC DUNSLEVES
|
MAC LEAYS
LIVINTSTONE
LEVENS

Murchard
MAC SWEENEY
|
Murchard Mar
Mac Sweeney
|
"The Galloglass"
Mercinary Soldiers

Descendants of DOMHNALL
King of Aileach, page 59.

Flan Tanist 900 A.D.
|
Mulrooney 935 A.D.
|
Malachy
|
Donal   Niall
| (King of Ulster)
Donal Oge
|
Muireadach
|
Lochlan 1020 A.D.
(King of Inishowen)
|
MAC LOCHLANN
of Derry
|
=
|
MAC LOUGHLIN
MAC LOCHLINN
MACKLIN
O'DONNELLY

Fergal
(King of Ulster)
|
Muireadhach
|
Cosrach

Conor 930 A.D.
|
Flaherity
(King of Ulster)

MORE CASTLE

MAC SWEENEY LAND

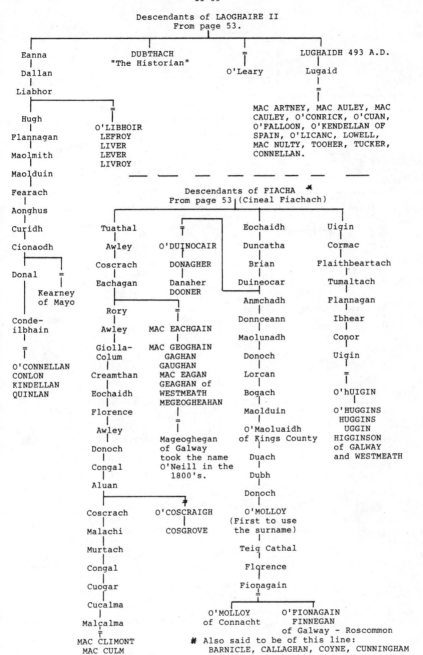

Descendants of LAOGHAIRE II
From page 53.

Eanna
Dallan
Liabhor

Hugh
Flannagan
Maolmith
Maolduin
Fearach
Aonghus
Curidh
Cionaodh

Donal = Kearney of Mayo

Conde-ilbhain
=
O'CONNELLAN
CONLON
KINDELLAN
QUINLAN

DUBTHACH
"The Historian"
=
O'LIBHOIR
LEFROY
LIVER
LEVER
LIVROY

O'Leary

LUGHAIDH 493 A.D.
Lugaid
=
MAC ARTNEY, MAC AULEY, MAC
CAULEY, O'CONRICK, O'CUAN,
O'FALLOON, O'KENDELLAN OF
SPAIN, O'LICANC, LOWELL,
MAC NULTY, TOOHER, TUCKER,
CONNELLAN.

Descendants of FIACHA ✳
From page 53 (Cineal Fiachach)

Tuathal
Awley
Coscrach
Eachagan
Rory
Awley
Giolla-Colum
Creamthan
Eochaidh
Florence
Awley
Donoch
Congal
Aluan
Coscrach
Malachi
Murtach
Congal
Cuogar
Cucalma
Malcalma
=
MAC CLIMONT
MAC CULM

O'DUINOCAIR
DONAGHER
Danaher
DOONER
=
MAC EACHGAIN
MAC GEOGHAIN
GAGHAN
GAUGHAN
MAC EAGAN
GEAGHAN of
WESTMEATH
MEGEOGHEAHAN
=
Mageoghegan
of Galway
took the name
O'Neill in the
1800's.

O'COSCRAIGH
COSGROVE

Eochaidh
Duncatha
Brian
Duineocar
Anmchadh
Donnceann
Maolunadh
Donoch
Lorcan
Bogach
Maolduin
O'Maoluaidh
of Kings County
Duach
Dubh
Donoch
O'MOLLOY
(First to use
the surname)
Teig Cathal
Florence
Fionagain
=

O'MOLLOY
of Connacht

O'FIONAGAIN
FINNEGAN
of Galway - Roscommon

✳ Also said to be of this line:
BARNICLE, CALLAGHAN, COYNE, CUNNINGHAM

Uigin
Cormac
Flaithbeartach
Tumaltach
Flannagan
Ibhear
Conor
Uigin
=
O'hUIGIN
O'HUGGINS
HUGGINS
UGGIN
HIGGINSON
of GALWAY
and WESTMEATH

Descendants of MAINE *
From page 53

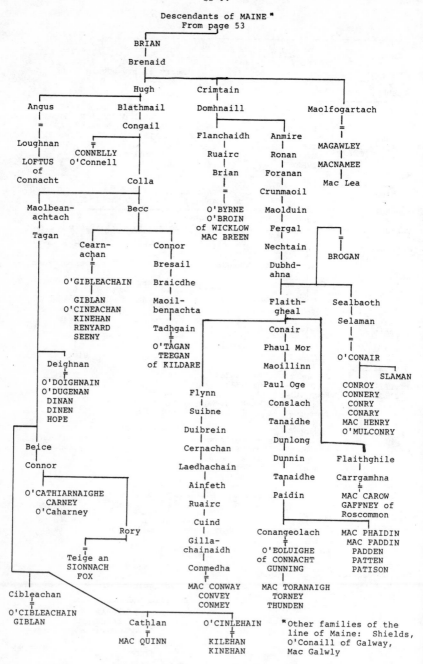

*Other families of the
 line of Maine: Shields,
 O'Conaill of Galway,
 Mac Galwly

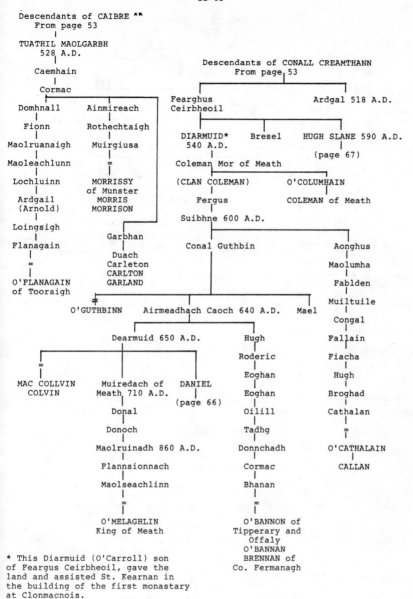

Descendants of CAIBRE **
   From page 53

TUATHIL MAOLGARBH
   528 A.D.

Caemhain

Cormac

Domhnall   Ainmireach

Fionn   Rothechtaigh

Maolruanaigh   Muirgiusa

Maoleachlunn   =

Lochluinn   MORRISSY
                  of Munster
Ardgail   MORRIS
(Arnold)   MORRISON

Loingsigh

Flanagain   Garbhan
   =
                  Duach
O'FLANAGAIN   Carleton
of Tooraigh   CARLTON
                  GARLAND

Descendants of CONALL CREAMTHANN
   From page 53

Fearghus   Ardgal 518 A.D.
Ceirbheoil

DIARMUID*   Bresel   HUGH SLANE 590 A.D.
540 A.D.
                          (page 67)
Coleman Mor of Meath

(CLAN COLEMAN)   O'COLUMHAIN

Fergus   COLEMAN of Meath

Suibhne 600 A.D.

Conal Guthbin   Aonghus

                               Maolumha

                               Fabiden

                               Muiltuile

O'GUTHBINN   Airmeadhach Caoch 640 A.D.   Mael   Congal

                                                     Fallain

Dearmuid 650 A.D.   Hugh   Fiacha

                           Roderic   Hugh

                           Eoghan   Broghad

MAC COLLVIN   Muiredach of   DANIEL   Eoghan   Cathalan
COLVIN   Meath 710 A.D.
                             (page 66) Oilill   =

              Donal   Tadhg   O'CATHALAIN

              Donoch   Donnchadh CALLAN

              Maolruinadh 860 A.D.   Cormac

              Flannsionnach   Bhanan

              Maolseachlinn |

                  | O'BANNON of
              O'MELAGHLIN   Tipperary and
              King of Meath   Offaly
                                        O'BANNAN
                                        BRENNAN of
                                        Co. Fermanagh

* This Diarmuid (O'Carroll) son
of Feargus Ceirbheoil, gave the
land and assisted St. Kearnan in
the building of the first monastary
at Clonmacnois.

                  Also descended from Caibre: **
                     O'NOWAN, SCANNELL

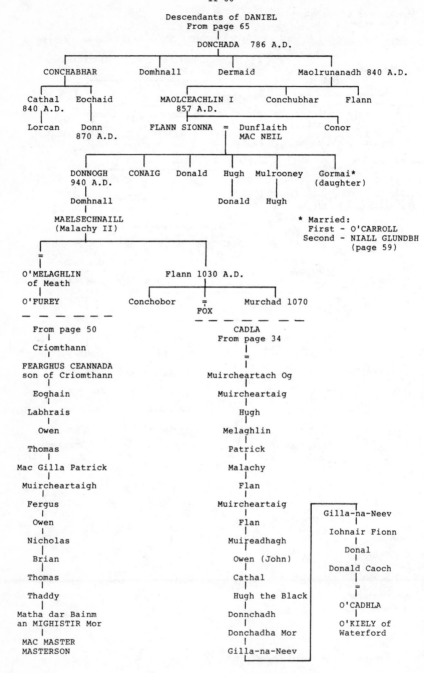

Descendants of DANIEL
From page 65

DONCHADA   786 A.D.

CONCHABHAR   Domhnall   Dermaid   Maolrunanadh 840 A.D.

Cathal   Eochaid   MAOLCEACHLIN I   Conchubhar   Flann
840 A.D.   857 A.D.

Lorcan   Donn   FLANN SIONNA = Dunflaith   Conor
          870 A.D.   MAC NEIL

DONNOGH   CONAIG   Donald   Hugh   Mulrooney   Gormai*
940 A.D.   (daughter)

Domhnall   Donald   Hugh

MAELSECHNAILL   * Married:
(Malachy II)   First - O'CARROLL
                                             Second - NIALL GLUNDBH
                                                      (page 59)

=   Flann 1030 A.D.

O'MELAGHLIN   Conchobor   =   Murchad 1070
of Meath   FOX

O'FUREY

From page 50   CADLA
                                      From page 34
Criomthann   =

FEARGHUS CEANNADA   Muircheartach Og
son of Criomthann
                                      Muircheartaig
Eoghain
                                      Hugh
Labhrais
                                      Melaghlin
Owen
                                      Patrick
Thomas
                                      Malachy
Mac Gilla Patrick
                                      Flan
Muircheartaigh
                                      Muircheartaig   Gilla-na-Neev
Fergus
                                      Flan   Iohnair Fionn
Owen
                                      Muireadhagh   Donal
Nicholas
                                      Owen (John)   Donald Caoch
Brian
                                      Cathal
Thomas
                                      Hugh the Black   =
Thaddy
                                      Donnchadh   O'CADHLA
Matha dar Bainm
an MIGHISTIR Mor   Donchadha Mor   O'KIELY of
                                                             Waterford
MAC MASTER   Gilla-na-Neev
MASTERSON

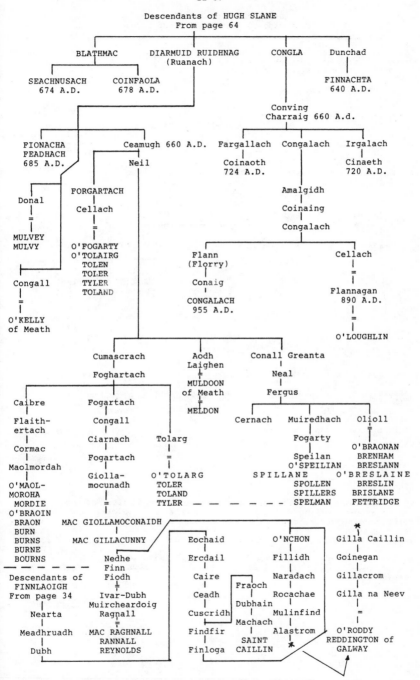

Descendants of HUGH SLANE
From page 64

Descendants of CONALL GULBAN
From page 53 (Conall of Mount Bulban)

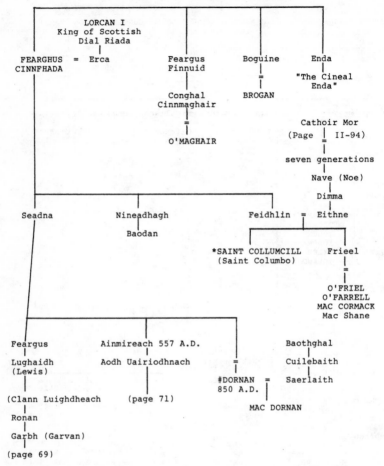

* SAINT COLUMBO (or Columbia) exiled himself to the Island of Iona off
the coast of Scotland to become a missionary to the picts. The reason
for his going was an argument over a copy of a book which he had made.
The heated debate exploded into a war between the occupants of his
monestary and that of the owner of the original book.

\# The book of MAC DORNAN is a beautifully illuminated manuscript now in
the Lambeth library in England. It was said to have been made for the
Dornan above.

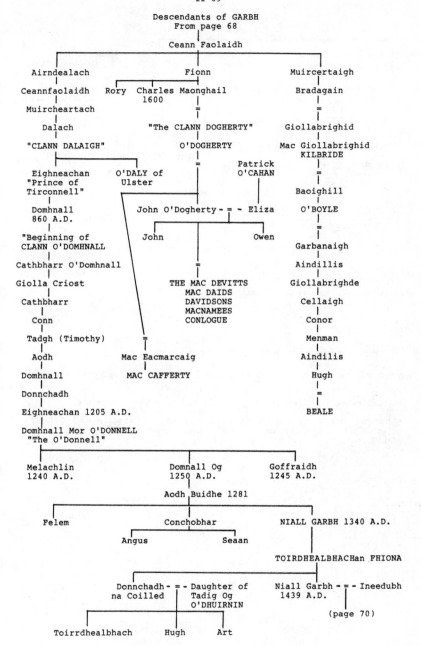

Descendants of GARBH
From page 68

Ceann Faolaidh

Airndealach   Fionn   Muircertaigh

Ceannfaolaidh   Rory   Charles Maonghail   Bradagain
                   1600

Muircheartach   =

Dalach   "The CLANN DOGHERTY"   Giollabrighid

"CLANN DALAIGH"   O'DOGHERTY   Mac Giollabrighid
                      =   Patrick   KILBRIDE
                O'DALY of   O'CAHAN   =

Eighneachan   Ulster   Baoighill
"Prince of
Tirconnell"   John O'Dogherty - = - Eliza   O'BOYLE

Domhnall   =
860 A.D.   John   Owen

"Beginning of   Garbanaigh
CLANN O'DOMHNALL

Cathbharr O'Domhnall   Aindillis

Giolla Criost   THE MAC DEVITTS   Giollabrighde
             MAC DAIDS
Cathbharr   DAVIDSONS   Cellaigh
            MACNAMEES
Conn   CONLOGUE   Conor

Tadgh (Timothy)   Menman

Aodh   Aindilis
          Mac Eacmarcaig
Domhnall   MAC CAFFERTY   Hugh

Donnchadh   =

Eighneachan 1205 A.D.   BEALE

Domhnall Mor O'DONNELL
"The O'Donnell"

Melachlin   Domnall Og   Goffraidh
1240 A.D.   1250 A.D.   1245 A.D.

Aodh Buidhe 1281

Felem   Conchobhar   NIALL GARBH 1340 A.D.

     Angus   Seaan

                         TOIRDHEALBHACHan FHIONA

Donnchadh - = - Daughter of   Niall Garbh - = - Ineedubh
na Coilled   Tadig Og   1439 A.D.
           O'DHUIRNIN   (page 70)

Toirrdhealbhach   Hugh   Art

Descendants of NIALL GARBH
From page 69

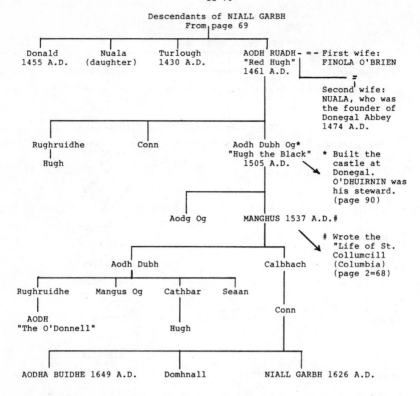

The following families are said to descend from the O'Donnells:

BALDWIN, O'BADGILL, O'BRACKEN of OFFALY, O'CANNON, MAC COLLVIN, O'DALLAGHAN, DEANE, DIAMOND, MAC LONS, O'MAOLMONY, O'MULLIGAN, MAC NERLIN, MULROY.

Descendants of AODH UAIRIODHNACH
From page 68

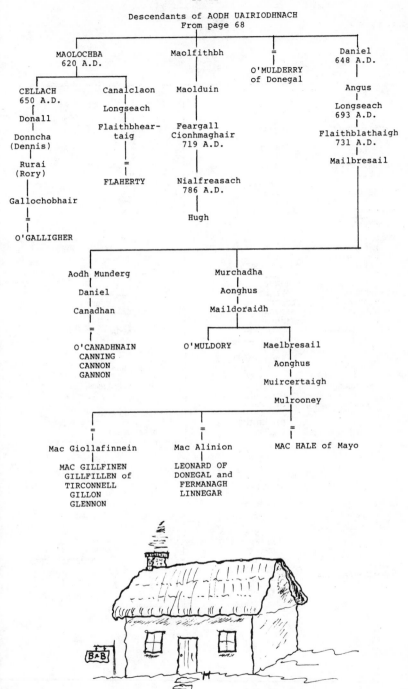

MAOLOCHBA
620 A.D.

Maolfithbh

=
O'MULDERRY
of Donegal

Daniel
648 A.D.

CELLACH
650 A.D.

Canalclaon

Maolduin

Angus

Donall

Longseach

Longseach
693 A.D.

Donncha
(Dennis)

Flaithbhear-
taig

Feargall
Cionhmaghair
719 A.D.

Flaithblathaigh
731 A.D.

Rurai
(Rory)

=

Mailbresail

Gallochobhair

FLAHERTY

Nialfreasach
786 A.D.

=

Hugh

O'GALLIGHER

Aodh Munderg

Murchadha

Daniel

Aonghus

Canadhan

Maildoraidh

=

O'CANADHNAIN
CANNING
CANNON
GANNON

O'MULDORY

Maelbresail

Aonghus

Muircertaigh

Mulrooney

=

Mac Giollafinnein

MAC GILLFINEN
GILLFILLEN of
TIRCONNELL
GILLON
GLENNON

=

Mac Alinion

LEONARD OF
DONEGAL and
FERMANAGH
LINNEGAR

=

MAC HALE of Mayo

Descendants of FIACHRATH
From page 45

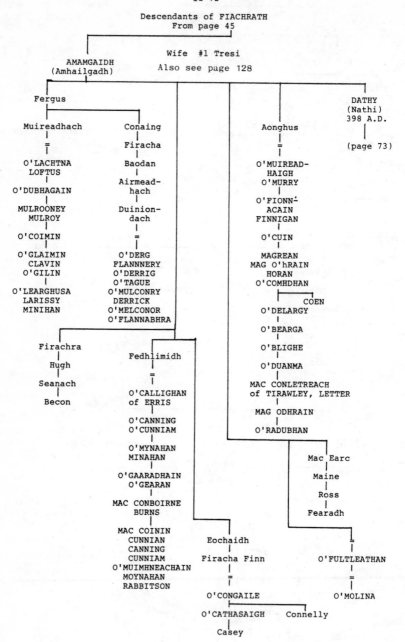

AMAMGAIDH
(Amhailgadh)

Wife #1 Tresi
Also see page 128

Fergus

DATHY
(Nathi)
398 A.D.

(page 73)

Muireadhach

O'LACHTNA
LOFTUS
|
O'DUBHAGAIN
|
MULROONEY
MULROY
|
O'COIMIN
|
O'GLAIMIN
CLAVIN
O'GILIN
|
O'LEARGHUSA
LARISSY
MINIHAN

Conaing
|
Firacha
|
Baodan
|
Airmead-
hach
|
Duinion-
dach
=
O'DERG
FLANNNERY
O'DERRIG
O'TAGUE
O'MULCONRY
DERRICK
O'MELCONOR
O'FLANNABHRA

Aonghus
=
O'MUIREAD-
HAIGH
O'MURRY
|
O'FIONN-
ACAIN
FINNIGAN
|
O'CUIN
|
MAGREAN
MAG O'hRAIN
HORAN
O'COMHDHAN
|
COEN
O'DELARGY
|
O'BEARGA
|
O'BLIGHE
|
O'DUANMA
|
MAC CONLETREACH
of TIRAWLEY, LETTER
|
MAG ODHRAIN
|
O'RADUBHAN

Firachra
|
Hugh
|
Seanach
|
Becon

Fedhlimidh
=
O'CALLIGHAN
of ERRIS
|
O'CANNING
O'CUNNIAM
|
O'MYNAHAN
MINAHAN
|
O'GAARADHAIN
O'GEARAN
|
MAC CONBOIRNE
BURNS
|
MAC COININ
CUNNIAN
CANNING
CUNNIAM
O'MUIMHNEACHAIN
MOYNAHAN
RABBITSON

Eochaidh
|
Firacha Finn
=
O'CONGAILE

Mac Earc
|
Maine
|
Ross
|
Fearadh

O'FULTLEATHAN
=
O'MOLINA

O'CATHASAIGH   Connelly
|
Casey

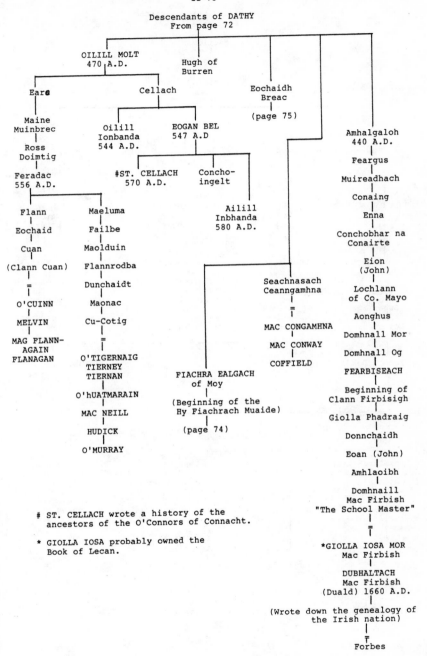

Descendants of DATHY
From page 72

OILILL MOLT
470 A.D.

Hugh of
Burren

Eare

Cellach

Eochaidh
Breac

(page 75)

Maine
Muinbrec

Oilill
Ionbanda
544 A.D.

EOGAN BEL
547 A.D

Amhalgaloh
440 A.D.

Ross
Doimtig

#ST. CELLACH
570 A.D.

Concho-
ingelt

Feargus

Feradac
556 A.D.

Muireadhach

Conaing

Flann

Maeluma

Ailill
Inbhanda
580 A.D.

Enna

Eochaid

Failbe

Conchobhar na
Conairte

Cuan

Maolduin

Eion
(John)

(Clann Cuan)

Flannrodba

Seachnasach
Ceanngamhna

Lochlann
of Co. Mayo

=

Dunchaidt

Aonghus

O'CUINN

Maonac

=

Domhnall Mor

MELVIN

Cu-Cotig

MAC CONGAMHNA

Domhnall Og

MAG FLANN-
AGAIN
FLANAGAN

=

MAC CONWAY

FEARBISEACH

O'TIGERNAIG
TIERNEY
TIERNAN

COFFIELD

Beginning of
Clann Firbisigh

O'hUATMARAIN

FIACHRA EALGACH
of Moy

Giolla Phadraig

MAC NEILL

(Beginning of the
By Fiachrach Muaide)

Donnchaidh

HUDICK

Eoan (John)

(page 74)

O'MURRAY

Amhlaoibh

Domhnaill
Mac Firbish
"The School Master"

ST. CELLACH wrote a history of the
ancestors of the O'Connors of Connacht.

=

* GIOLLA IOSA probably owned the
Book of Lecan.

*GIOLLA IOSA MOR
Mac Firbish

DUBHALTACH
Mac Firbish
(Duald) 1660 A.D.

(Wrote down the genealogy of
the Irish nation)

=

Forbes

Descendants of FIACHRA EALGACH *
From page 73

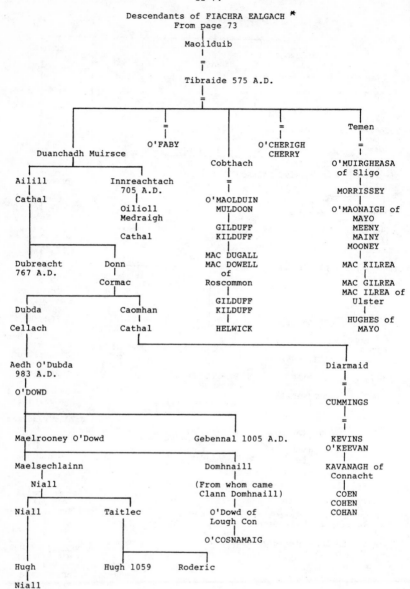

* Descendants of Fiachra Ealgach also of this line - O'DOOGAN.

Descendants of EOCHAIDH BREAC
From page 73

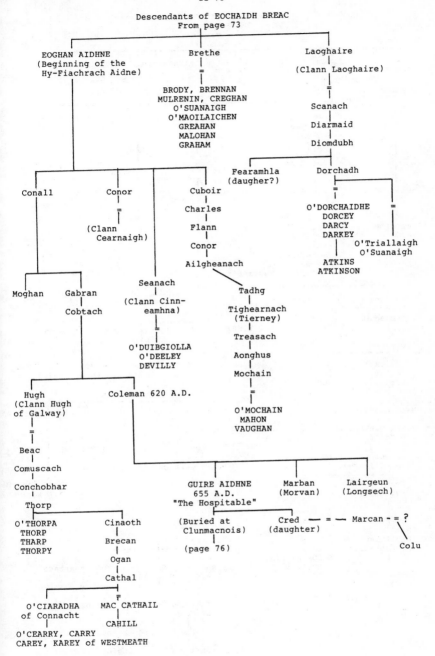

EOGHAN AIDHNE
(Beginning of the
Hy-Fiachrach Aidne)

Brethe
=
BRODY, BRENNAN
MULRENIN, CREGHAN
O'SUANAIGH
O'MAOILAICHEN
GREAHAN
MALOHAN
GRAHAM

Laoghaire
(Clann Laoghaire)
=
Scanach

Diarmaid

Diomdubh

Fearamhla
(daugher?)

Dorchadh
=
O'DORCHAIDHE
DORCEY
DARCY
DARKEY

ATKINS
ATKINSON

=
O'Triallaigh
O'Suanaigh

Conall

Conor
=
(Clann
Cearnaigh)

Cuboir

Charles

Flann

Conor

Ailgheanach

Moghan   Gabran

Cobtach

Seanach
(Clann Cinn-
eamhna)
=
O'DUIBGIOLLA
O'DEELEY
DEVILLY

Tadhg

Tighearnach
(Tierney)

Treasach

Aonghus

Mochain
=
O'MOCHAIN
MAHON
VAUGHAN

Hugh
(Clann Hugh
of Galway)
=
Beac

Comuscach

Conchobhar

Coleman 620 A.D.

GUIRE AIDHNE
655 A.D.
"The Hospitable"

(Buried at
Clunmacnois)

(page 76)

Marban
(Morvan)

Lairgeun
(Longsech)

Cred
(daughter)

— = — Marcan - = ?

Colu

Thorp

O'THORPA
THORP
THARP
THORPY

Cinaoth

Brecan

Ogan

Cathal

O'CIARADHA
of Connacht

O'CEARRY, CARRY
CAREY, KAREY of WESTMEATH

MAC CATHAIL
=
CAHILL

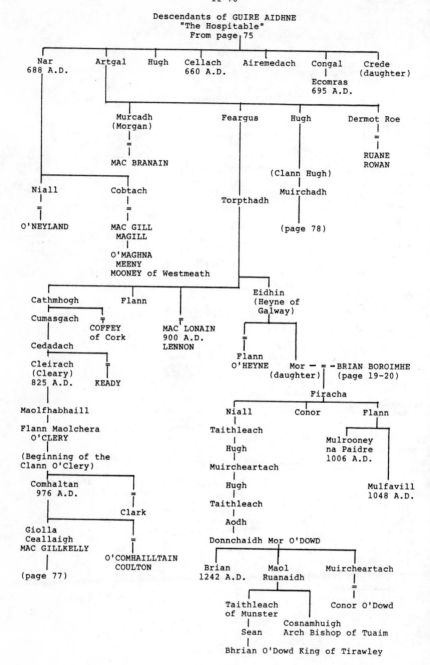

Descendants of GUIRE AIDHNE
"The Hospitable"
From page 75

Descendants of GIOLLA CELLAIGH
From page 76

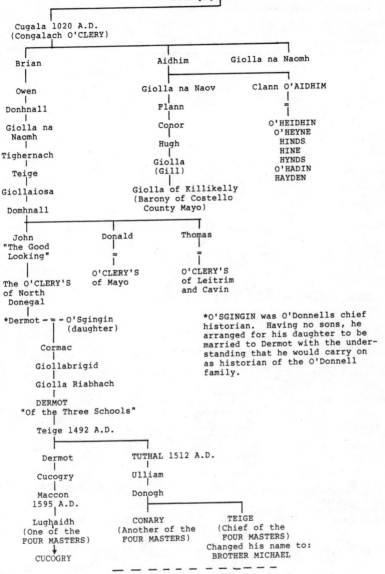

Cugala 1020 A.D.
(Congalach O'CLERY)

Brian   Aidhim   Giolla na Naomh

Owen   Giolla na Naov   Clann O'AIDHIM

Donhnall   Flann

Giolla na   Conor   O'HEIDHIN
Naomh   O'HEYNE
      Hugh   HINDS
Tighernach   HINE
      Giolla   HYNDS
Teige   (Gill)   O'HADIN
                HAYDEN
Giollaiosa   Giolla of Killikelly
      (Barony of Costello
Domhnall   County Mayo)

John   Donald   Thomas
"The Good
Looking"   O'CLERY'S   O'CLERY'S
      of Mayo   of Leitrim
The O'CLERY'S   and Cavin
of North
Donegal

*Dermot - = - O'Sgingin
         (daughter)

Cormac

Giollabrigid

Giolla Riabhach

DERMOT
"Of the Three Schools"

Teige 1492 A.D.

Dermot   TUTHAL 1512 A.D.

Cucogry   Ulliam

Maccon   Donogh
1595 A.D.

Lughaidh   CONARY   TEIGE
(One of the   (Another of the   (Chief of the
FOUR MASTERS)   FOUR MASTERS)   FOUR MASTERS)
                         Changed his name to:
CUCOGRY   BROTHER MICHAEL

*O'SGINGIN was O'Donnells chief
historian. Having no sons, he
arranged for his daughter to be
married to Dermot with the understanding that he would carry on
as historian of the O'Donnell
family.

Other families descended from EOCHAIDH BREAC (page 73):

COMMON, COWAN, HURLEY of CORK, O'LAVERTY, O'LENNAN of CORK,
LEONARD, LINNEEN, MORAN, MULDOON, O'MULFOVER.

Descendants of MUIRCHADH
From page 76

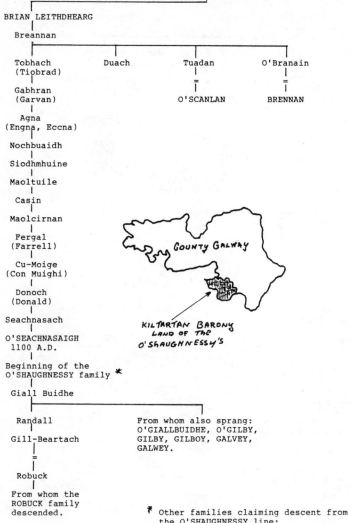

BRIAN LEITHDHEARG
|
Breannan
|

| | | |
Tobhach | Duach | Tuadan | O'Branain |
(Tiobrad) | | = | = |
| | | O'SCANLAN | BRENNAN |
Gabhran
(Garvan)
|
Agna
(Engna, Eccna)
|
Nochbuaidh
|
Siodhmhuine
|
Maoltuile
|
Casin
|
Maolcirnan
|
Fergal
(Farrell)
|
Cu-Moige
(Con Muighi)
|
Donoch
(Donald)
|
Seachnasach
|
O'SEACHNASAIGH
1100 A.D.
|
Beginning of the
O'SHAUGHNESSY family *
|
Giall Buidhe
|

KILTARTAN BARONY
LAND OF THE
O'SHAUGHNESSY'S

COUNTY GALWAY

Randall   From whom also sprang:
| O'GIALLBUIDHE, O'GILBY,
Gill-Beartach GILBY, GILBOY, GALVEY,
| GALWEY.
=
|
Robuck
|
From whom the
ROBUCK family
descended.

* Other families claiming descent from
  the O'SHAUGHNESSY line:

  O'CAFFY, O'CANNON, CREGHAN, CREIGH?,
  O'CROCAN, O'DOWEL, MAC EAGIN, O'FAHY,
  O'KEADY, O'KERIN, LIERAN, O'NENY,
  SHIEBY, MACKLAFLIN.

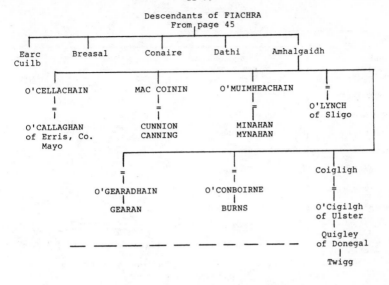

Descendants of FIACHRA
From page 45

Earc Cuilb — Breasal — Conaire — Dathi — Amhalgaidh

O'CELLACHAIN
=
O'CALLAGHAN
of Erris, Co.
Mayo

MAC COININ
CUNNION
CANNING

O'MUIMHEACHAIN
MINAHAN
MYNAHAN

=
O'LYNCH
of Sligo

=
O'GEARADHAIN
GEARAN

=
O'CONBOIRNE
BURNS

Coigligh
O'Cigilgh
of Ulster
Quigley
of Donegal
Twigg

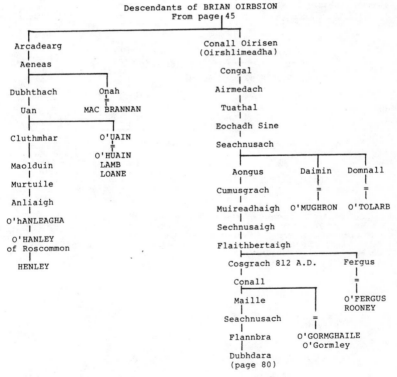

Descendants of BRIAN OIRBSION
From page 45

Arcadearg
Aeneas

Dubhthach
Uan

Onah
=
MAC BRANNAN

Cluthmhar
Maolduin
Murtuile
Anliaigh
O'hANLEAGHA
O'HANLEY
of Roscommon
HENLEY

O'UAIN
=
O'HUAIN
LAMB
LOANE

Conall Oirisen
(Oirshlimeadha)
Congal
Airmedach
Tuathal
Eochadh Sine
Seachnusach

Aongus
Cumusgrach
Muireadhaigh
Sechnusaigh
Flaithbertaigh
Cosgrach 812 A.D.
Conall
Maille
Seachnusach
Flannbra
Dubhdara
(page 80)

Daimin
=
O'MUGHRON

Domnall
=
O'TOLARB

Fergus
=
O'FERGUS
ROONEY

=
O'GORMGHAILE
O'Gormley

Descendants of DUBHDARA
From page 79

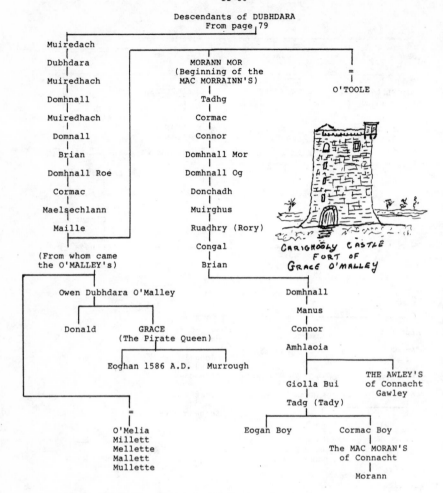

Muiredach

Dubhdara

Muiredhach   MORANN MOR
                          (Beginning of the
Domhnall   MAC MORRAINN'S)   =
                                                          |
Muiredhach   Tadhg   O'TOOLE

Domnall   Cormac

Brian   Connor

Domhnall Roe   Domhnall Mor

Cormac   Domhnall Og

Maelsechlann   Donchadh

Maille   Muirghus

                              Ruadhry (Rory)
(From whom came
the O'MALLEY's)   Congal   CARIGHOOLY CASTLE
                                                      FORT OF
                              Brian   GRACE O'MALLEY

        Owen Dubhdara O'Malley   Domhnall

                                            Manus

    Donald   GRACE   Connor
               (The Pirate Queen)
                                            Amhlaoia

        Eoghan 1586 A.D.   Murrough
                                                              THE AWLEY'S
                                                              of Connacht
                                            Giolla Bui   Gawley

                                            Tadg (Tady)
                    =
            O'Melia   Eogan Boy   Cormac Boy
            Millett
            Mellette   The MAC MORAN'S
            Mallett   of Connacht
            Mullette
                                                      Morann

GRACE O'MALLEY was one of the more colorful ladies in Irish
history. This may be one reason why more than one version
of traditional relationships exist for this family. The
one given above was collected from several sources and
cannot be fully documented.

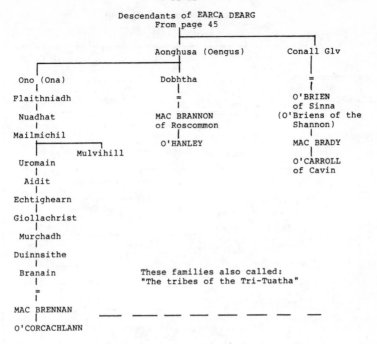

Descendants of EARCA DEARG
From page 45

Aonghusa (Oengus)   Conall Glv

Ono (Ona)   Dobhtha
| =
Flaithniadh |
| MAC BRANNON
Nuadhat   of Roscommon
|
Mailmichil   O'HANLEY
|
Uromain   Mulvihill
|
Aidit
|
Echtighearn
|
Giollachrist
|
Murchadh
|
Duinnsithe
|
Branain
|
=
|
MAC BRENNAN
|
O'CORCACHLANN

Conall Glv
=
O'BRIEN
of Sinna
(O'Briens of the
Shannon)

MAC BRADY

O'CARROLL
of Cavin

These families also called:
"The tribes of the Tri-Tuatha"

Descendants of CONALL
From page 45

It has already been shown that the MAC MORUINNS
(MORRIANS) were a branch of the O'MALLEY'S.
Others believe them to have descended from
CONALL, so this line is repeated below as
collected.

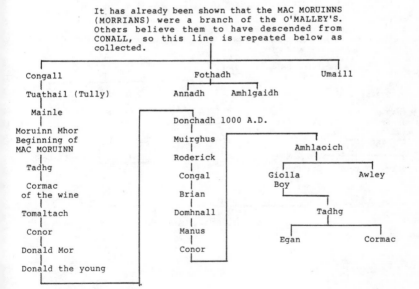

Congall   Fothadh   Umaill
|
Tuathail (Tully)   Annadh   Amhlgaidh
|
Mainle
|
Moruinn Mhor   Donchadh 1000 A.D.
Beginning of |
MAC MORUINN   Muirghus
| |
Tadhg   Roderick   Amhlaoich
| | |
Cormac   Congal   Giolla   Awley
of the wine | Boy
| Brian
Tomaltach | Tadhg
| Domhnall |
Conor | Egan   Cormac
| Manus
Donald Mor |
| Conor
Donald the young

Descendants of DUALACH GALACH*
Twenty-fourth son of Brian
From page 45

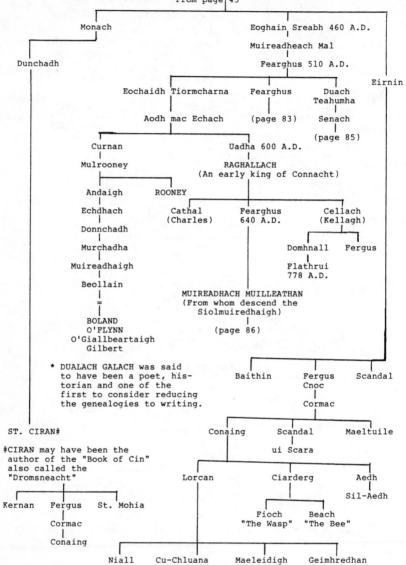

Monach

Dunchadh

Eoghain Sreabh 460 A.D.

Muireadheach Mal

Fearghus 510 A.D.

Eirnin

Eochaidh Tiormcharna   Fearghus   Duach
                                    Teahumha

Aodh mac Echach   (page 83)   Senach

                                (page 85)

Curnan   Uadha 600 A.D.

Mulrooney   RAGHALLACH
                (An early king of Connacht)

Andaigh   ROONEY

Echdhach   Cathal   Fearghus   Cellach
            (Charles)   640 A.D.   (Kellagh)

Donnchadh

Murchadha   Domhnall   Fergus

Muireadhaigh   Flathrui
                             778 A.D.
Beollain

   =   MUIREADHACH MUILLEATHAN
            (From whom descend the
BOLAND   Siolmuiredhaigh)
O'FLYNN
O'Giallbeartaigh   (page 86)
Gilbert

* DUALACH GALACH was said
  to have been a poet, his-   Baithin   Fergus   Scandal
  torian and one of the   Cnoc
  first to consider reducing
  the genealogies to writing.   Cormac

ST. CIRAN#   Conaing   Scandal   Maeltuile

#CIRAN may have been the   ui Scara
author of the "Book of Cin"
also called the
"Dromsneacht"   Lorcan   Ciarderg   Aedh

                                                     Sil-Aedh
Kernan   Fergus   St. Mohia
                              Fioch   Beach
          Cormac   "The Wasp" "The Bee"

          Conaing

              Niall   Cu-Chluana   Maeleidigh   Geimhredhan

Descendants of FEARGUS
From page 82

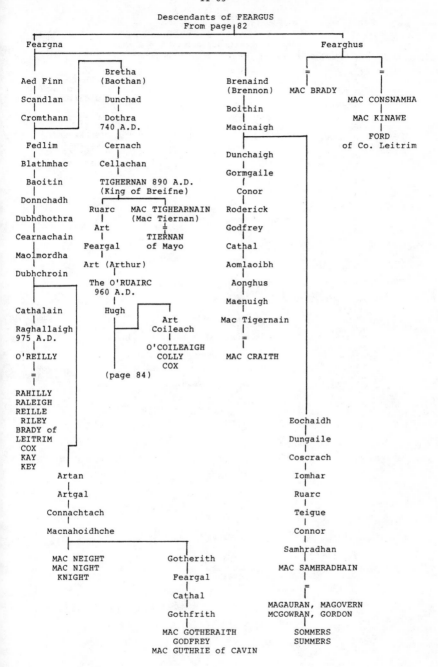

Descendants of O'RUAIRC
From page 83

Art Uallach

| Niall | UI BRIUIN EOLA | UI BRIUIN na SIONNA (Tribe name of the O'Beirnes) |

Ualgarg

=

O'LEE, LEECH

=

O'BEIRNE, of Roscommon
O'MANAHAN of Roscommon

(See P. 85)

Domnall
(UI BRIUIN of BREIFNE, tribe name of the O'Ruairc's)

Tigernan

=

MAC TIGHERNAIN
Tierney

Murchadh MAC FLYNN
King of Meath

Donnchadh

Tigernan
O'RUAIRC   =   Dearbforgail
1170 A.D.

=

BRODY, BRODIE
BRUODIN,
MAC MURRAY
MAC HUGH
MAC NEILL
NEILSON
NELSON

CLANN
MAOLMOLDHA

Taidhg Mor

Conchubhair

Catail

TAIDHG an EACHGHIL

Aodha an Ghabhearnaigh

Rugraighe

Turlough
(Terence)

Eoghin
(Owen)

Maonghus

Roderic
(Rory)

=

O'EOGHAIN

EWING
OWENS
HOYNE
HYNES
O'HOWE
in County
Fermanagh
MAC MASTER

COLES CASTLE
CO. FERMANAGH.

Descendants of SENACH
From page 82

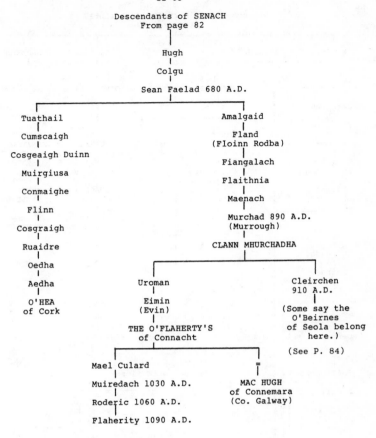

Hugh

Colgu

Sean Faelad 680 A.D.

Tuathail   Amalgaid

Cumscaigh   Fland
                              (Floinn Rodba)
Cosgeaigh Duinn
                              Fiangalach
Muirgiusa
                              Flaithnia
Conmaighe
                              Maenach
Flinn
                              Murchad 890 A.D.
Cosgraigh   (Murrough)

Ruaidre   CLANN MHURCHADHA

Oedha

Aedha   Uroman   Cleirchen
                                        910 A.D.
O'HEA   Eimin
of Cork   (Evin)   (Some say the
                                     O'Beirnes
               THE O'FLAHERTY'S   of Seola belong
                 of Connacht   here.)

                                    (See P. 84)

Mael Culard

Muiredach 1030 A.D.   MAC HUGH
                              of Connemara
Roderic 1060 A.D.   (Co. Galway)

Flaherity 1090 A.D.

AUGHNANURE CASTLE
THE O'FLAHERTY'S
CO. GALWAY

Descendants of MUIREADHACH MUILLEATHAN
From page 82

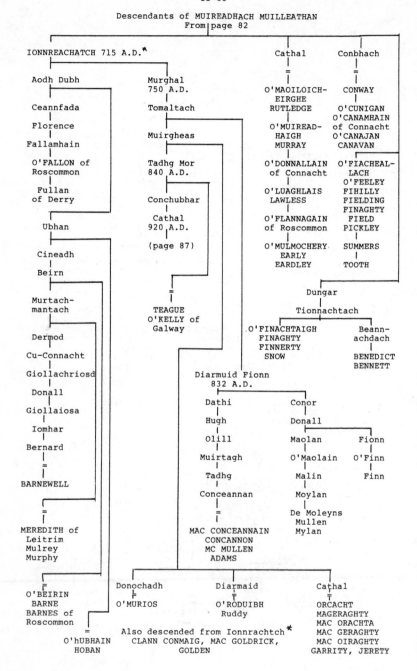

IONNREACHATCH 715 A.D. *

Aodh Dubh

Ceannfada

Florence

Fallamhain

O'FALLON of
Roscommon

Fullan
of Derry

Ubhan

Cineadh

Beirn

Murtach-
mantach

Dermod

Cu-Connacht

Giollachriosd

Donall

Giollaiosa

Iomhar

Bernard
|
=
|
BARNEWELL
|
=
|
MEREDITH of
Leitrim
Mulrey
Murphy

Murghal
750 A.D.

Tomaltach

Muirgheas

Tadhg Mor
840 A.D.

Conchubhar

Cathal
920 A.D.

(page 87)

=
|
TEAGUE
O'KELLY of
Galway

Cathal
=
O'MAOILOICH-
EIRGHE
RUTLEDGE

O'MUIREAD-
HAIGH
MURRAY

O'DONNALLAIN
of Connacht

O'LUAGHLAIS
LAWLESS

O'FLANNAGAIN
of Roscommon

O'MULMOCHERY
EARLY
EARDLEY

Conbhach
=
CONWAY

O'CUNIGAN
O'CANAMHAIN
of Connacht
O'CANAJAN
CANAVAN

O'FIACHEAL-
LACH
O'FEELEY
FIHILLY
FIELDING
FINAGHTY
FIELD
PICKLEY

SUMMERS

TOOTH

Dungar

Tionnachtach

O'FINACHTAIGH
FINAGHTY
FINNERTY
SNOW

Beann-
achdach

BENEDICT
BENNETT

Diarmuid Fionn
832 A.D.

Dathi

Hugh

Olill

Muirtagh

Tadhg

Conceannan
|
=
|
MAC CONCEANNAIN
CONCANNON
MC MULLEN
ADAMS

Conor

Donall

Maolan

O'Maolain

Malin

Moylan

De Moleyns
Mullen
Mylan

Fionn

O'Finn

Finn

O'BEIRIN
BARNE
BARNES of
Roscommon

=
|
O'hUBHAIN
HOBAN

Donochadh
=
O'MURIOS

Diarmaid
=
O'RODUIBH
Ruddy

Cathal
=
ORCACHT
MAGERAGHTY
MAC ORACHTA
MAC GERAGHTY
MAC OIRAGHTY
GARRITY, JERETY

Also descended from Ionnrachtch *
CLANN CONMAIG, MAC GOLDRICK,
GOLDEN

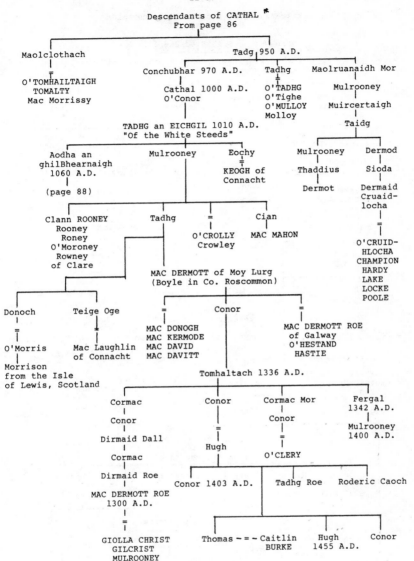

Descendants of CATHAL *
From page 86

Maolclothach

O'TOMHAILTAIGH
TOMALTY
Mac Morrissy

Tadg 950 A.D.

Conchubhar 970 A.D.

Cathal 1000 A.D.
O'Conor

Tadhg

O'TADHG
O'Tighe
O'MULLOY
Molloy

Maolruanaidh Mor

Mulrooney

Muircertaigh

Taidg

TADHG an EICHGIL 1010 A.D.
"Of the White Steeds"

Aodha an
ghilBhearnaigh
1060 A.D.

(page 88)

Mulrooney

Eochy

KEOGH of
Connacht

Mulrooney

Thaddius

Dermot

Dermod

Sioda

Dermaid
Cruaid-
locha

Clann ROONEY
Rooney
Roney
O'Moroney
Rowney
of Clare

Tadhg   =

O'CROLLY
Crowley

Cian

MAC MAHON

O'CRUID-
HLOCHA
CHAMPION
HARDY
LAKE
LOCKE
POOLE

MAC DERMOTT of Moy Lurg
(Boyle in Co. Roscommon)

Donoch

=

O'Morris

Morrison
from the Isle
of Lewis, Scotland

Teige Oge

Mac Laughlin
of Connacht

=

MAC DONOGH
MAC KERMODE
MAC DAVID
MAC DAVITT

Conor

=

MAC DERMOTT ROE
of Galway
O'HESTAND
HASTIE

Tomhaltach 1336 A.D.

Cormac

Conor

Dirmaid Dall

Cormac

Dirmaid Roe

MAC DERMOTT ROE
1300 A.D.

=

GIOLLA CHRIST
GILCRIST
MULROONEY

Conor

=

Hugh

Cormac Mor

Conor

=

O'CLERY

Fergal
1342 A.D.

Mulrooney
1400 A.D.

Conor 1403 A.D.

Tadhg Roe

Roderic Caoch

Thomas – = – Caitlin
BURKE

Hugh
1455 A.D.

Conor

Other Descendants of Cathal are: *

FANAGHEY, FEENAHY, FENTON, O'MAOILBREANAINN, MULREANNAN.

Descendants of AODH an gHILBHEARNAIGH
From page 87

RUADIHRI na SOIGHE BUIDHE 1118 A.D.

Conor — Tadg — TOIRDHEALBHACH MOR O'CONNOR — Nial Aithclerech
(Turlough Mor)   1150 A.D.

Conor O'Connor
of Dublin
│
Gilbert
(Who changed his
surname to DENOGENT
│
NUGENT

Brian
Breifneach
1155 A.D.
│
Urgan 1190 A.D.
│
Cathal Migaran

Aodh Dall
"Hugh the blind"
│
Maelsechlainn
│
Fingin
│
Donnchad
=
O'MALLONE of
OFFALY
│
O'GILBY
OGILVY
Gilboy

=
O'DOLLE
DOYLE

RUADHE
O'CONCHUBHAIR
1150 A.D.
│
(page 89)
│
Domhnaill
1155 A.D.
│
BRIAN
LUIGHNEACH
1181 A.D.
│
(page 91)
│
CATHAL
CROIBHOHEARG
1220
│
(page 92)

Dermot
│
Donogh

Mor (Daughter)

Melsa
1220 A.D.
=
Maoleoin
│
O'MAOILEON
MALONE

Tadgh
Aluinn

(Hugh)

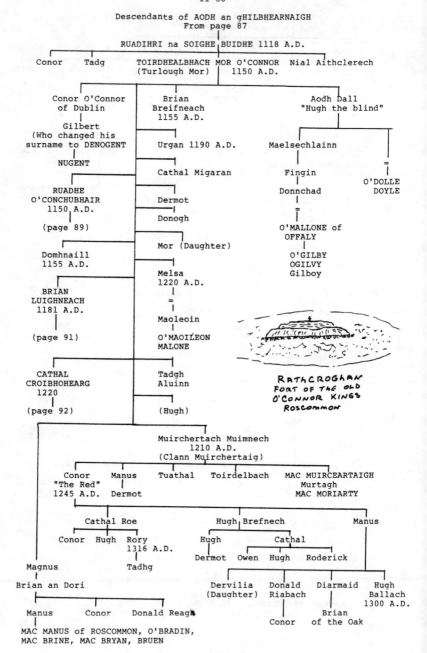

RATHCROGHAN
FORT OF THE OLD
O'CONNOR KINGS
ROSCOMMON

Muirchertach Muimnech
1210 A.D.
(Clann Muirchertaig)

Conor
"The Red"
1245 A.D.
│
Cathal Roe

Manus
│
Dermot

Tuathal

Toirdelbach

MAC MUIRCEARTAIGH
Murtagh
MAC MORIARTY

Conor Hugh Rory
1316 A.D.

Hugh Brefnech

Manus

Magnus
│
Brian an Dori

Tadhg

Hugh
│
Dermot

Cathal
│
Owen Hugh Roderick

Manus Conor Donald Reagh

MAC MANUS of ROSCOMMON, O'BRADIN,
MAC BRINE, MAC BRYAN, BRUEN

Dervilia
(Daughter)

Donald
Riabach
│
Conor

Diarmaid
│
Brian
of the Oak

Hugh
Ballach
1300 A.D.

Descendants of RUADHE O'CONCHUBHAIR
(Roderic O'Connor)
From page 88

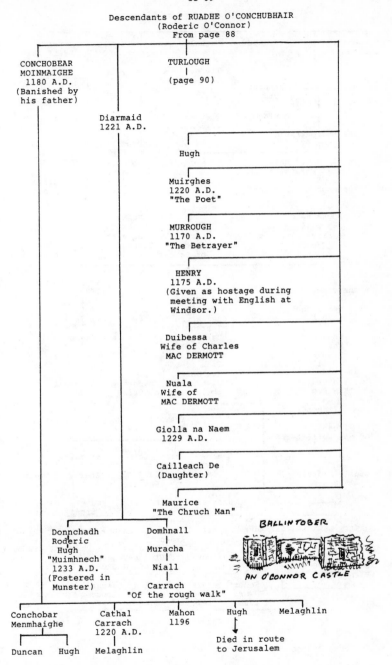

CONCHOBEAR
MOINMAIGHE
1180 A.D.
(Banished by
his father)

TURLOUGH

(page 90)

Diarmaid
1221 A.D.

Hugh

Muirghes
1220 A.D.
"The Poet"

MURROUGH
1170 A.D.
"The Betrayer"

HENRY
1175 A.D.
(Given as hostage during
meeting with English at
Windsor.)

Duibessa
Wife of Charles
MAC DERMOTT

Nuala
Wife of
MAC DERMOTT

Giolla na Naem
1229 A.D.

Cailleach De
(Daughter)

Maurice
"The Chruch Man"

BALLINTOBER

Donnchadh
Roderic
Hugh
"Muimhnech"
1233 A.D.
(Fostered in
Munster)

Domhnall

Muracha

Niall

Carrach
"Of the rough walk"

AN O'CONNOR CASTLE

Conchobar
Menmhaighe

Cathal
Carrach
1220 A.D.

Mahon
1196

Hugh

Melaghlin

Duncan   Hugh   Melaghlin

Died in route
to Jerusalem

Descendants of TURLOUGH O'CONNOR
From page 89

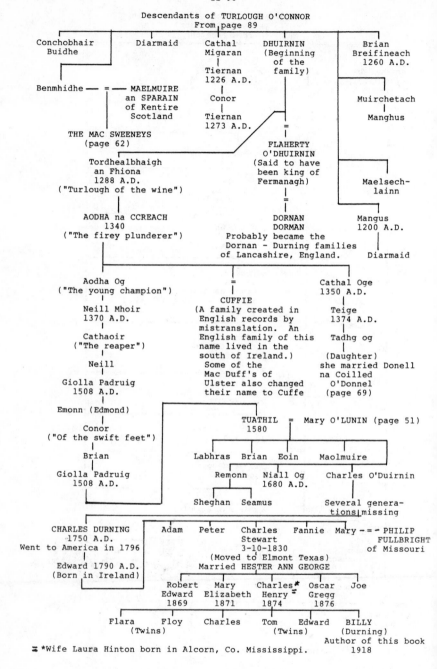

Conchobhair Buidhe — Diarmaid — Cathal Migaran | Tiernan 1226 A.D. | Conor | Tiernan 1273 A.D.

DHUIRNIN (Beginning of the family)

Brian Breifineach 1260 A.D. | Muirchetach | Manghus

Benmhidhe = MAELMUIRE an SPARAIN of Kentire Scotland

THE MAC SWEENEYS (page 62)

Tordhealbhaigh an Fhiona 1288 A.D. ("Turlough of the wine")

= FLAHERTY O'DHUIRNIN (Said to have been king of Fermanagh)

Maelsech-lainn

AODHA na CCREACH 1340 ("The firey plunderer")

= DORNAN DORMAN
Probably became the Dornan - Durning families of Lancashire, England.

Mangus 1200 A.D. | Diarmaid

Aodha Og ("The young champion") | Neill Mhoir 1370 A.D. | Cathaoir ("The reaper") | Neill | Giolla Padruig 1508 A.D. | Emonn (Edmond) | Conor ("Of the swift feet") | Brian | Giolla Padruig 1508 A.D.

= CUFFIE
(A family created in English records by mistranslation. An English family of this name lived in the south of Ireland.) Some of the Mac Duff's of Ulster also changed their name to Cuffe

Cathal Oge 1350 A.D. | Teige 1374 A.D. | Tadhg og | (Daughter) she married Donell na Coilled O'Donnel (page 69)

TUATHIL = Mary O'LUNIN (page 51)
1580

Labhras   Brian   Eoin   Maolmuire

Remonn   Niall Og 1680 A.D.

Charles O'Duirnin

Sheghan   Seamus

Several generations missing

CHARLES DURNING 1750 A.D. Went to America in 1796 | Edward 1790 A.D. (Born in Ireland)

Adam   Peter   Charles Stewart 3-10-1830 (Moved to Elmont Texas) Married HESTER ANN GEORGE   Fannie   Mary = PHILIP FULLBRIGHT of Missouri

Robert Edward 1869   Mary Elizabeth 1871   Charles* Henry = 1874   Oscar Gregg 1876   Joe

Flara   Floy (Twins)   Charles   Tom   Edward (Twins)   BILLY (Durning) Author of this book 1918

= *Wife Laura Hinton born in Alcorn, Co. Mississippi.

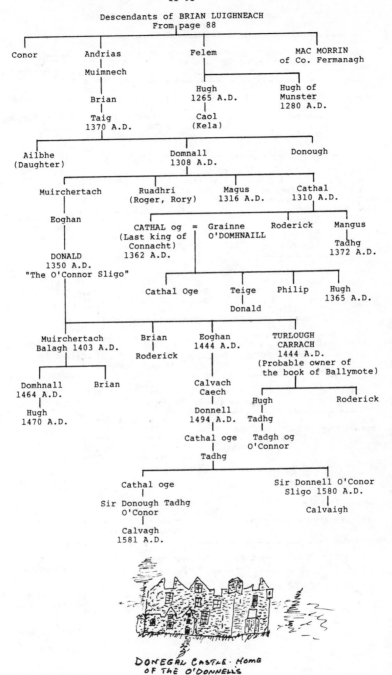

Descendants of BRIAN LUIGHNEACH
From page 88

Conor   Andrias   Felem   MAC MORRIN
of Co. Fermanagh

Muimnech

Hugh
1265 A.D.   Hugh of
Munster
1280 A.D.

Brian

Taig
1370 A.D.   Caol
(Kela)

Ailbhe
(Daughter)   Domnall
1308 A.D.   Donough

Muirchertach   Ruadhri
(Roger, Rory)   Magus
1316 A.D.   Cathal
1310 A.D.

Eoghan

CATHAL og = Grainne
(Last king of   O'DOMHNAILL
Connacht)
1362 A.D.   Roderick   Mangus

DONALD
1350 A.D.
"The O'Connor Sligo"   Tadhg
1372 A.D.

Cathal Oge   Teige   Philip   Hugh
1365 A.D.

Donald

Muirchertach
Balagh 1403 A.D.   Brian   Eoghan
1444 A.D.   TURLOUGH
CARRACH
1444 A.D.
(Probable owner of
the book of Ballymote)

Roderick

Domhnall
1464 A.D.   Brian   Calvach
Caech   Hugh   Roderick

Hugh
1470 A.D.   Donnell
1494 A.D.   Tadhg

Cathal oge   Tadgh og
O'Connor

Tadhg

Cathal oge   Sir Donnell O'Conor
Sligo 1580 A.D.

Sir Donough Tadhg
O'Conor   Calvaigh

Calvagh
1581 A.D.

DONEGAL CASTLE. HOME
OF THE O'DONNELLS

Descendants of CATHAL CROIBHOHEARG*
From page 88

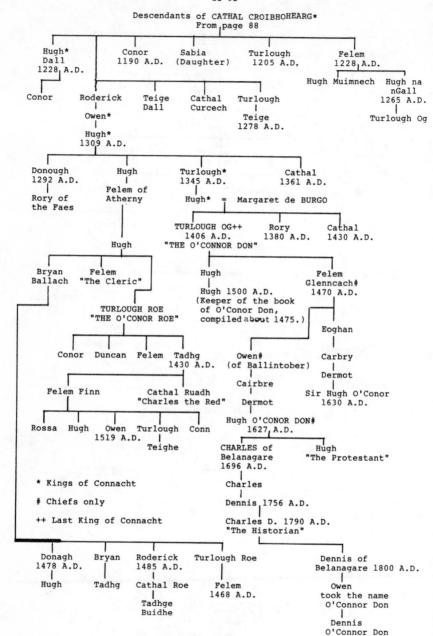

* Kings of Connacht

Chiefs only

++ Last King of Connacht

Descendants of LOGAIRE LORC
From page 40

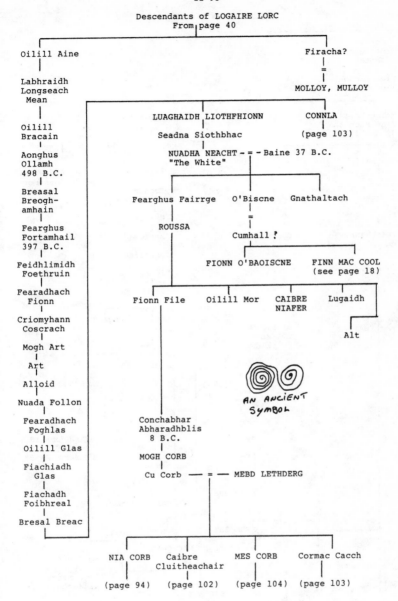

Oilill Aine

Labhraidh
Longseach
Mean

Oilill
Bracain

Aonghus
Ollamh
498 B.C.

Breasal
Breogh-
amhain

Fearghus
Fortamhail
397 B.C.

Feidhlimidh
Foethruin

Fearadhach
Fionn

Criomyhann
Coscrach

Mogh Art

Art

Alloid

Nuada Follon

Fearadhach
Foghlas

Oilill Glas

Fiachiadh
Glas

Fiachadh
Foibhreal

Bresal Breac

Firacha?
=
MOLLOY, MULLOY

LUAGHAIDH LIOTHFHIONN   CONNLA
                              (page 103)
Seadna Siothbhac

NUADHA NEACHT - = - Baine 37 B.C.
"The White"

Fearghus Fairrge   O'Biscne   Gnathaltach
                        =
ROUSSA   Cumhall ?

            FIONN O'BAOISCNE   FINN MAC COOL
                                (see page 18)

Fionn File   Oilill Mor   CAIBRE   Lugaidh
                            NIAFER

                                      Alt

AN ANCIENT
SYMBOL

Conchabhar
Abharadhblis
8 B.C.

MOGH CORB

Cu Corb — = — MEBD LETHDERG

NIA CORB   Caibre   MES CORB   Cormac Cacch
            Cluitheachair

(page 94)   (page 102)   (page 104)   (page 103)

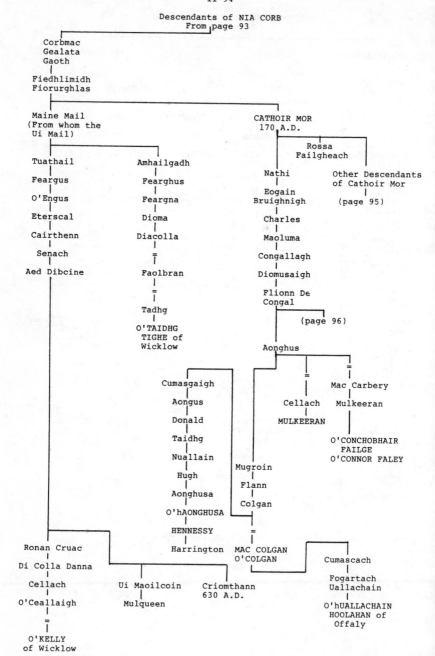

Descendants of NIA CORB
From page 93

Corbmac
Gealata
Gaoth

Fiedhlimidh
Fiorurghlas

Maine Mail
(From whom the
Ui Mail)

CATHOIR MOR
170 A.D.

Rossa
Failgheach

Tuathail

Amhailgadh

Nathi

Other Descendants
of Cathoir Mor

Feargus

Fearghus

Eogain
Bruighnigh

(page 95)

O'Engus

Feargna

Charles

Eterscal

Dioma

Maoluma

Cairthenn

Diacolla

Congallagh

Senach

=

Diomusaigh

Aed Dibcine

Faolbran

Flionn De
Congal

=

(page 96)

Tadhg

Aonghus

O'TAIDHG
TIGHE of
Wicklow

Cumasgaigh

=

Mac Carbery

Aongus

Cellach

Mulkeeran

Donald

MULKEERAN

Taidhg

O'CONCHOBHAIR
FAILGE
O'CONNOR FALEY

Nuallain

Hugh

Aonghusa

Mugroin

O'hAONGHUSA

Flann

HENNESSY

Colgan

Ronan Cruac

Harrington

=

Di Colla Danna

MAC COLGAN
O'COLGAN

Cellach

Cumascach

O'Ceallaigh

Ui Maoilcoin

Criomthann
630 A.D.

Fogartach
Uallachain

=

Mulqueen

O'hUALLACHAIN
HOOLAHAN of
Offaly

O'KELLY
of Wicklow

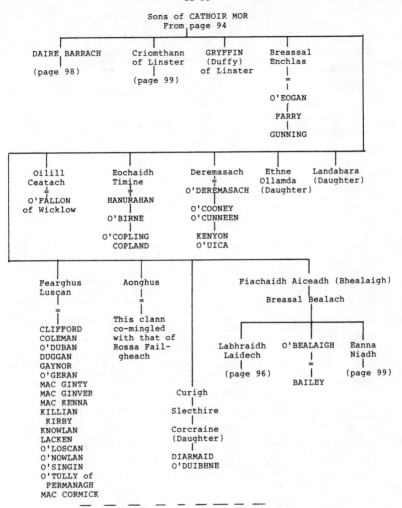

Sons of CATHOIR MOR
From page 94

DAIRE BARRACH

(page 98)

Criomthann
of Linster

(page 99)

GRYFFIN
(Duffy)
of Linster

Breassal
Enchlas
=

O'EOGAN

FARRY

GUNNING

Oilill
Ceatach
=
O'FALLON
of Wicklow

Eochaidh
Timine
=
HANURAHAN

O'BIRNE

O'COPLING
COPLAND

Deremasach
=
O'DEREMASACH

O'COONEY
O'CUNNEEN

KENYON
O'UICA

Ethne
Ollamda
(Daughter)

Landabara
(Daughter)

Fearghus
Luscan

=

CLIFFORD
COLEMAN
O'DUBAN
DUGGAN
GAYNOR
O'GERAN
MAC GINTY
MAC GINVER
MAC KENNA
KILLIAN
KIRBY
KNOWLAN
LACKEN
O'LOSCAN
O'NOWLAN
O'SINGIN
O'TULLY of
  FERMANAGH
MAC CORMICK

Aonghus
=
This clann
co-mingled
with that of
Rossa Fail-
gheach

Fiachaidh Aiceadh (Bhealaigh)

Breasal Bealach

Labhraidh
Laidech

(page 96)

O'BEALAIGH

BAILEY

Eanna
Niadh

(page 99)

Curigh

Slecthire

Corcraine
(Daughter)

DIARMAID
O'DUIBHNE

The following families are said to descend from CATHOIR MOR
page 94: ALLIAN, O'CULLEN, MAC DONAGH, O'DONDON, ENNIS,
O'FINN, FORAN, O'FORANAN, HARTAGAN, MAC LEAN, O'MAINE,
MORGAN.

Descendants of LABHRAIDH LAIDECH
From page 95

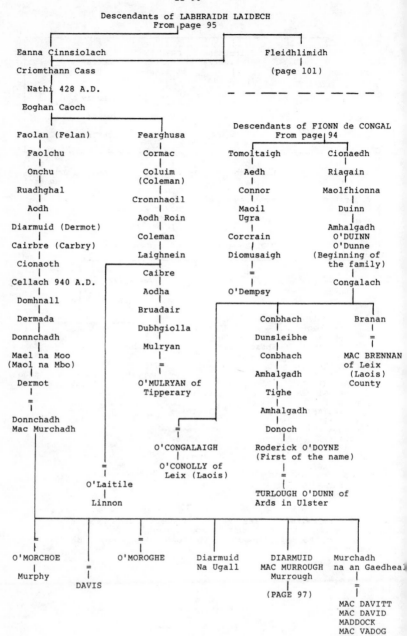

Eanna Cinnsiolach

Criomthann Cass

Nathi 428 A.D.

Eoghan Caoch

Fleidhlimidh

(page 101)

Faolan (Felan)

Faolchu

Onchu

Ruadhghal

Aodh

Diarmuid (Dermot)

Cairbre (Carbry)

Cionaoth

Cellach 940 A.D.

Domhnall

Dermada

Donnchadh

Mael na Moo
(Maol na Mbo)

Dermot
=

Donnchadh
Mac Murchadh

Fearghusa

Cormac

Coluim
(Coleman)

Cronnhaoil

Aodh Roin

Coleman

Laighnein

Caibre

Aodha

Bruadair

Dubhgiolla

Mulryan
=

O'MULRYAN of
Tipperary

Descendants of FIONN de CONGAL
From page 94

Tomoltaigh

Aedh

Connor

Maoil
Ugra

Corcrain

Diomusaigh
=

O'Dempsy

Cionaedh

Riagain

Maolfhionna

Duinn

Amhalgadh
O'DUINN
O'Dunne
(Beginning of
the family)

Congalach

Conbhach

Dunsleibhe

Conbhach

Amhalgadh

Tighe

Amhalgadh

Donoch

Roderick O'DOYNE
(First of the name)
=

TURLOUGH O'DUNN of
Ards in Ulster

Branan
=

MAC BRENNAN
of Leix
(Laois)
County

O'CONGALAIGH

O'CONOLLY of
Leix (Laois)

=
O'Laitile

Linnon

O'MORCHOE

Murphy

=
DAVIS

O'MOROGHE

Diarmuid
Na Ugall

DIARMUID
MAC MURROUGH
Murrough

(PAGE 97)

Murchadh
na an Gaedheal

=
MAC DAVITT
MAC DAVID
MADDOCK
MAC VADOG
WADDICK

Descendants of DIARMUID MAC MURROUGH
From page 96

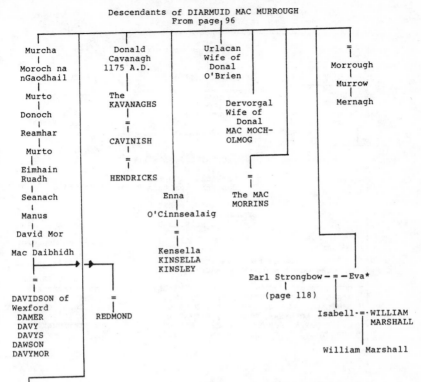

Murcha
|
Moroch na
nGaodhail
|
Murto
|
Donoch
|
Reamhar
|
Murto
|
Eimhain
Ruadh
|
Seanach
|
Manus
|
David Mor
|
Mac Daibhidh

DAVIDSON of
Wexford
DAMER
DAVY
DAVYS
DAWSON
DAVYMOR

Donald
Cavanagh
1175 A.D.

The
KAVANAGHS

CAVINISH

HENDRICKS

REDMOND

Urlacan
Wife of
Donal
O'Brien

Dervorgal
Wife of
Donal
MAC MOCH-
OLMOG

Enna
O'Cinnsealaig

Kensella
KINSELLA
KINSLEY

The MAC
MORRINS

Morrough
Murrow
Mernagh

Earl Strongbow — = — Eva*
(page 118)

Isabell - = - WILLIAM
MARSHALL

William Marshall

CONOR - This son was blinded by an enemy in 1168. He was later given
as hostage to hi-king Roderic O'Connor. His father broke the
treaty with O'Connor, who had Conor put to death.

* Much has been written about Eva and her fathers promise
of her as bride to Earl Strongbow. Under Irish law the
land did not belong to the king but to the people.
Norman law, however, said that the king owned the land
and all in it. Thus, by marriage, Strongbow came into
possession of Irish land.

CASHEL

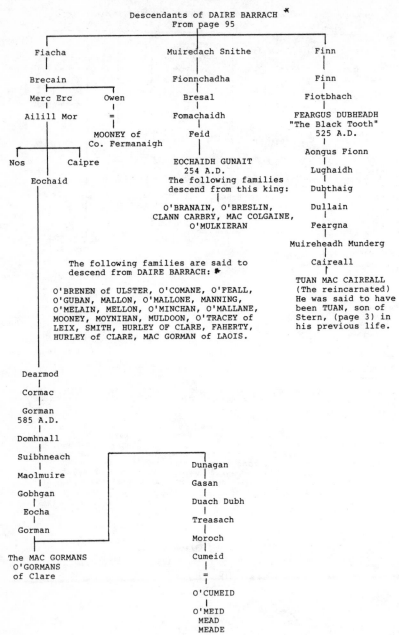

Descendants of DAIRE BARRACH *
From page 95

Fiacha
|
Brecain
|
Merc Erc   Owen
| =
Ailill Mor
              MOONEY of
              Co. Fermanaigh

Nos   Caipre
|
Eochaid

Muiredach Snithe
|
Fionnchadha
|
Bresal
|
Fomachaidh
|
Feid
|
EOCHAIDH GUNAIT
254 A.D.
The following families
descend from this king:

O'BRANAIN, O'BRESLIN,
CLANN CARBRY, MAC COLGAINE,
O'MULKIERAN

Finn
|
Finn
|
Fiotbhach
|
FEARGUS DUBHEADH
"The Black Tooth"
525 A.D.
|
Aongus Fionn
|
Lughaidh
|
Dubthaig
|
Dullain
|
Feargna
|
Muireheadh Munderg
|
Caireall

TUAN MAC CAIREALL
(The reincarnated)
He was said to have
been TUAN, son of
Stern, (page 3) in
his previous life.

The following families are said to
descend from DAIRE BARRACH: *

O'BRENEN of ULSTER, O'COMANE, O'FEALL,
O'GUBAN, MALLON, O'MALLONE, MANNING,
O'MELAIN, MELLON, O'MINCHAN, O'MALLANE,
MOONEY, MOYNIHAN, MULDOON, O'TRACEY of
LEIX, SMITH, HURLEY OF CLARE, FAHERTY,
HURLEY of CLARE, MAC GORMAN of LAOIS.

Dearmod
|
Cormac
|
Gorman
585 A.D.
|
Domhnall
|
Suibhneach
|
Maolmuire
|
Gobhgan
|
Eocha
|
Gorman

The MAC GORMANS
O'GORMANS
of Clare

Dunagan
|
Gasan
|
Duach Dubh
|
Treasach
|
Moroch
|
Cumeid
|
=
|
O'CUMEID
|
O'MEID
MEAD
MEADE

Descendants of CRIOMTHANN
Of Linster, page 95

Aenghusa

Eochach

Criomthann

Nastair

Nainedh

Cormack

Cobthaigh

Eoghain

Mailochtaigh

Dubhdacrioch

Conqalaigh

Dunqhaile

Cinnfaeladh

Murchadh

Dubfel

Uchbuidh

O'CRIOMTHAIN

CRAMTON
GRIFFIN

Noinnean

Maoloctrach

Flaithreach

Marcam

Dubh
=

O'DUIBHE
DOWLING of
Offaly

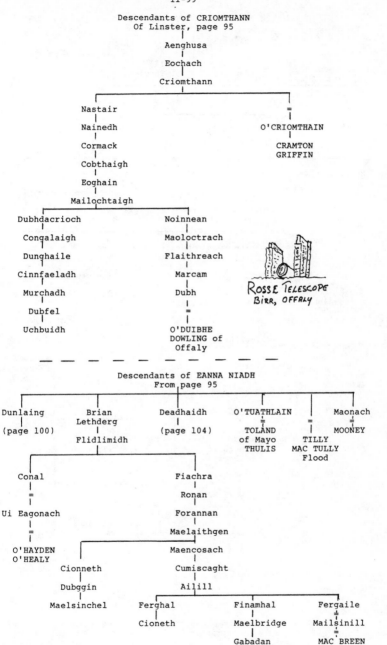

ROSSE TELESCOPE
BIRR, OFFALY

— — — — — — — —

Descendants of EANNA NIADH
From page 95

Dunlaing
(page 100)

Brian
Lethderg

Flidlimidh

Deadhaidh
(page 104)

O'TUATHLAIN
=
TOLAND
of Mayo
THULIS

=
TILLY
MAC TULLY
Flood

Maonach
=
MOONEY

Conal
=
Ui Eagonach
=
O'HAYDEN
O'HEALY

Fiachra

Ronan

Forannan

Maelaithgen

Maencosach

Cumiscaght

Ailill

Cionneth

Dubggin

Maelsinchel

Ferghal

Cioneth

Finamhal

Maelbridge

Gabadan

Fergaile
=
Mailsinill
=
MAC BREEN
MAC BRAOIN of OSSORY

Descendants of DUNLAING
From page 99

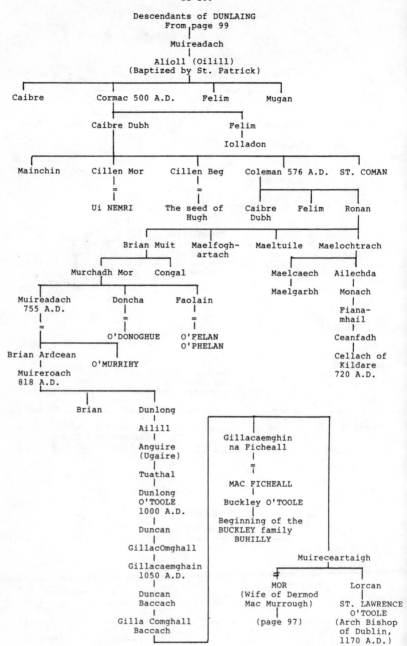

Muireadach
|
Alioll (Oilill)
(Baptized by St. Patrick)

Caibre   Cormac 500 A.D.   Felim   Mugan

Caibre Dubh   Felim
|
Iolladon

Mainchin Cillen Mor Cillen Beg Coleman 576 A.D. ST. COMAN
=   =
Ui NEMRI   The seed of Caibre Felim Ronan
         Hugh   Dubh

Brian Muit Maelfogh- Maeltuile Maelochtrach
         artach

Murchadh Mor Congal   Maelcaech Ailechda

                     Maelgarbh Monach

Muireadach Doncha Faolain   Fiana-
755 A.D.   mhail
=   =   =
      O'DONOGHUE O'FELAN   Ceanfadh
                 O'PHELAN
Brian Ardcean   Cellach of
| O'MURRIHY   Kildare
Muireroach   720 A.D.
818 A.D.

Brian Dunlong
      Ailill   Gillacaemghin
      | na Ficheall
      Anguire   =
      (Ugaire)   MAC FICHEALL
      Tuathal   Buckley O'TOOLE
      Dunlong   Beginning of the
      O'TOOLE   BUCKLEY family
      1000 A.D.   BUHILLY
      Duncan
      GillacOmghall
      Gillacaemghain   Muireceartaigh
      1050 A.D.
      Duncan   =
      Baccach   MOR   Lorcan
            (Wife of Dermod |
    Gilla Comghall Mac Murrough) ST. LAWRENCE
    Baccach   O'TOOLE
           (page 97) (Arch Bishop
                    of Dublin,
                    1170 A.D.)

Descendants of FLEIDHLIMIDH
From page 96

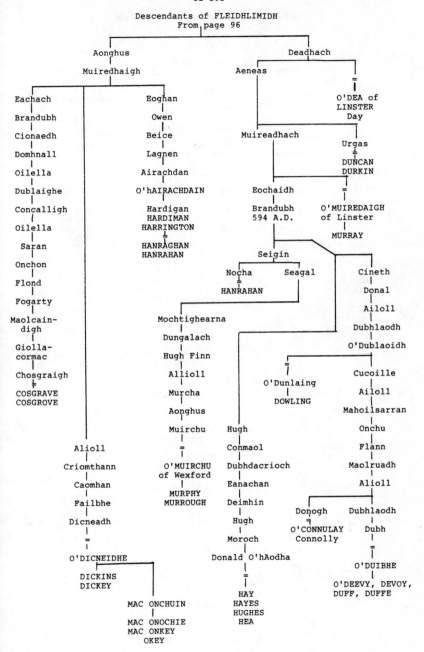

Descendants of CAIRBRE CLUITHEACHAIR
From page 93

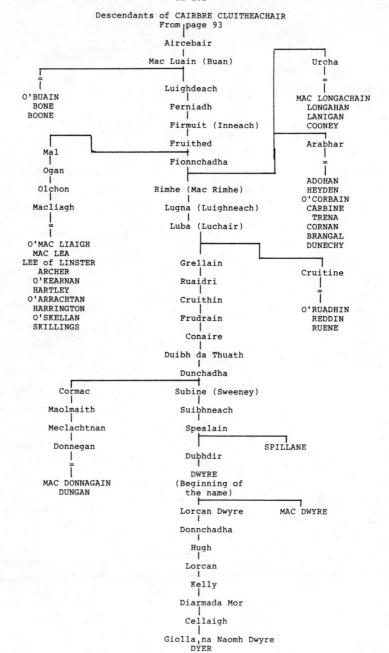

Aircebair

Mac Luain (Buan)

Urcha

O'BUAIN
BONE
BOONE

Luighdeach

Ferniadh

Firmuit (Inneach)

MAC LONGACHAIN
LONGAHAN
LANIGAN
COONEY

Fruithed

Arabhar

Mal

Fionnchadha

Ogan

Olchon

Macliagh

Rimhe (Mac Rimhe)

Lugna (Luighneach)

Luba (Luchair)

ADOHAN
HEYDEN
O'CORBAIN
CARBINE
TRENA
CORNAN
BRANGAL
DUNECHY

O'MAC LIAIGH
MAC LEA
LEE of LINSTER
ARCHER
O'KEARNAN
HARTLEY
O'ARRACHTAN
HARRINGTON
O'SKELLAN
SKILLINGS

Grellain

Cruitine

Ruaidri

Cruithin

O'RUADHIN
REDDIN
RUENE

Frudrain

Conaire

Duibh da Thuath

Dunchadha

Cormac

Subine (Sweeney)

Maolmaith

Suibhneach

Meclachtnan

Spealain

SPILLANE

Donnegan

Dubhdir

DWYRE
(Beginning of
the name)

MAC DONNAGAIN
DUNGAN

Lorcan Dwyre

MAC DWYRE

Donnchadha

Hugh

Lorcan

Kelly

Diarmada Mor

Cellaigh

Giolla na Naomh Dwyre
DYER

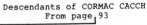

Descendants of CORMAC CACCH
From page 93

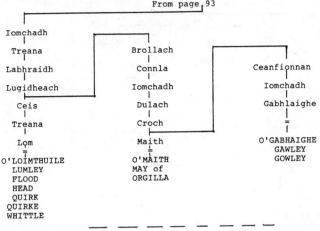

Iomchadh
Treana
Labhraidh
Lugidheach
Ceis
Treana
Lom
=
O'LOIMTHUILE
LUMLEY
FLOOD
HEAD
QUIRK
QUIRKE
WHITTLE

Brollach
Connla
Iomchadh
Dulach
Croch
Maith
=
O'MAITH
MAY of
ORGILLA

Ceanfionnan
Iomchadh
Gabhlaighe
=
O'GABHAIGHE
GAWLEY
GOWLEY

Descendants of CONNLA
From page 93

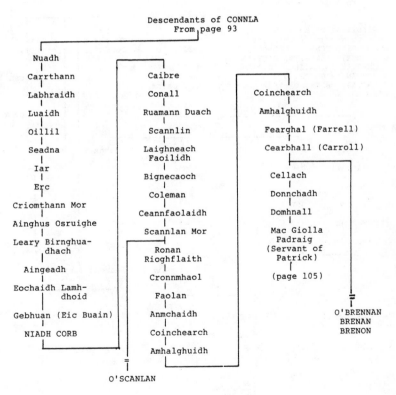

Nuadh
Carrthann
Labhraidh
Luaidh
Oillil
Seadna
Iar
Erc
Criomthann Mor
Ainghus Osruighe
Leary Birnghua-dhach
Aingeadh
Eochaidh Lamh-dhoid
Gebhuan (Eic Buain)
NIADH CORB

Caibre
Conall
Ruamann Duach
Scannlin
Laighneach Faoilidh
Bignecaoch
Coleman
Ceannfaolaidh
Scannlan Mor
Ronan Rioghflaith
Cronnmhaol
Faolan
Anmchaidh
Coinchearch
Amhalghuidh
=
O'SCANLAN

Coinchearch
Amhalghuidh
Fearghal (Farrell)
Cearbhall (Carroll)
Cellach
Donnchadh
Domhnall
Mac Giolla Padraig (Servant of Patrick)
(page 105)
=
O'BRENNAN
BRENAN
BRENON

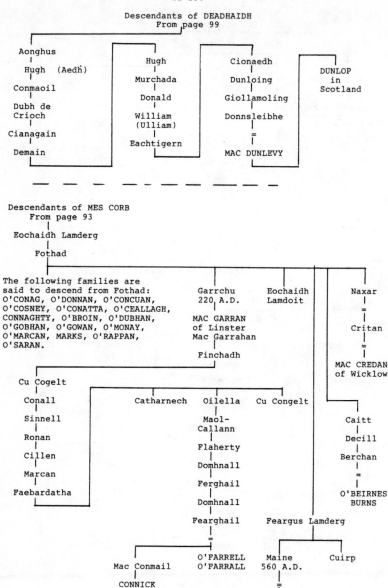

Descendants of DEADHAIDH
From page 99

Aonghus
|
Hugh (Aedh)
|
Conmaoil
|
Dubh de
Crioch
|
Cianagain
|
Demain

Hugh
|
Murchada
|
Donald
|
William
(Ulliam)
|
Eachtigern

Cionaedh
|
Dunloing
|
Giollamoling
|
Donnsleibhe
=
MAC DUNLEVY

DUNLOP
in
Scotland

Descendants of MES CORB
From page 93

Eochaidh Lamderg
|
Fothad

The following families are
said to descend from Fothad:
O'CONAG, O'DONNAN, O'CONCUAN,
O'COSNEY, O'CONATTA, O'CEALLAGH,
CONNAGHTY, O'BROIN, O'DUBHAN,
O'GOBHAN, O'GOWAN, O'MONAY,
O'MARCAN, MARKS, O'RAPPAN,
O'SARAN.

Garrchu
220 A.D.
|
MAC GARRAN
of Linster
Mac Garrahan
|
Finchadh

Eochaidh
Lamdoit

Naxar
=
Critan
=
MAC CREDAN
of Wicklow

Cu Cogelt
|
Conall
|
Sinnell
|
Ronan
|
Cillen
|
Marcan
|
Faebardatha

Catharnech

Oilella
|
Maol-
Callann
|
Flaherty
|
Domhnall
|
Ferghail
|
Domhnall
|
Fearghail
=

Cu Congelt

Caitt
|
Decill
|
Berchan
=
O'BEIRNES
BURNS

Mac Conmail
|
CONNICK

O'FARRELL
O'FARRALL

Feargus Lamderg

Maine
560 A.D.
=
O'SLEIGHAN
of Kilshine
Shine

Cuirp

Descendants of GIOLLA PADRAIG
From page 103

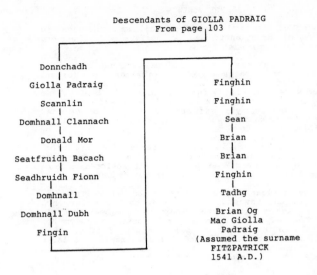

Donnchadh
|
Giolla Padraig
|
Scannlin
|
Domhnall Clannach
|
Donald Mor
|
Seatfruidh Bacach
|
Seadhruidh Fionn
|
Domhnall
|
Domhnall Dubh
|
Fingin

Finghin
|
Finghin
|
Sean
|
Brian
|
Brian
|
Finghin
|
Tadhg
|
Brian Og
Mac Giolla
Padraig
(Assumed the surname
FITZPATRICK
1541 A.D.)

THE ASH TREE BY THE CABIN

By an old mountain cabin there grows a wild ash
　　Twas planted by Nature I'm told
The storms of Winter may rave and may lash
　　But it's roots firmly anchored still hold

When trees and flowers have strung into leaf
　　And wild birds sing sweet song on the spray
From the cabin you hear the shrill notes of the fife
　　While rambling the hillside and brae

Quite often with comrades I rambled along
　　And sheltered neath the old ash tree
Then repaired to the cabin where music and song
　　Whiled way the night with mirthmaking glee

Long years have rolled by since last strolling that hill
　　And the cabin I oft loved to see
Now lies there in ruins, what sadness it brings
　　As I stand now neath the old Ash tree

Billy Durning, farmer, poet, 1885-1979
Dunfanagh, Co. Donegal, Ireland

THE VIKINGS

We can only speculate on the date when sailors first began to
brave the fury of the Atlantic, but by the late 700's a new era
dawned in mans struggle with the sea.

In Norway, probably near the site of present day Bergan, a
brilliant designer of ships sailed the first of a new design.
It was destined to be an instrument of change in Europe. This
new ship had wide, gracefully curving sides and a keel. Made
of long wood boards, it had the flexibility to withstand the
fury of the Atlantic, yet was light enough to be carried
overland by it's crew. This was the ship which made the Viking
raids possible.

The origin of the Vikings is still a matter of speculation.
Some think their ancestors were the Fomorians and the Tuatha de
Dannan of Irish history.   Some believe their anticedants were
the Phonecians (who in turn may have been the Fomorians).

Tradition doesn't clearly spearate 'Viking gods from ancestors.
At the time of the invasion of Ireland, they were staunch
worshippers of the god Thor (who appears to have been an early
ancestor). They were a rejected people. Choosing exile rather
than submittig to their king who had become Christian. Oden
(Woden) was their chief ancestor god. Their writers of a later
period, and other sources, seem to agree that the tables which
follow show a combination of gods and humanity.

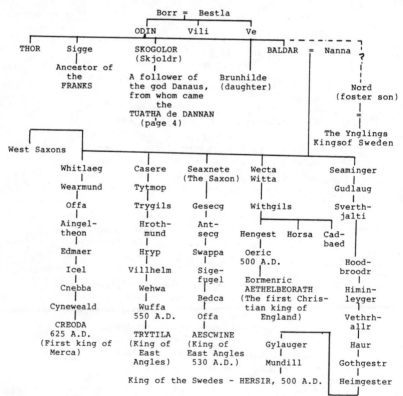

EARLY VIKINGS IN IRISH HISTORY

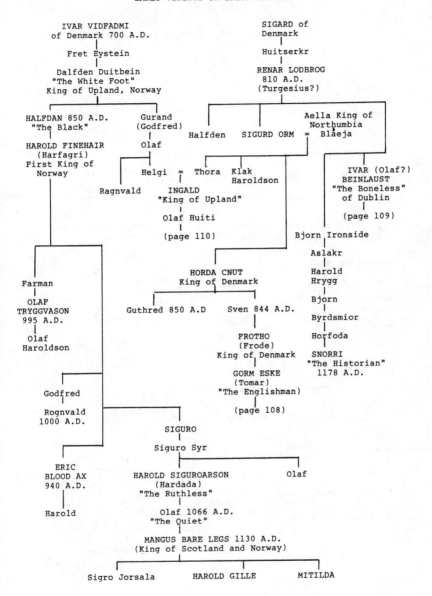

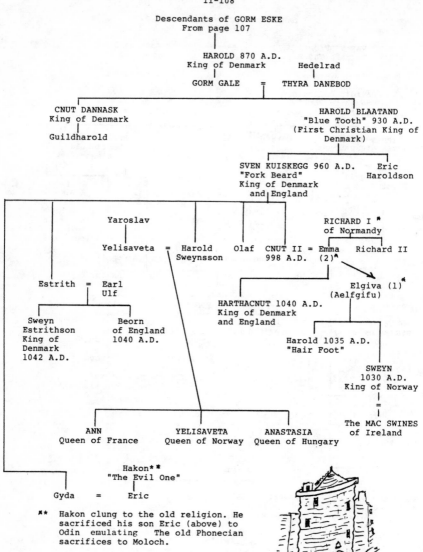

Descendants of GORM ESKE
From page 107

HAROLD 870 A.D.
King of Denmark   Hedelrad

GORM GALE   =   THYRA DANEBOD

CNUT DANNASK
King of Denmark

Guildharold

HAROLD BLAATAND
"Blue Tooth" 930 A.D.
(First Christian King of
Denmark)

SVEN KUISKEGG 960 A.D.   Eric
"Fork Beard"   Haroldson
King of Denmark
and England

Yaroslav

RICHARD I *
of Normandy

Yelisaveta   =   Harold   Olaf   CNUT II = Emma   Richard II
Sweynsson   998 A.D.   (2) *

Estrith   =   Earl
Ulf

Elgiva (1) *
(Aelfgifu)

Sweyn   Beorn
Estrithson   of England
King of   1040 A.D.
Denmark
1042 A.D.

HARTHACNUT 1040 A.D.
King of Denmark
and England

Harold 1035 A.D.
"Hair Foot"

SWEYN
1030 A.D.
King of Norway
|
=
The MAC SWINES
of Ireland

ANN   YELISAVETA   ANASTASIA
Queen of France   Queen of Norway   Queen of Hungary

Hakon* *
"The Evil One"

Gyda   =   Eric

**   Hakon clung to the old religion. He
sacrificed his son Eric (above) to
Odin emulating The old Phonecian
sacrifices to Moloch.

REGINALDS TOWER
WATERFORD

Descendants of IVAR BEINLAUST
From page 107

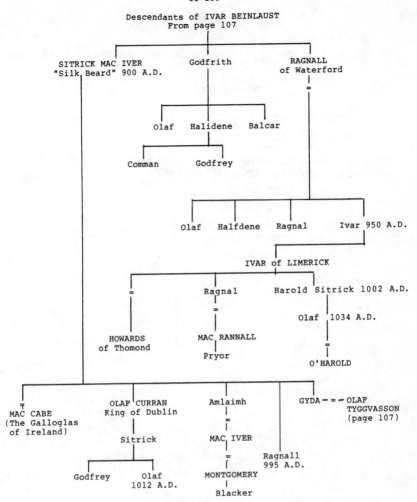

SITRICK MAC IVER
"Silk Beard" 900 A.D.

Godfrith

RAGNALL
of Waterford
=

Olaf   Halidene   Balcar

Comman   Godfrey

Olaf   Halfdene   Ragnal   Ivar 950 A.D.

IVAR of LIMERICK

=   Ragnal   Harold Sitrick 1002 A.D.

=   Olaf 1034 A.D.

HOWARDS
of Thomond

MAC RANNALL
=
Pryor

O'HAROLD
=

MAC CABE
(The Galloglas
of Ireland)
T

OLAF CURRAN
King of Dublin

Amlaimh
=
MAC IVER
=
MONTGOMERY
Blacker

GYDA — = — OLAF
TYGGVASSON
(page 107)

Sitrick

Ragnall
995 A.D.

Godfrey   Olaf
1012 A.D.

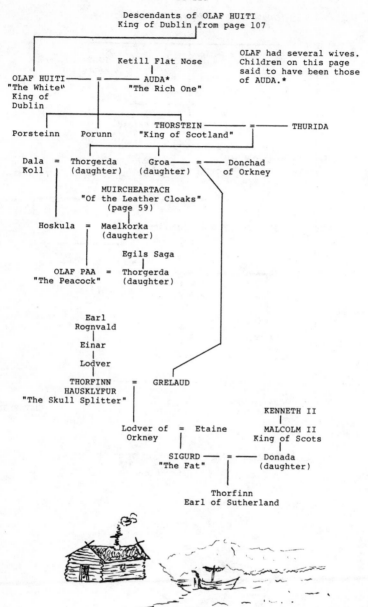

Descendants of OLAF HUITI
King of Dublin from page 107

Ketill Flat Nose

OLAF had several wives.
Children on this page
said to have been those
of AUDA.*

OLAF HUITI ———— = ———— AUDA*
"The White"   "The Rich One"
King of
Dublin

Porsteinn   Porunn   THORSTEIN ———— = ———— THURIDA
                          "King of Scotland"

Dala = Thorgerda   Groa ———— = ———— Donchad
Koll   (daughter)   (daughter)   of Orkney

              MUIRCHEARTACH
              "Of the Leather Cloaks"
              (page 59)

Hoskula = Maelkorka
            (daughter)

              Egils Saga

OLAF PAA = Thorgerda
"The Peacock" (daughter)

Earl
Rognvald

Einar

Lodver

THORFINN   = GRELAUD
HAUSKLYFUR
"The Skull Splitter"

                          KENNETH II

Lodver of = Etaine   MALCOLM II
Orkney   King of Scots

        SIGURD ———— = ———— Donada
        "The Fat"   (daughter)

              Thorfinn
              Earl of Sutherland

The Vikings in Iceland and America

When the Vikings reached Iceland they found Irish Monks
already living there. The Irish, loving solitude, packed
and departed.

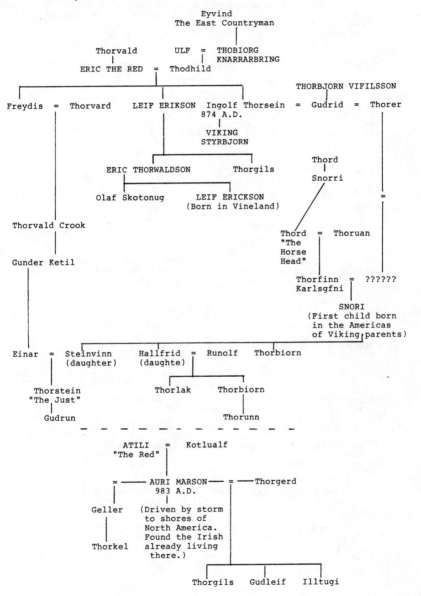

THE NORMANS IN IRELAND

In the late 1100's, Mac Murrough, an Irish King, was ejected by Hi-King Roderick O'Connor for misconduct. He appealed to the King of England for help. This king in turn permitted some of his Welch-Norman vassels to assist Mac Murrough. Thus began the uneasy association between England and Ireland which has continued in varied forms to the present.

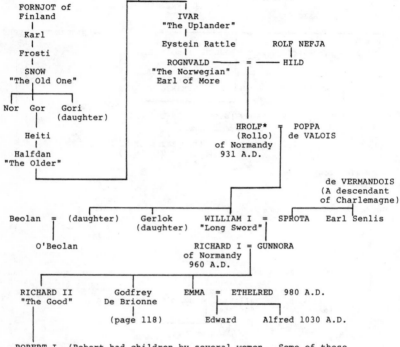

ROBERT I   (Robert had children by several women. Some of these
1020 A.D.   are listed below.)

1. = MATILDA = Richard de la Rule, from whom the RULES of Ire.

2. = HELUIN = ODO, Bishop of Bayeux & Earl of Kent.

3. = ARLETTA* = WILLIAM, "The Conquoror" (page 113)

  +The daughter of the village tanner, William was an
   illegitimate child. Norman Fuedal Lords owning the
   tenents as well as the land observed this right by
   spending the first night with a newly married woman.

  * HRolf plundered territory belonging to king Harold.
    He was "outlawed" and fled the country moving to
    France.

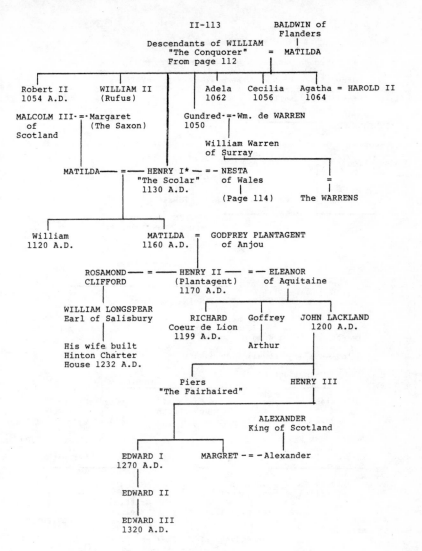

II-113

BALDWIN of
Flanders
|
Descendants of WILLIAM
"The Conquorer"   = MATILDA
From page 112

Robert II   WILLIAM II   Adela   Cecilia   Agatha = HAROLD II
1054 A.D.   (Rufus)   1062   1056   1064

MALCOLM III·=·Margaret   Gundred·=·Wm. de WARREN
    of   (The Saxon)   1050
Scotland
                                       William Warren
                                       of Surray

        MATILDA——— = ——— HENRY I* —— = – NESTA   =
                    "The Scolar"   of Wales
                    1130 A.D.   The WARRENS
                                    (Page 114)

   William   MATILDA = GODFREY PLANTAGENT
   1120 A.D.   1160 A.D.   of Anjou

        ROSAMOND——— = ——— HENRY II —— = — ELEANOR
        CLIFFORD   (Plantagent)   of Aquitaine
                            1170 A.D.

        WILLIAM LONGSPEAR   RICHARD   Goffrey   JOHN LACKLAND
        Earl of Salisbury   Coeur de Lion   1200 A.D.
                                   1199 A.D.
        His wife built   Arthur
        Hinton Charter
        House 1232 A.D.

                           Piers   HENRY III
                        "The Fairhaired"

                                       ALEXANDER
                                       King of Scotland

                EDWARD I   MARGRET – = –Alexander
                1270 A.D.

                EDWARD II

                EDWARD III
                1320 A.D.

* HENRY I is said to have been the first English king to
  use and grant the use of "A Coat of Arms."

THE WELCH AND THE IRISH

As noted on page 112, NESTA had children by HENRY
I of England. She also had children by others,
many of whom founded the most powerful families in
Ireland under the Normans. Thus the origins of
this family follow.

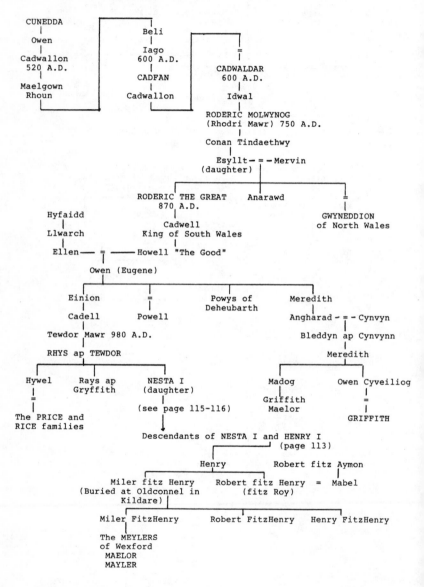

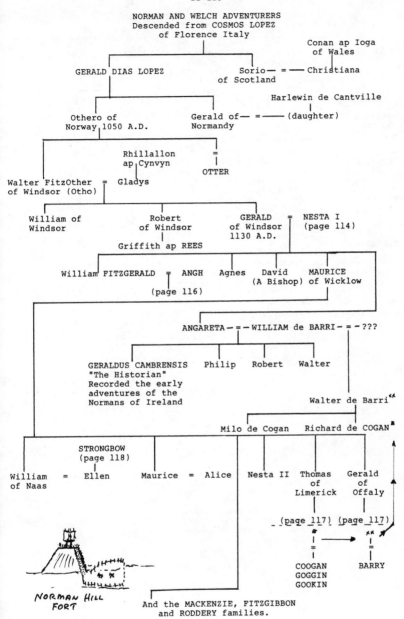

NORMAN AND WELCH ADVENTURERS
Descended from COSMOS LOPEZ
of Florence Italy

Conan ap Ioga
of Wales

GERALD DIAS LOPEZ

Sorio— = ——Christiana
of Scotland

Harlewin de Cantville

Othero of
Norway 1050 A.D.

Gerald of— = ——(daughter)
Normandy

Rhillallon
ap Cynvyn

=

OTTER

Walter FitzOther = Gladys
of Windsor (Otho)

William of
Windsor

Robert
of Windsor

GERALD = NESTA I
of Windsor   (page 114)
1130 A.D.

Griffith ap REES

William FITZGERALD = ANGH   Agnes   David   MAURICE
                                      (A Bishop) of Wicklow
        (page 116)

ANGARETA— = —WILLIAM de BARRI— = −???

GERALDUS CAMBRENSIS   Philip   Robert   Walter
"The Historian"
Recorded the early
adventures of the
Normans of Ireland

Walter de Barri

Milo de Cogan   Richard de COGAN

STRONGBOW
(page 118)

William = Ellen   Maurice = Alice   Nesta II   Thomas   Gerald
of Naas   of   of
                                                   Limerick   Offaly

(page 117) (page 117)

=   =

COOGAN   BARRY
GOGGIN
GOOKIN

NORMAN HILL
FORT

And the MACKENZIE, FITZGIBBON
and RODDERY families.

Descendants of WILLIAM FITZGERALD
From page 115

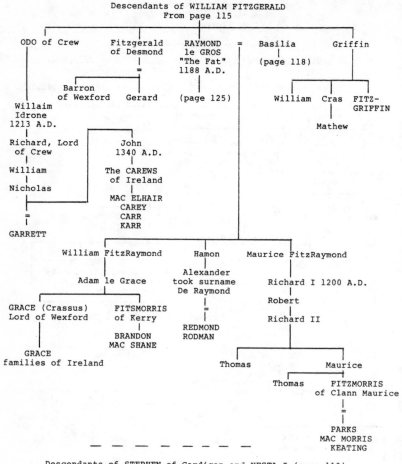

ODO of Crew   Fitzgerald of Desmond   RAYMOND le GROS "The Fat" 1188 A.D.   =   Basilia (page 118)   Griffin

Barron of Wexford   Gerard

=

(page 125)

William Cras FITZ-GRIFFIN

Mathew

Willaim Idrone 1213 A.D.

Richard, Lord of Crew

William

Nicholas

=

GARRETT

John 1340 A.D.

The CAREWS of Ireland

MAC ELHAIR
CAREY
CARR
KARR

William FitzRaymond   Hamon   Maurice FitzRaymond

Adam le Grace

Alexander took surname De Raymond

Richard I 1200 A.D.

Robert

Richard II

GRACE (Crassus) Lord of Wexford   FITSMORRIS of Kerry

=

REDMOND
RODMAN

BRANDON
MAC SHANE

GRACE families of Ireland

Thomas   Maurice

Thomas   FITZMORRIS of Clann Maurice

=

PARKS
MAC MORRIS
KEATING

— — — — — — — — —

Descendants of STEPHEN of Cardigan and NESTA I (page 113)

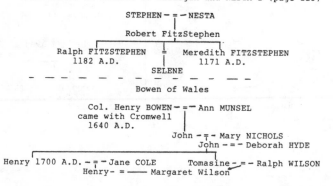

STEPHEN — = — NESTA

Robert FitzStephen

Ralph FITZSTEPHEN 1182 A.D.   =   Meredith FITZSTEPHEN 1171 A.D.

SELENE

— — — — — — — — — — — — —

Bowen of Wales

Col. Henry BOWEN — = — Ann MUNSEL
came with Cromwell
1640 A.D.

John — = — Mary NICHOLS
John — = — Deborah HYDE

Henry 1700 A.D. — = — Jane COLE   Tomasine — = — Ralph WILSON
Henry — = —— Margaret Wilson

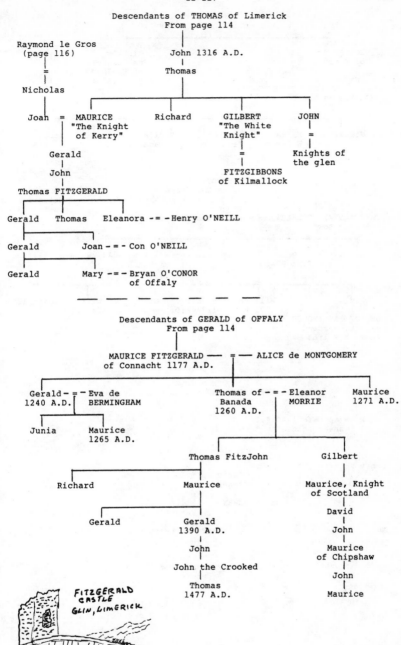

Descendants of THOMAS of Limerick
From page 114

Raymond le Gros
(page 116)
=
Nicholas

John 1316 A.D.
Thomas

Joan = MAURICE   Richard   GILBERT   JOHN
        "The Knight   "The White
         of Kerry"   Knight"
                                              =   =
        Gerald   FITZGIBBONS   Knights of
         John   of Kilmallock   the glen

Thomas FITZGERALD

Gerald   Thomas   Eleanora - = - Henry O'NEILL

Gerald   Joan - = - Con O'NEILL

Gerald   Mary - = - Bryan O'CONOR
                              of Offaly

— — — — — — —

Descendants of GERALD of OFFALY
From page 114

MAURICE FITZGERALD —— = —— ALICE de MONTGOMERY
of Connacht 1177 A.D.

Gerald - = - Eva de   Thomas of - = - Eleanor   Maurice
1240 A.D.   BERMINGHAM   Banada   MORRIE   1271 A.D.
                             1260 A.D.

Junia   Maurice
         1265 A.D.   Thomas FitzJohn   Gilbert

Richard   Maurice   Maurice, Knight
                                  of Scotland

Gerald   Gerald   David
                1390 A.D. |
                  | John
                John |
                  | Maurice
            John the Crooked   of Chipshaw
                  | |
                Thomas   John
                1477 A.D. |
                                 Maurice

FITZGERALD
CASTLE
GLIN, LIMERICK

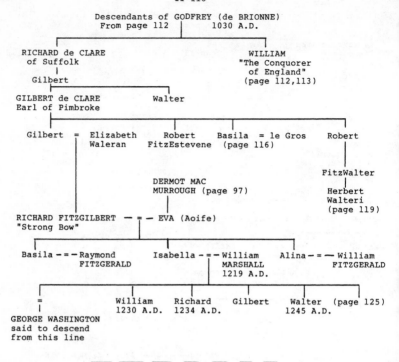

Descendants of GODFREY (de BRIONNE)
From page 112   1030 A.D.

RICHARD de CLARE
of Suffolk
|
Gilbert

WILLIAM
"The Conquerer
of England"
(page 112,113)

GILBERT de CLARE   Walter
Earl of Pimbroke

Gilbert = Elizabeth   Robert   Basila = le Gros   Robert
          Waleran   FitzEstevene   (page 116)

FitzWalter
|
Herbert
Walteri
(page 119)

DERMOT MAC
MURROUGH (page 97)
|
RICHARD FITZGILBERT — = — EVA (Aoife)
"Strong Bow"

Basila — = — Raymond   Isabella — = — William   Alina — = — William
           FITZGERALD   MARSHALL   FITZGERALD
                                          1219 A.D.

=   William   Richard   Gilbert   Walter (page 125)
| 1230 A.D.   1234 A.D.   1245 A.D.
GEORGE WASHINGTON
said to descend
from this line

THE BOWENS
Of Wales and Bowens Court

MORGAN ap OWEN 1440 A.D.
  of Swansea Wales
|
Richard
|
Henry ap Owen — = — Eliza
                    HOPKIN
|
Thomas — = — David ap EVAN
             Janet
|
Henry BOWEN - = - Ellen
1580   FRANKLIN
|
Harry — = — Margaret
1650 A.D.   HOLLAND
|
HENRY — = — Ann MUNSEL
founder of
Bowens
Court
|
John Bowen
1700 A.D.

THE BUTLERS of IRELAND

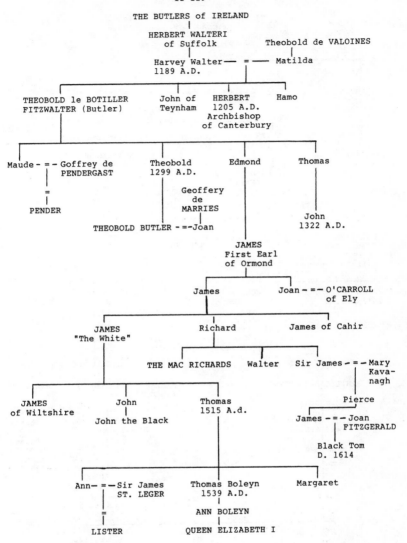

Note: Some BUTLERS changed their name to KENTON in the U.S.

The deBURGO (Burks) of Ireland
said to descend from Charlemagne

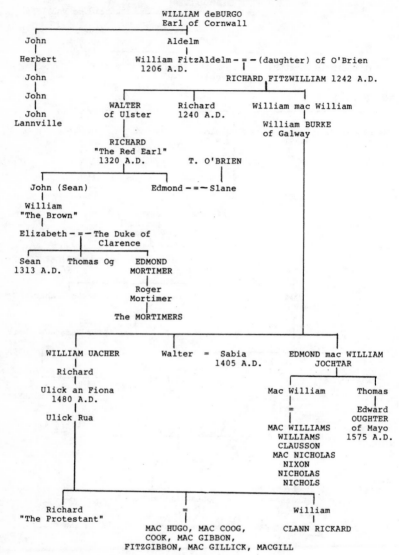

```
                              WILLIAM deBURGO
                               Earl of Cornwall
         ┌─────────────────────────┴──────────┐
      John                               Aldelm
         |                                   |
     Herbert            William FitzAldelm─ ═ ─(daughter) of O'Brien
         |                    1206 A.D.
      John                            RICHARD FITZWILLIAM 1242 A.D.
         |              ┌──────────────┴───────────┬──────────────────┐
      John          WALTER              Richard          William mac William
         |        of Ulster             1240 A.D.                |
      John                                              William BURKE
   Lannville                                              of Galway
                    RICHARD
                 "The Red Earl"              T. O'BRIEN
                   1320 A.D.
         ┌──────────────┴──────────────┐
    John (Sean)                  Edmond ─ ═ ─ Slane
         |
     William
   "The Brown"
         |
   Elizabeth ─ ═ ─ The Duke of
                     Clarence
    ┌──────────┬─────────────┐
  Sean     Thomas Og       EDMOND
1313 A.D.                  MORTIMER
                              |
                            Roger
                           Mortimer
                              |
                        The MORTIMERS
```

```
   ┌──────────────────────────┬──────────────────────────────┐
WILLIAM UACHER          Walter  =  Sabia          EDMOND mac WILLIAM
     |                         1405 A.D.                JOCHTAR
  Richard                                       ┌───────────┴────────┐
     |                                    Mac William           Thomas
Ulick an Fiona                                 |                    |
 1480 A.D.                                      =                 Edward
     |                                                           OUGHTER
 Ulick Rua                                MAC WILLIAMS           of Mayo
     |                                     WILLIAMS             1575 A.D.
     |                                     CLAUSSON
     |                                   MAC NICHOLAS
     |                                     NIXON
     |                                    NICHOLAS
     |                                    NICHOLS
     |
  Richard                =                       William
"The Protestant"                                    |
                  MAC HUGO, MAC COOG,         CLANN RICKARD
                  COOK, MAC GIBBON,
              FITZGIBBON, MAC GILLICK, MACGILL
```

Other families who are a branch of the BURKS: MAC DAVID,
MAC DAVY, JENNINGS, MAC PHILBIN, MAC SHONEEN, MAC
SEOININ, MAC WALTE, MANDEVILLE, MAC CULLEN, CULLEN, GAULE
of KILKENNY.

THE BOUCHERS
from Essex, England

le BURSER = BOSSER = BOURCHIER = BUTCHER = BUSHER = BOUCHER

RICHARD le BURSER - = - Emma
From Essex, England

Walter of Colechester

John 1300

Sir Thomas PRAER

Robert — = — Margaret

William = Eleanor
BOUCHER de LOVAINE

— — — — — — — — — —

HERBERT de MONTCHENSEY - = - Alice

Peter de VALLERIES

Warine

Herbert - = - Muriel

William le MARECHALE
of Pimbroke
Marshall

Warine - = - Joan

John de SOMERY
of Stansted, England

* Normans, French and Scotch
were often known by the name
of the lands they held.

Herbert - = - Ela

Joan - = - Walter de
COLCHESTER *

— — — — — — — — — — — —

THE ROTHE FAMILY
of Kilkenny

WILLIAM

John Rothe FitzWilliam - = - BRENERTON
of Norton Rothe, Co.   (daughter)
Lancashire, Eng. 1172

Walter Rothe FitzJohn - = - PENDERGAST
(daughter)

Walte Rothe
Fitzwalter — = - PRESTON
(daughter)

Gilbert Rothe - = - Eleanor W.
FitzJohn

Walter Rothe - = - Elizabeth BLANCHVILLE

Thomas Rothe of - = - ELLEN BALLYFOYLE
Kilkenny

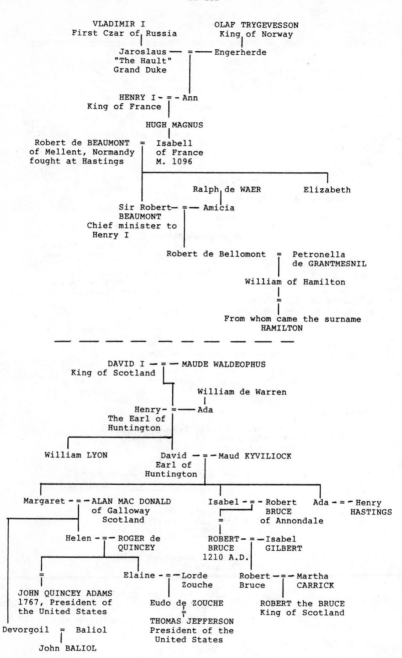

VLADIMIR I
First Czar of Russia

OLAF TRYGEVESSON
King of Norway

Jaroslaus — = — Engerherde
"The Hault"
Grand Duke

HENRY I - = - Ann
King of France

HUGH MAGNUS

Robert de BEAUMONT = Isabell
of Mellent, Normandy   of France
fought at Hastings   M. 1096

Ralph de WAER   Elizabeth

Sir Robert— = — Amicia
BEAUMONT
Chief minister to
Henry I

Robert de Bellomont = Petronella
                       de GRANTMESNIL

William of Hamilton
=
From whom came the surname
HAMILTON

DAVID I — = — MAUDE WALDEOPHUS
King of Scotland

William de Warren

Henry- = — Ada
The Earl of
Huntington

William LYON   David — = — Maud KYVILIOCK
                      Earl of
                      Huntington

Margaret - = — ALAN MAC DONALD   Isabel - = - Robert   Ada - = - Henry
               of Galloway   BRUCE   HASTINGS
               Scotland   of Annondale
                                               =
Helen - = — ROGER de   ROBERT- = —Isabel
            QUINCEY   BRUCE   GILBERT
                                   1210 A.D.
=   Elaine - = —Lorde   Robert - = — Martha
                             Zouche   Bruce   CARRICK
JOHN QUINCEY ADAMS
1767, President of   Eudo de ZOUCHE   ROBERT the BRUCE
the United States   ╤   King of Scotland
                           THOMAS JEFFERSON
Devorgoil = Baliol   President of the
                           United States
John BALIOL

THE STEWARTS of HORNHEAD

This family came to Ireland from Lennox in
Scotland. They were stewards to the Earl of
Darnley.

In 1700 Capt. CHARLES STEWART, an officer in
King Williams army at the battle of the
Boyne, purchased Horn Head from Captain John
Forward and Capt. William Simpson.

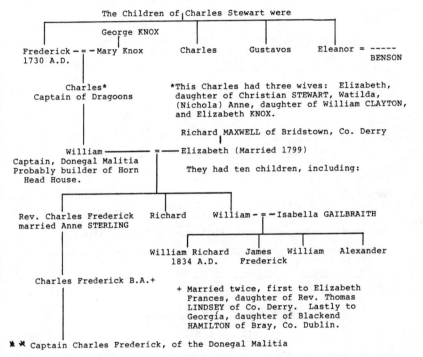

The Children of Charles Stewart were

George KNOX

Frederick – = – Mary Knox   Charles   Gustavos   Eleanor = -----
1730 A.D.   BENSON

Charles*
Captain of Dragoons

*This Charles had three wives: Elizabeth,
daughter of Christian STEWART, Watilda,
(Nichola) Anne, daughter of William CLAYTON,
and Elizabeth KNOX.

Richard MAXWELL of Bridstown, Co. Derry

William ——————— = —— Elizabeth (Married 1799)
Captain, Donegal Malitia
Probably builder of Horn   They had ten children, including:
Head House.

Rev. Charles Frederick   Richard   William – = – Isabella GAILBRAITH
married Anne STERLING

William Richard   James   William   Alexander
1834 A.D.   Frederick

Charles Frederick B.A.+

+ Married twice, first to Elizabeth
Frances, daughter of Rev. Thomas
LINDSEY of Co. Derry. Lastly to
Georgia, daughter of Blackend
HAMILTON of Bray, Co. Dublin.

✱ ✱ Captain Charles Frederick, of the Donegal Malitia

✱ ✱ This Charles was the last of the Stewarts to live on Horn
Head. Following the formation of the Republic, he moved to
England. Shortly thereafter, the property was acquired by
BILLY DURNING. Hornhead house, near Dunfanaghy, in Co.
Donegal, is still owned by the Durning family.

FULKE de BELESME
Lord of Nogent le Rotrov
(Said to have taken part in
the battle at Hastings.)
|
=
|
NOGENT
A surname taken by later generations
|
               Richard de Lachapelle
=
|
Gilbert de Nugent
(Changed surname to Nugent.)

The family name came to Ireland with de Lacy.
The family settled in Westmeath.

(see page 126)

— — — — — — — — — — — — — —

de LEIS *   KING RODERICK
(de Lacy)   O'CONNOR
|
=
|
Gilbert de LACY - = - Rose O'Connor

Hugh de Lacy, Earl of Ulster   Walter de Lacy
|
(daughter) —— = —— ------
        de BURGO, Earl of Ulster
        (BURKE)

(Elizabeth?) Ellen - = - ROBERT BRUCE, King of Scotland 1306 A.D.

* The De Lacys had title to 13 manors in Co. Lancashire, England
near Liverpool.

— — — — — — — — — — — — —

DE LINCE
The LYNCH Family
Said to have come from Austria
=
William de Lince
came to Ireland in 1185

— — — — — — — — — —

POWER
LE POER
|
Origin of this family is somewhat uncertain. Some claim
Irish origin while others declare they are Norman.
=
Bened Le Poer
(Claimed by some to be a branch of
the EUSTICE family.)

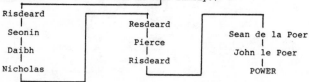

Risdeard   Resdeard
| | Sean de la Poer
Seonin   Pierce |
| | John le Poer
Daibh   Risdeard |
| POWER
Nicholas

Grandchildren of STRONGBOW
(see page 118)

Strongbow had a daughter named Isabella who
was married to Willliam le Mareschal. It is said
they had ten children, including the following:

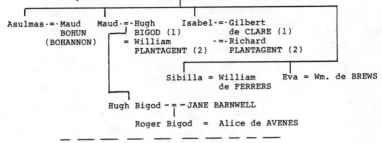

Asulmas -=- Maud   Maud -=- Hugh   Isabel -=- Gilbert
         BOHUN   BIGOD (1)   de CLARE (1)
        (BOHANNON)   = William   -=- Richard
                         PLANTAGENT (2)   PLANTAGENT (2)

                    Sibilla = William   Eva = Wm. de BREWS
                            de FERRERS

            Hugh Bigod -=- JANE BARNWELL

            Roger Bigod = Alice de AVENES

— — — — — — — — — — — — — —

The MEADE Family

John MIAGH of Cork
|
John
|
William 1480 A.D.
|
John 1488 A.D.
|
William MEAGH
|
John MEADE of Cork, 1560 A.D.
|
John
|
Sir John MEADE of Ballintubber

William = Elizabeth GRAVES   John
                                          |
                              Andrew who went to America
                                          |
                               David = Suzanna EVERHARD
                               1731 A.D.   of Virginia

— — — — — — — — — — — — — —

The DORMEYS of Cork

James DORMEY -=- Catherine MAHONY
              of Macroom 1802 A.D.

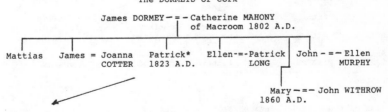

Mattias   James = Joanna   Patrick*   Ellen-=-Patrick   John -=- Ellen
                  COTTER   1823 A.D.   LONG   MURPHY

                                          Mary -=- John WITHROW
                                          1860 A.D.

* Patrick was first to come to America. The others followed and
settled in Knox, Co. Missouri.

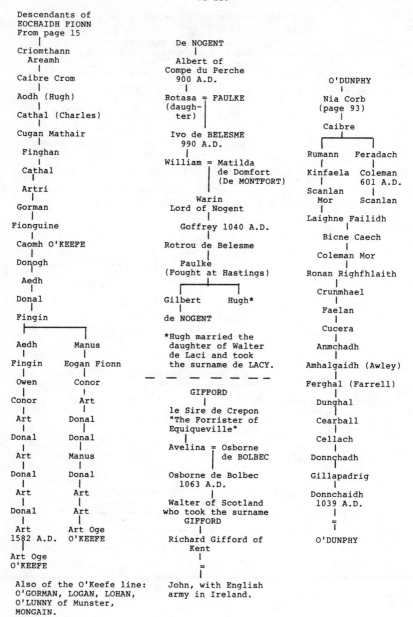

Descendants of
EOCHAIDH FIONN
From page 15
|
Criomthann
Areamh
|
Caibre Crom
|
Aodh (Hugh)
|
Cathal (Charles)
|
Cugan Mathair
|
Finghan
|
Cathal
|
Artri
|
Gorman
|
Fionguine
|
Caomh O'KEEFE
|
Donogh
|
Aedh
|
Donal
|
Fingin
┌─────────┴─────────┐
Aedh   Manus
| |
Fingin   Eogan Fionn
| |
Owen   Conor
| |
Conor   Art
| |
Art   Donal
| |
Donal   Donal
| |
Art   Manus
| |
Donal   Donal
| |
Art   Art
| |
Donal   Art
| |
Art   Art Oge
1582 A.D.   O'KEEFE
|
Art Oge
O'KEEFE

Also of the O'Keefe line:
O'GORMAN, LOGAN, LOHAN,
O'LUNNY of Munster,
MONGAIN.

De NOGENT
|
Albert of
Compe du Perche
900 A.D.
|
Rotasa = FAULKE
(daugh-
ter)
|
Ivo de BELESME
990 A.D.
|
William = Matilda
          de Domfort
          (De MONTFORT)
|
Warin
Lord of Nogent
|
Goffrey 1040 A.D.
|
Rotrou de Belesme
|
Faulke
(Fought at Hastings)
┌───────────┴───────────┐
Gilbert   Hugh*
|
de NOGENT

*Hugh married the
daughter of Walter
de Laci and took
the surname de LACY.

— — — — — — —

GIFFORD
|
le Sire de Crepon
"The Forrister of
Equiqueville"
|
Avelina = Osborne
          de BOLBEC
|
Osborne de Bolbec
1063 A.D.
|
Walter of Scotland
who took the surname
GIFFORD
|
Richard Gifford of
Kent
|
=
|
John, with English
army in Ireland.

O'DUNPHY
|
Nia Corb
(page 93)
|
Caibre
┌──────────┴──────────┐
Rumann   Feradach
| |
Kinfaela   Coleman
| 601 A.D.
Scanlan |
Mor   Scanlan
|
Laighne Failidh
|
Bicne Caech
|
Coleman Mor
|
Ronan Righfhlaith
|
Crunmhael
|
Faelan
|
Cucera
|
Anmchadh
|
Amhalgaidh (Awley)
|
Ferghal (Farrell)
|
Dunghal
|
Cearball
|
Cellach
|
Donnchadh
|
Gillapadrig
|
Donnchaidh
1039 A.D.
|
=
|
O'DUNPHY

Descendants of EOCHAIDH MOR
From page 13

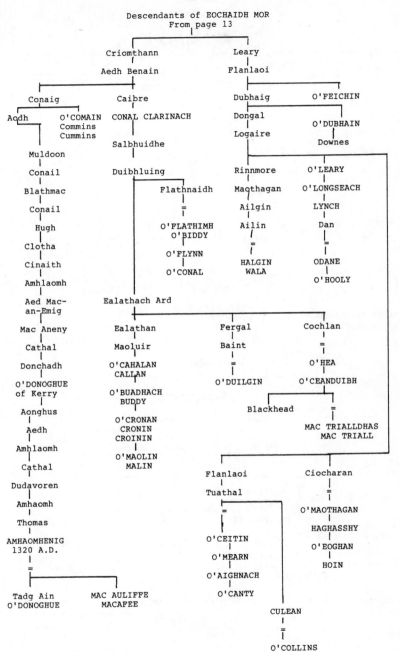

From page 72

Descendants of AMAMGAIDH
by 2nd wife EARCA

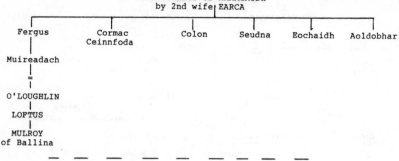

Fergus — Cormac Ceinnfoda — Colon — Seudna — Eochaidh — Aoldobhar

Fergus
  |
Muireadach
  |
  =
  |
O'LOUGHLIN
  |
LOFTUS
  |
MULROY
of Ballina

Descendants of AMAMGAIDH
by 3rd wife MUIRENN

Cairpri
  |
Ninnidh
  |
  =
  |
SAINT TIGHEARNAN
of Lough Con

Aongus Fionn
  |
  =
  |
GAUGHAN
  |
O'GAIBHTHEACHAIN
  |
O'FLYNN
  |
O'MAOILFHIONA
  |
O'MOLINA

Aodh
  |
Seanach
  |
Coman
  |
  =
  |
BACON
of Meath

The PENN Family

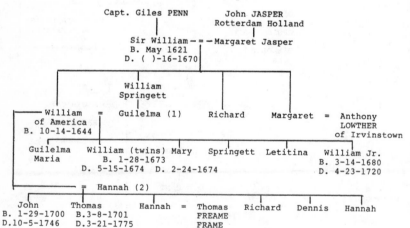

Capt. Giles PENN   John JASPER
                          Rotterdam Holland

Sir William — = — Margaret Jasper
B. May 1621
D. ( )-16-1670

William
Springett

William   Richard   Margaret = Anthony
of America = Guilelma (1)   LOWTHER
B. 10-14-1644   of Irvinstown

Guilelma   William (twins) Mary Springett Letitina William Jr.
Maria   B. 1-28-1673   B. 3-14-1680
            D. 5-15-1674 D. 2-24-1674   D. 4-23-1720

= Hannah (2)

John   Thomas   Hannah = Thomas   Richard Dennis Hannah
B. 1-29-1700 B.3-8-1701   FREAME
D.10-5-1746   D.3-21-1775   FRAME

```
COLLEY                        NIDDRIE                       HAY (LE)
of Barbery Castle            of Ireland                |
in Ireland                       |                     Robert de HAIA
    |                        Archibald                 of Sussex, Eng.
  BOURDET                 ┌──────┴──────────┐      ┌──────┴──────┐
of Cuilly in           Gilbert  Robert George   Richard      Ralf
  Normandie                     Archbishop of   LE HAY
  1066 A.D.                     Armagh          ─ ─ ─ ─ ─
Came to Eng.                    1405 A.D.
with William              ─ ─ ─ ─ ─ ─                 The MASSEY's
┌──────┴──────┐                                       of Ireland
Robert       Hugh             WAHAB                        |
  |            |           of Co. Down            de MASXI of
DeCuleio     Burdett           |                  Cheshire, 1086 A.D.
(After the     |           WAUCHOPEDALE                |
prop. in       =           of Eskdale in Dum-        MACI
Norm.)       The           fresshire, Scot.            |
  =          BURDETTS      1200 A.D.               MASSEY in Ireland
Ancestor of  of Ireland        |                  ─ ─ ─ ─ ─ . ─
the follow-               Gilbert WAUCHOPE
ing famil-                of Niddire Scot.             The MINER'S
ies                       1500 A.D.                    of Ireland
CULEY                          |                           |
  |                   ┌────────┼────────┐          DE MINERIIS of
CULLY                William  Gilbert  John        Cambridge became
  |                                    Who              |
COLLEY                                changed his   Miner in Ireland
  |                        name to WAHAB in Co.
CULAI                                     Down.
CUILYS                    ─ ─ ─ ─ ─ ─ ─
  |                                                    Roger DE BEAUMONT
CALEY                     The WALLS of IRELAND         Count of Meulan
CAILEY                         |                       in Normandie 1086
  |                        The Marquess of                 |
CAYLE                      de Fontenall in         Robert of England
  |        ┌──────────    Normandie                who became Earl
COLLEY     WELLESLEY           |                   of Leicester.
                          Sieur Duvall Dary
─ ─ ─ ─ ─ ─ ─ ─           Came to Eng. 1066 A.D.   ─ ─ ─ ─ ─
                               |
The STONEYS               Name became DE VALLE         Roger BIGOT
of Ireland                in Ireland which in turn     of Calvados, Norm.
   |                           became               came to Suffolk, Eng.
Original home                  |
Warfield York-             Walls                    ─ ─ ─ ─ ─
shire, Eng.
   |                      ─ ─ ─ ─ ─ ─ ─                The BISET'S of
George = Mary                                             Ireland
         MOOREHOUSE        The GREENVILLE's                |
         of Rilston            |                   Manasser Biset 1150
         1650 A.D.         Ralph de GRANVILLA       Steward to Henry II
   |                      of Normandie came to   ┌─────┴──────────┐
Thomas of Grayfort        Eng. after William.    M. Biset = Alice
   |                           |                            de CANY │
George of Ireland         Was ancestor of the                  ┌────┴──────┐
                          EUSTICE families,                        Gilbert
                          Grenville of Buckingham                  de FALAISE
                          and Grenville, Grain-
                          ville, Greinville in     Henry Biset came to
                          Ireland and GREENVILLE   Ireland with King
                          in U.S.                        John
```

The MAC LEODS

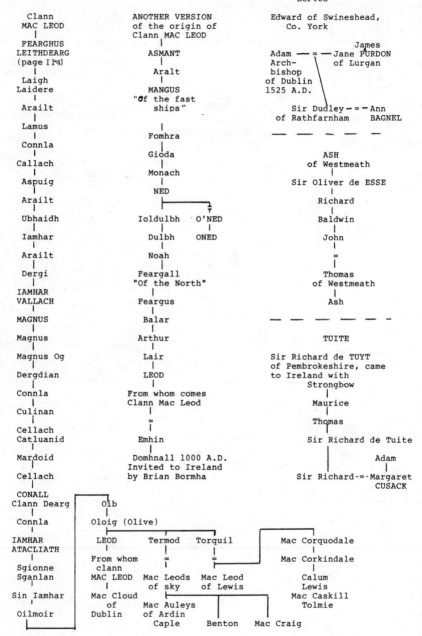

Clann MAC LEOD	ANOTHER VERSION of the origin of Clann MAC LEOD	LOFTUS Edward of Swineshead, Co. York
FEARGHUS LEITHDEARG (page II4)	ASMANT	Adam ——=—— James Arch- Jane PURDON bishop of Lurgan of Dublin 1525 A.D.
Laigh Laidere	Aralt	
Arailt	MANGUS "Of the fast ships"	Sir Dudley —=— Ann of Rathfarnham BAGNEL
Lamus		— — — —
Connla	Fomhra	
Callach	Gioda	ASH of Westmeath
Aspuig	Monach	Sir Oliver de ESSE
Arailt	NED	Richard
Ubhaidh	Ioldulbh O'NED	Baldwin
Iamhar	Dulbh ONED	John
Arailt	Noah	=
Dergi	Feargall "Of the North"	Thomas of Westmeath
IAMHAR VALLACH	Feargus	Ash
MAGNUS	Balar	— — — —
Magnus	Arthur	TUITE
Magnus Og	Lair	Sir Richard de TUYT of Pembrokeshire, came to Ireland with Strongbow
Dergdian	LEOD	Maurice
Connla	From whom comes Clann Mac Leod	Thomas
Culinan	=	Sir Richard de Tuite
Cellach Catluanid	Emhin	Adam
Mardoid	Domhnall 1000 A.D. Invited to Ireland by Brian Bormha	Sir Richard —=— Margaret CUSACK
Cellach		

CONALL
Clann Dearg — Oib
|
Connla — Oloig (Olive)
|
IAMHAR   LEOD   Termod   Torquil   Mac Corquodale
ATACLIATH | =   = |
| From whom   Mac Leods Mac Leod Mac Corkindale
Sgionne   clann   of sky   of Lewis |
Sganlan   MAC LEOD   Calum
| | Mac Auleys   Lewis
Sin Iamhar Mac Cloud of Ardin   Mac Caskill
| of   Caple   Tolmie
Oilmoir   Dublin   Benton   Mac Craig

```
        WHITTY
       of Wexford
    |
  Walter Whitty
    |
    |_____
    |                                        |
  Richard - = - Jane DEVEREUX      Margaret - = - Michael KEATING
  1546 A.D.    |
               |
       Walter - = - Eleanor STAFFORD
       1603 A.D. |
                 |
                 |_____
                 |                            |
          Richard - = - Catherine DEVEREUX    Catherine - = - James
          1623 A.D.     1646 A.D.                             BRYAN
            ___  ___  ___
```

The Irish Mac Faoitigh family took the surname MAC WHITTY.
___ ___ ___ ___ ___ ___ ___ ___

```
     CLEBOURNE _____ BODINE              DE LA HIDE
                 |                              |
              THORFIN                    Roger De La Hide of
                 |                             Wales
                 =                              |
     _____|_____                 John
    |                        |                  |
  Bardolph                  Bodin             Henry
 of Yorkshire                |                  |
  1080 A.D.                  =              John 1295 A.D.
    |                        |                  |
  Acarius                O'Buadain         Walter De La HIDE
 Fitzbardolph             BODEN            of Ballymadun in
    |                     BODINE              Ireland
  Harvey                                        |
 Fitzakaris                                    Hyde
    |                        ___  ___  ___  ___  ___
  Alan
    |                   DELMORE  -  HERBERT
  Harvey                         |
    |                   Herbert DE LAMARE
  Geoffrey              _____|_____
 Fitzharvey            |                        |
    |                William                 Mac Ebebeirt
  Robert               |                         =
    |                 John                   MAC HERBERT
  John               Deleamare                   |
    |                   =                      HERBERT
  Rowland            DELMORE
    |              of Westmeath
  John                DELMER
    |               Delamer
  Thomas             ___  ___  ___  ___  ___  ___
    |
  Robert              BLENNERHASSETT
    |                 from Cumberland
  Edward              Thomas _____ = _____ Elizabeth SANDYS
    |                 settled in      |            of Dublin
  Richard             Kerry           |
  of York                             |
    |               Leonard - = - Deborah MERVYN
  Edmond                        |
    |                   Henry - = - Phoebe HUME
  Thomas                        |
who was transplanted from  Deborah - = - James COLQUHOUN
Cumberland to Roscommon               |      (Colhoun)
    =                                  |
  William CLEBOURNE            James  =  Catherine
    CLIBORNE                             CHIDEOCK
    CLEBURNE
```

HAZARD
of Co. Fermanagh

Le duc de Charante
of Switzerland, a
Crusader, 1060 A.D.
|
Duke de Charante
|
Hazard of Hazard
|
Reginald Hazard
of Bristol 1216
|
Robert Hazard
|
John
|
Thomas
|
Alexander
|
Thomas of
Wiltshire
|
John
|
Robert
| John
Robert   PARROTT
| (father)
|
John = Thomasine
|
John
|
George, a Captain
in Col. Coles regiment
in Ireland
|
Jason of Mullymusker
Co. Farm. 1617 A.D.
He became Hi-Sheriff
— — — — — —

The WARRENS

Thomas Warren
|
Sir Henry
| Adam LOFTUS
|
Sir Henry = Alicia
of Warrentown |
|
Capt. John = Catherine
WARREN   ROWE
of Dublin
— — — — — —

SWIFT

Bryan Swyfte
of Durham, England
|
Humphrey
|
John - = - Marie Hedworth

ROCHFORT

Boucard I
|
Thibauld
|
Surname to here
was:
|
DE RUPE FORTI
|
Sir John
de Rochfort
|
Sir William
de Rochfort of
Kilbride, Ire.
|
Edmond
|
Sir John 1384 A.D.

— — — — — —

SARSFIELD
of Porte Banniere
in France
|
=
|
Roger Sarsfield
of Sarsfieldtown,
Westmeath
|
John, Mayor
of Dublin
|
Patrick
|
Sir William
|
John
|
Patrick,
deprived of his
land by Cromwell.
|
Patrick
Earl of Lucan and
and a commander in
King James II army.
Died 1693.
— — — — — — —

PILKINGTON

Of Pilkington
Lancashire, Eng.
|
Richard of Tore in
Co. Westmeath
|
Abraham - = - Elizabeth
1756 A.D. | WEST
|
Mary - = - Duke
TYRRELL
|
Edmond - = - Margaret Trollope

AYLMER
of Co. Meath
|
Richard Aylmer
of Lyons, Co. Meath
|
John
|
Richard = Catherine
| PETTITT
|
=
|
Bartholomew =
CHEEVERS
— — — —

HORN

According to tradition,
the original family name
was LITTLEBURYE. Sir Wm.
on the staff of Edward
III was the best of the
horn blowers on the hunt.
The king renamed him "the
HORN."
— — — — — —

BLENNERHASSETT
of Kerry

Jenkin CONWAY
|
Robert - = - Elizabeth
of Cumberland |
1575 A.D.
|
John   Arthur   Edward
All of Co. Kerry

MAC ELLIGOTT
Originally of Scotland
|
Came to Ireland about
1550 A.D.
|
Name also spelled:
MAC ELYOT, MAC ELGOTE
— — —

Geoffrey DE MONTMORENCY
of Hertshire, England
|
Piers
|
Sir Simon de Mauteby
|
Sir Walter
|
Sir Robert 1200 A.D
|
Sir Walter - = - Christian
MABEY   de
BASSINGHAM
|
=
|
Johathan Swift
1700 A.D.

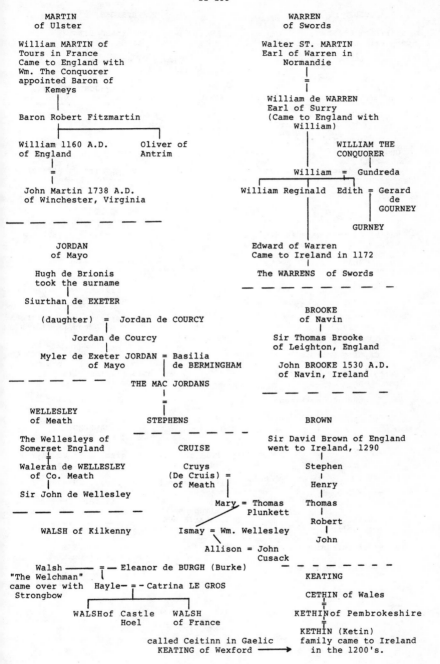

```
MARTIN                              WARREN
of Ulster                           of Swords

William MARTIN of                   Walter ST. MARTIN
Tours in France                     Earl of Warren in
Came to England with                   Normandie
Wm. The Conquorer                          |
appointed Baron of                         |
   Kemeys                                   |
      |                             William de WARREN
Baron Robert Fitzmartin             Earl of Surry
      |                             (Came to England with
      |                                  William)
  _____|_____                        |
 |                 |                        |
William 1160 A.D.  Oliver of                          WILLIAM THE
of England         Antrim                             CONQUORER
 |                                    William = Gundreda
 =                          William Reginald  Edith = Gerard
 |                                                      de
John Martin 1738 A.D.                                 GOURNEY
of Winchester, Virginia
                                                    GURNEY

—  —  —  —  —  —  —               Edward of Warren
                                  Came to Ireland in 1172

        JORDAN                     The WARRENS  of Swords
        of Mayo
                                  —  —  —  —  —  —  —
    Hugh de Brionis
    took the surname
          |                               BROOKE
   Siurthan de EXETER                     of Navin
          |                                  |
    (daughter) = Jordan de COURCY     Sir Thomas Brooke
          |                           of Leighton, England
     Jordan de Courcy                        |
          |                           John BROOKE 1530 A.D.
   Myler de Exeter JORDAN = Basilia   of Navin, Ireland
        of Mayo          | de BERMINGHAM
 —  —  —  —  —  —        |             —  —  —  —  —  —
                   THE MAC JORDANS
                        |
                        |                  BROWN
WELLESLEY               |
of Meath             STEPHENS        Sir David Brown of England
                                     went to Ireland, 1290
The Wellesleys of   —  —  —  —  —          |
Somerset England                         Stephen
     |                CRUISE                |
Waleran de WELLESLEY                       Henry
of Co. Meath          Cruys                 |
     |               (De Cruis) =         Thomas
Sir John de Wellesley of Meath              |
                           Mary = Thomas  Robert
 —  —  —  —  —  —  —             Plunkett    |
                                           John
      WALSH of Kilkenny   Ismay = Wm. Wellesley
                                             —  —  —  —  —  —
      Walsh ——— = — Eleanor de BURGH (Burke)
 "The Welchman"          Allison = John       KEATING
came over with   Hayle— = - Catrina LE GROS   Cusack
Strongbow                                    CETHIN of Wales
      WALSHof Castle    WALSH                      =
             Hoel       of France         KETHINof Pembrokeshire
                  called Ceitinn in Gaelic        =
                  KEATING of Wexford  ——→   KETHIN (Ketin)
                                            family came to Ireland
                                            in the 1200's.
```

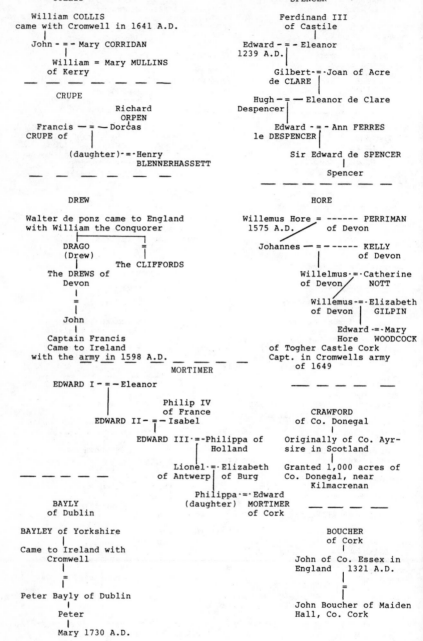

COLLIS

William COLLIS
came with Cromwell in 1641 A.D.
|
John - = - Mary CORRIDAN
|
William = Mary MULLINS
of Kerry

— — — — — — — —

CRUPE

Richard
ORPEN
Francis — = — Dorcas
CRUPE of |
|
(daughter) - = - Henry
BLENNERHASSETT

— — — — — — —

DREW

Walter de ponz came to England
with William the Conquorer
|
DRAGO   =
(Drew) |
| The CLIFFORDS
The DREWS of
Devon
|
=
|
John
|
Captain Francis
Came to Ireland
with the army in 1598 A.D.

SPENCER

Ferdinand III
of Castile
|
Edward - = - Eleanor
1239 A.D.|
|
Gilbert - = - Joan of Acre
de CLARE |
|
Hugh - = — Eleanor de Clare
Despencer|
|
Edward - = - Ann FERRES
le DESPENCER|
|
Sir Edward de SPENCER
|
Spencer

— — — — — —

HORE

Willemus Hore = ------ PERRIMAN
1575 A.D.| of Devon
|
Johannes — = - ----- KELLY
| of Devon
|
Willelmus - = - Catherine
of Devon/   NOTT
|
Willemus - = - Elizabeth
of Devon | GILPIN
|
Edward - = - Mary
Hore   WOODCOCK
of Togher Castle Cork
Capt. in Cromwells army
of 1649

— — — — —

MORTIMER

EDWARD I - = — Eleanor
|
Philip IV
of France
EDWARD II - = — Isabel
|
EDWARD III - = - Philippa of
Holland
|
Lionel - = - Elizabeth
of Antwerp| of Burg
|
Philippa - = - Edward
(daughter) MORTIMER
of Cork

CRAWFORD
of Co. Donegal
|
Originally of Co. Ayr-
sire in Scotland
|
Granted 1,000 acres of
Co. Donegal, near
Kilmacrenan

— — — —

BAYLY
of Dublin

BAYLEY of Yorkshire
|
Came to Ireland with
Cromwell
|
=
|
Peter Bayly of Dublin
|
Peter
|
Mary 1730 A.D.

BOUCHER
of Cork
|
John of Co. Essex in
England   1321 A.D.
|
=
|
John Boucher of Maiden
Hall, Co. Cork

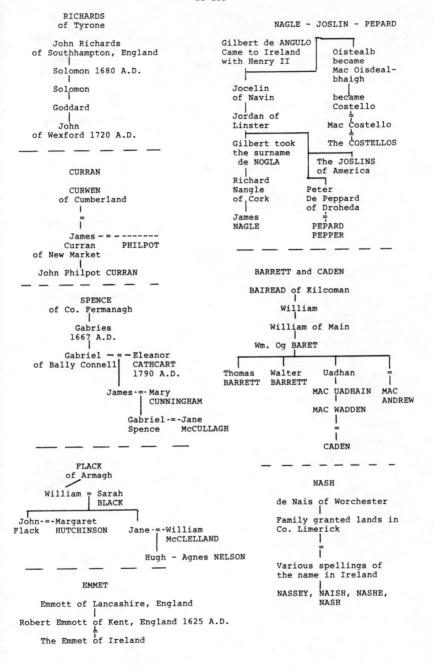

RICHARDS
of Tyrone

John Richards
of Southhampton, England
|
Solomon 1680 A.D.
|
Solomon
|
Goddard
|
John
of Wexford 1720 A.D.

— — — — — —

CURRAN

CURWEN
of Cumberland
|
=
|
James — = — — — — — —
Curran   PHILPOT
of New Market
|
John Philpot CURRAN

— — — — — —

SPENCE
of Co. Fermanagh
|
Gabries
1667 A.D.
|
Gabriel — = — Eleanor
of Bally Connell| CATHCART
                    1790 A.D.
|
James — = — Mary
          | CUNNINGHAM
|
Gabriel — = — Jane
Spence   McCULLAGH

— — — — — —

FLACK
of Armagh
|
William = Sarah
         BLACK
|
John — = — Margaret |
Flack   HUTCHINSON   Jane — = — William
                            | McCLELLAND
                     Hugh — Agnes NELSON

— — — — — —

EMMET

Emmott of Lancashire, England
|
Robert Emmott of Kent, England 1625 A.D.
|
The Emmet of Ireland

NAGLE - JOSLIN - PEPARD

Gilbert de ANGULO   Oistealb
Came to Ireland   became
with Henry II   Mac Oisdeal-
| bhaigh
Jocelin   became
of Navin   Costello
| |
Jordan of   Mac Costello
Linster |
| The COSTELLOS
Gilbert took
the surname   The JOSLINS
de NOGLA   of America
|
Richard   Peter
Nangle   De Peppard
of Cork   of Droheda
| |
James   PEPARD
NAGLE   PEPPER

— — — — — —

BARRETT and CADEN

BAIREAD of Kilcoman
|
William
|
William of Main
|
Wm. Og BARET
|
Thomas   Walter   Uadhan   =
BARRETT   BARRETT |
                    MAC UADHAIN   MAC
                    | ANDREW
                    MAC WADDEN
                    |
                    =
                    |
                    CADEN

— — — — — —

NASH

de Nais of Worchester
|
Family granted lands in
Co. Limerick
|
|
Various spellings of
the name in Ireland
|
NASSEY, NAISH, NASHE,
NASH

PETIT - LYNCH

William LE PETITO
of Wales 1210 A.D.
Migrated to Westmeath

```
            |
    James           Nicholas
    took the            =
    surname        This family
    PETIT          later took
                   the surname
                      LYNCH
                    of Galway
```

— — — — — — —

TRENCH
of France

Frederic DE LA TRANCHE
Became a Protestant and
moved to Northumberland
in England

```
        |
    William = Mary SUTTON
        |
Thomas -=- Catherine    James
          BROOKE
        |
    Frederick   =  Anna 1613 A.D.
    of Ireland
        |
Frederick  John   William
1633 A.D. "The Huguenots"
```

— — — — — — —

YARDLEY

John Yardley of
Staffordshire, Eng.

```
        |
      John
        |
   John -=- Margaret
        |
    John -=- Elizabeth
           BIRKES
        |
    William 1580 A.D.
        |
   William -=- Dorothy
              DRAKE
        |
    William YARDLEY
    Went to America
```

AGNEW

From Agneau in
Normandie

The de AGNEAUS came
to England, moved to
Wales then to Ireland
with Strongbow.
Settled in Ulster.

— — — — —

STEEL

Originally of
Scotland, James
STEILE came to
Raphoe, Co.
Donegal - 1665 A.D.

```
        |
      James
        |
    William = Mary
             HUGHES
```

Hugh Montgomery
of Ayershire
= Margaret
MONTGOMERY
of Ards

— — — — — — —

DALTON

Sir Walter DE ALITON
of France came to
Ireland about 1200 A.D.

```
        |
      Philip
        |
     Nicholas
        |
     Philbug
        |
    Piersdubh
        |
     Maurice
   DE ALITON changed
   his name to the
   English form
      DALTON
```

ARMSTRONG

The family was given
this name by the King
        Scotland.
```
        |
```
A branch of the family
moved to Ulster, where
some took the sur-
names:

LAVERY and TRAYNOR

— — — — — — —

COURTNEY

A French family.
```
        |
```
William Courtney
became Earl of Devon
in England.
```
        |
```
A branch of the
family moved to Co.
Antrim prior to 1670.

— — — — — — —

KNOLLE - KNOWLES

The NOLLY family of Norfolk,
England moved to Co. Cork,
where the family name was
changed to KNOLLE & KNOWLES.

— — — — — — —

GLENN

The GLENNE family are
said to have come from
Ayre in Scotland.

David GLENNY (Glenn)
resided in Co. Down.

— — — — — —

CLIFFE

John CLIFFE was a
member of Cromwell's
army. He came to
Ireland in 1649 A.D.

— — — — — —

BURNELL

Said to have come
from Shropshire in
England to Dublin.

ALEXANDER

Descendants of
Alexander MAC DONALD
took the surname:
|
Alexander

— — — — —

BELSCHE

Of Roxburghire in
Scotland, in Ireland
had the following names:
|
BELASIS, BELASES,
BELSHIES, BELSHAES
BELSHES

— — — —

BOYD

A branch of the
STEWARTS
of Scotland
|
Allen
|
Simon
|
Robert BOYT who's
descendants took
the surname:
BOYD

— — — — —

CHIDEOCK

An English family who
moved to Co. Fermanagh
|
=
|
Henry
|
Thomas CHIDEOCK

— — — — —

DEVEREUX

DE HEDING
of Adamstown
|
----- = Alice
Devereux |
=
|
The DEVEREUX
family of
Wexford and
later of
New York.

GAVIN

GAVINE of Berwick, Scotland
came to Ulster about 1600 A.D.
|
=
|
Robert of Antrim, 1790 A.D.
|
John
|
Samuel GIVEN   =
|
GAVIN   GEVIN   GIVIN

— — — — —

RINTOUL (Rintous)

deRINTOUL of Scotland
|
=
|
James RINTOUL = Ann REED
went to Ireland
|
Alexander Rintoul = Erminda
CHIDEOCK

— — — — -

MILLER

This family migrated from
Scotland to Co. Tyrone

Gayden MILLER = Margaret
of Tyrone | HENDERSON
1650 A.D. | of Scotland
|
James = Catherine
| LIGHTFOOT
|
Descendants of this
family migrated to
Pennsylvania.

— — — — -

HATCHELL

This family from
Devon, England
migrated to Wexford.

ALLARD

ALWARD of Bristol
moved to Waterford.

— — — — —

LATHOM

Part of this family
from Co. Lancashire
England, took up
residence in Co.
Tipperary, Ireland.

— = SIR WARHAM ST. LEGER = —
Sir Walter RALEIGH* |
1553 A.D.   Humphrey GILBERT
Born at Hayes Barton
Devonshire, England.

* Planted the first potato in Ireland, 1596 A.D.
Sallinger also branches from St. Leger.

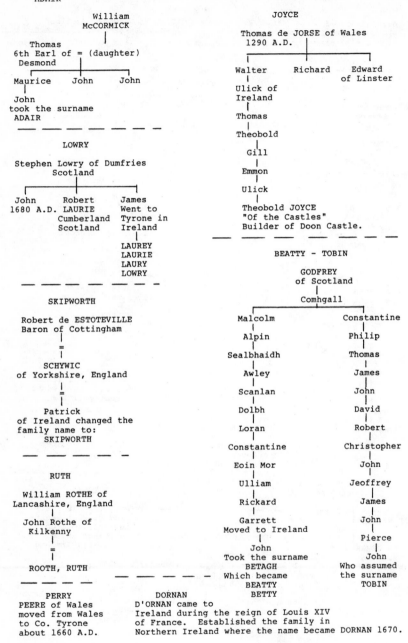

ADAIR

```
                    William
                    McCORMICK
                        |
    Thomas
    6th Earl of = (daughter)
    Desmond         |
    _____|_____
    |              |                |
  Maurice        John             John
    |
   John
took the surname
   ADAIR
```

JOYCE

```
        Thomas de JORSE of Wales
             1290 A.D.
    _____|_____
    |            |              |
  Walter      Richard        Edward
    |                       of Linster
  Ulick of
  Ireland
    |
  Thomas
    |
  Theobold
    |
   Gill
    |
  Emmon
    |
  Ulick
    |
  Theobold JOYCE
  "Of the Castles"
  Builder of Doon Castle.
```

LOWRY

```
    Stephen Lowry of Dumfries
           Scotland
    _____|_____
    |          |           |
  John       Robert      James
1680 A.D.    LAURIE     Went to
           Cumberland   Tyrone in
            Scotland    Ireland
                           |
                        LAUREY
                        LAURIE
                        LAURY
                        LOWRY
```

SKIPWORTH

```
    Robert de ESTOTEVILLE
    Baron of Cottingham
           |
           =
           |
        SCHYWIC
    of Yorkshire, England
           |
           =
           |
        Patrick
    of Ireland changed the
    family name to:
        SKIPWORTH
```

BEATTY - TOBIN

```
              GODFREY
            of Scotland
                |
             Comhgall
        _____|_____
        |               |
     Malcolm        Constantine
        |               |
      Alpin           Philip
        |               |
   Sealbhaidh         Thomas
        |               |
      Awley            James
        |               |
     Scanlan            John
        |               |
      Dolbh            David
        |               |
      Loran           Robert
        |               |
   Constantine      Christopher
        |               |
     Eoin Mor          John
        |               |
     Ulliam          Jeoffrey
        |               |
     Rickard           James
        |               |
     Garrett            John
    Moved to Ireland     |
        |              Pierce
       John              |
    Took the surname    John
      BETAGH          Who assumed
    Which became      the surname
      BEATTY            TOBIN
      BETTY
```

RUTH

```
    William ROTHE of
    Lancashire, England
           |
    John Rothe of
      Kilkenny
           |
           =
           |
      ROOTH, RUTH
```

PERRY
PEERE of Wales
moved from Wales
to Co. Tyrone
about 1660 A.D.

DORNAN
D'ORNAN came to
Ireland during the reign of Louis XIV
of France. Established the family in
Northern Ireland where the name became DORNAN 1670.

Descendants of
CHARLEMAGNE

ANTENOR king of
the Cimmerians
in Russia 443 B.C.
|
Marcomir
|
Antenor
|
Priamus
|
Hellenus
|
DIOCLES 294 B.C.
|
Bassanus
Magnus
|
Clodomir
|
Nicanor
|
Marcomir
|
CLODIUS I
|
Antenor II
|
Clodimir II
123 B.C.
|
Merodacus
|
Cassander
|
Antharius
|
FRANKUIS of
the West
Franks 9 B.C.
|
Clodius
|
Marcomir
|
Clodomir
|
Antenor IV
69 A.D.
|
Ratherius
|
Richemour
|
Odemir
|
MARCOMIR IV =
who married
|
ATHILDIS of
Britian

Coldomir IV
|
Farabert
|
Sunno
|
Hilderic 253 A.D.
|
Bartherus
|
Coldius III
298 A.D.
|
Walter
|
Dagobert
|
Clodius
|
MARCOMIR of
the East
Franks
|
Pharamond
|
Clodius
|
Sigmerius
|
Ferreolus
|
Asopert
|
Arnold
|
ST. ARNOLD
married Dodo
of Saxony.
|
Ansegius
|
PEPIN duke
of Brabant

CHARLES MARTEL
|
PEPIN
|
                    Gertrude
CHARLEMAGNE =
Married HILDEGARDE
|
LOUIS "Le Debonnair"
|
CHARLES "The Bald"
|
(page 140)

Childerbrand
|
Nivelon
|
Theodoret
|
Childebrand II
(Hildebrand)
|
Eccard
|
Nivelon II
879 A.D.
|
Terril
|
Waleran Count
of Vexin
|
Walter I
Count of
Vexin and
Valois
|
Ralf
|
Fulke de Tirel
|
SIR WALTER
de TIREL was
at battle of
Hastings.
|
Walter II
|
Walter III
founded Priory
of St. Denis
1116 A.D.
|
Hugh Tirel of
Essex 1146 A.D.
a Crusader.
|
SIR HUGH II
1st Baron of
Castle Rock.
|
Went to Ireland
with Strongbow,
was Gov. of Trim
1183 A.D.
|
TIRRILL
|
TERRAL
|
TYRRELL

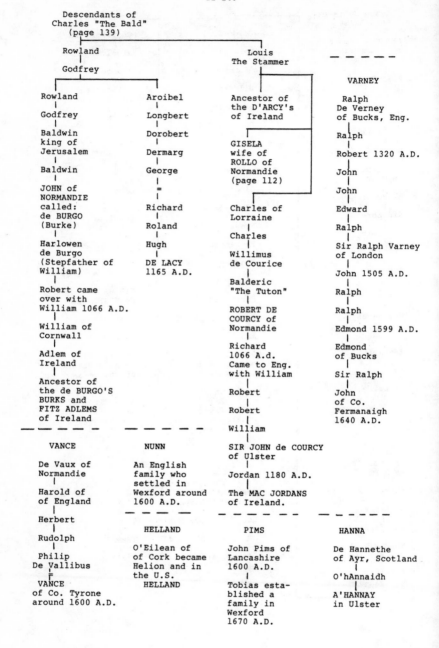

```
            Descendants of
          Charles "The Bald"
             (page 139)

      Rowland              Louis              — — — —
        |              The Stammer
      Godfrey                |                   VARNEY

  Rowland      Aroibel     Ancestor of          Ralph
    |            |          the D'ARCY's       De Verney
  Godfrey     Longbert     of Ireland         of Bucks, Eng.
    |            |                                |
  Baldwin     Dorobert                          Ralph
  king of        |          GISELA                |
  Jerusalem    Dermarg      wife of             Robert 1320 A.D.
    |            |          ROLLO of              |
  Baldwin      George       Normandie           John
    |            |          (page 112)            |
  JOHN of        =                               John
  NORMANDIE                                        |
  called:      Richard     Charles of           Edward
  de BURGO       |         Lorraine               |
  (Burke)      Roland         |                  Ralph
    |            |          Charles                |
  Harlowen     Hugh           |               Sir Ralph Varney
  de Burgo       |          Willimus           of London
  (Stepfather  DE LACY      de Courice            |
  of           1165 A.D.      |                 John 1505 A.D.
  William)                  Balderic              |
    |                       "The Tuton"         Ralph
  Robert came                 |                   |
  over with                 ROBERT DE           Ralph
  William 1066 A.D.         COURCY of             |
    |                       Normandie           Edmond 1599 A.D.
  William of                  |                   |
  Cornwall                  Richard             Edmond
    |                       1066 A.d.           of Bucks
  Adlem of                  Came to Eng.          |
  Ireland                   with William        Sir Ralph
    |                         |                   |
  Ancestor of               Robert              John
  the de BURGO'S              |                 of Co.
  BURKS and                 Robert              Fermanaigh
  FITZ ADLEMS                 |                 1640 A.D.
  of Ireland                William
 — — — — —                    |
                          SIR JOHN de COURCY
   VANCE        NUNN       of Ulster
                            |
 De Vaux of   An English  Jordan 1180 A.D.
 Normandie    family who     |
    |         settled in   The MAC JORDANS
 Harold of    Wexford around of Ireland.
 of England   1600 A.D.
    |         — — — —      — — — — — — —      — — — — —
 Herbert
    |          HELLAND       PIMS              HANNA
 Rudolph
    |         O'Eilean of   John Pims of     De Hannethe
 Philip       of Cork became Lancashire      of Ayr, Scotland
 De Vallibus  Helion and in  1600 A.D.          |
    |         the U.S.         |              O'hAnnaidh
 VANCE        HELLAND        Tobias esta-       |
 of Co. Tyrone              blished a         A'HANNAY
 around 1600 A.D.          family in         in Ulster
                           Wexford
                           1670 A.D.
```

WHITE

```
de PITCHE of
   Normandie
       |
Came to England with
   William
       |
       =
       |
    Rudolph
Moved to Ireland 1172 A.D.
       |
  John PITCHFORD
       |
   Rudolph 1285 A.D.
       |
    Thomas
       |
  James of Trim
       |
  ┌────────────────┐
Christopher      Thomas
                   |
                  John
               took the
               surname
                WHYTE
                   |
            Walter WHITE
```
— — — — —

STEWARD

William Stewart served
in Danish and Swedish armies.
Came to Ireland from Whithorn,
Wigtonshire,with 200 mercinaries
in 1608. On 11-30-1610 he was
granted land near Kilmacrenan,
Co. Donegal.
— — — —

VAUS

This family came to Ireland
from Barnbarroch, Wigtonshire.
— — — ——

DEGERNON
of Wales

Roger De Gurnon
came over with Strongbow.
Now Garland. — — — —

ORMSBY
```
   Ormsby — = — Rose
of Lincolnshire |  Woodforde

          Edward = Elizabeth
          of Essex | Moffett

               Henry
               of Sligo
            came with Cromwell
```

HEGUENOTS

Some came directly from mainland
Europe, others as soldiers in
Cromwells army.

Name	Resided in this Irish County
Addis	Westmeath
Alland	Cavin
Aungier	Cavin
Ballard	Cavin
Basil	Dublin
Bedell	Cavin
Borr	Monaghan
Chapelin (Chaplin)	Cavin
Casaubon	Cork
Chartres	Cork
Covert	Cork
Cramer	Kilkenny
Croizier	Fermanagh
Cuppaidge	Dublin
Cornick	Kilkenny
De La Cour (Dilworth)	Cork
Delaune (Delaney)	Dublin
de Lapp (Lappin)	Fermanagh
Everis	Donegal
Frizelle	Monaghan
Grolier	Dublin
Herrick	Cork
Holland	Monaghan
Jaques	Roscommon
Jerome	Kilkenny
Lemon	Dublin
Lynegar	Dublin
Mamon	Kilkenny
Mussenden	Down
Obin (Hobin)	Armagh
Pineau (Dinean)	Mayo
Sisson	Dublin
Termond	Cavin
Valentine	Tipperary
Van Homrigh	Dublin
Vernloe	Leitrim
Viner	Meath
Vigor	Carlow
Voss (Vaus)	Cavin
Westerna	Limerick
Wibrant	Kilkenny
Wishard	Monaghan
Yarner	Wicklow

— — — — —

ORPEN
```
   Orpen   =   Agnes
of Sumerset |  Edwards 1490 A.D.

            John
       Henry of Salsbury
            Robert
        Robert — = — Mary
        of Dorset  |  Ley
        1600 A.D.  Henry
                     |
              Robert of Kerry
```

NORMANS NOT OTHERWISE ACCOUNTED FOR:

BACON - Little known of them in Ireland. Arrived about 1175.

BATES - A Somerset, England, family, found in English records.

BISSETT - A family of French descent who moved to Scotland. A branch continued on to Co. Antrim, some took the surname MAC EOIN which was later translated as JOHNSON.

BLAKE - Originally CADDELL of Wales. The Galway branch took Blake as their surname.

BLACKWELL - This English family probably took their name from the community they lived near in England.

BRANNICK - A Welsh family who came over with Strongbow.

BRAY-BREE - An English family of Co. Wicklow. Now impossible to separate from Irish families who took this surname.

BROWN - An English family of Norman heritage who came to Ireland around 1180. Following them, other families of the same name settled in other parts of the country.

BRUCE - This family took their name from Brousse in France. Came to England with William. Robert Bruce is the best known family member.

CAREW - A Norman family from Pembrokeshire in Wales. Arrived in Ireland in the early 1200's. Some took the Irish name Carey.

CLAYTON - Better known in Lancashire than in Ireland. May have arrived in Ireland as one of Cromwells officers.

CONDON - A Norman family arriving probably in the late 1500's.

COTTON - An English family mostly around Cork.

CROFTON - An English family from Yorkshire or Lancastershire.

DALAMARA - From Normandie, came to Ireland via England. Settled in Westmeath. One branch took the surname MAC HERBERT, another DELMER.

DATON - From Autun, Normandy.

DEVEREUX - From Evereus in Normandie. To England 1066 and Ireland in the 1170's.

FAY - A Norman family who came to Ireland in the 1200's and were granted lands in Westmeath. The Irish O'Feic family have the same English translation of Fay.

GASKIN - Originally from Southern France. Date of arrival uncertain.

GRANT - In the South of Ireland they were Normans. In the North the Grants were Scotch.

GREEN - Most Greens are Irish but a few in the South are of English descent.

HAYDON - English, as distinct from from the Irish family which took this English name.

HOUGHTON - Said to be an English place name taken as a family surname, 1200 A.D.

L'ESTRANGE - An Irish family who changed their Gaelic name by translating it into French.

LOFTIS - Of Yorkshire, came to Ireland and settled in Wexford.

NEVILLE - Normans who came over about 1180 and aren't related to the Irish Nevill's.

PRATT - Arrived from England in the early 1200's.

RIDDLE - An old English family who are long time residents of Co. Limerick.

SARSFIELD - An English family from Herefordshire who came shortly after 1170.

SEAGRAVE - An English family from Leicestershire. Settled in Ireland in the early 1300's.

STOKES - An English name of uncertain origin. Settled around Dublin after 1300.

STAUNTON - This family was in Ireland by 1171. In later times formed a close association with the BURKES. One branch took the surname MAC EVILLY.

SCOTLAND

1. ABERDEEN	16. EAST LOTHIAN	31. ROSS & CROMARTY
2. KINCARDINE	17. BERWICK	32. SKYE
3. ANGUS	18. PEEBLES	33. SUTHERLAND
4. PERTH	19. SELKIRK	34. CATHNESS
5. INVERNESS	20. ROXBURGH	35. ORKNEY
6. ARGYLL	21. DUMFRIES	36. LEWIS
7. FIFE	22. KIRKCUDBRIGHT	37. HARRIS
8. KINROSS	23. WIGTON	38. NORTH UIST
9. STERLING	24. MIDLOTHIAN	39. SOUTH UIST
10. DUNBARTON	25. BUTE	40. IONA
11. RENFREW	26. KINTYRE	41. CLACAMANNAN
12. AYR	27. ISLAY	42. NAIRN
13. LANARK	28. JURA	43. MORAY
14. WEST LOTHIAN	29. MULL	44. BANFF
15. EDINBURGH CITY	30. MORUEN	

THE SCOT-IRISH

Protestant English and Scots who came to Ireland and later moved to the New World where they were called "Scot-Irish". **P** = Presbyterian **Q** = Quaker

NAME	RELIGION	IRE. MAPS	SCOT.	NAME	RELIGION	IRE. MAPS	SCOT.
Achison Acheson	P	(1)	[17]	Barnet		(2-28)	[15]
Adair Mac Daraich		9		Barney			
Adams	Q	5		Barton		7	24
Agnew	Q	3-5	22	Barnwell		12	15
Alan		3	10	Barr		1	11-12
Alexander, Mac Alasdair		4		Baxter		3	4
Allen, Mac Ailean	Q	8	17	Bacon		27-28	
Mac Allister			21	Bedford		25	11
Alton		30		Beecher		27	
Anderson	Q	4-7	21	Begg		12	15
Andrews	Q	3-5	21	Bell		3-4	21
Arbuckle		3-6	13	Bellew		12	1
Archdale		7	21	Benson		6	15
Armour		2-6	11-13	Berry		6-11-19	7
Armstrong, Mac Ghille-Laidir	Q	7-8	21	Bertram			15
Ashe		2-11		Best		13	15
Atchison		1	15	Betty		7	21
Atherton		5	7	Biddle		1	
Atkinson	Q	4-5	11	Biggin		5	13
Audley,		3-4	11	Birney		4	15
Mac Aulay		3	10	Black		3	13
McAulla		1	11	Blakley		3-6-8	
Austin		2	15	Blackwood		6	21
Bacon		2-27-28		Blair		3-6	7-12
Bagnoll		18	11	Boggas		7	21
Bain		3		Bolton		2-9	21
Baird		3-6-12		Bond		5	
Balfour			7	Bone		3	12
Ballantine	Q	6	20	Bomby		1	12-21
Bankhead		2	12	Bothwick			20-21
Barber		2-4-5	12	Boylan		26	21
Barclay		1	7	Boyd		3-6	21
Barnes		1	1	Bradshaw	Q	5	

Name			Name		
McBride	(6)		Clifton		[15]
Brougham	1-20		Coach	(6)	
Brown	2-3	[17]	Cokley	26-27	
Brownlowe	1		Coates	6	
Bruce		19	Cobert	6	10-11
Buchanan		9	Colvin Q	5	9
Bullock Q	5	10-18	Comb (Mc)	3	23
Burley	7		Comiskey (Mc)		12
Busby		11	Cooke Q	3	17
Burnside	4	9	Cooper Q	26	7
Byers	6	24	Cope Q		
Caddon (Mc)	4	24	Copeland	26	11
Caldwell	1-3	11	Colthart	6-9	22
Callaway			Courtney	26	
Calley	3	7	Coutts		1-15
McCallum	1-2	12	Cowan (Mc)		12
Calvert	7	7	Cranston		15
Cameron		7	Crawford	3	12
Candless (Mc)		23	Cracken (Mc)	1	22
McCannell (Mc)	6	6	Craig	3	17
Carnes		Eng.	Crispie		26
Carr	4	9	Croskey (Mc)	6	
Carson	3-4	22	Cudbert	6-18	21
McCartney (Mc)	6	22-23	Cuddy	6	21
Cathcart	4-7	11	Cullock (Mc)	1	22
Caruthers	4-5	21	Cunningham	1-2	12
Chalmers Q	4-5-6	12-13	Cully (Mc)	6	5
Chandler		17	Cummin	6-8	5
Chapman	5	4	Curry	1-3-6	12
Cherry Q		12	Cusker (Mc)	19	11
Christy Q	6	7	Dalrymple		7
Cleave (Mc)		23	Daniel Q	5	1
Clernon (Mc)	6	4	Davidson	3-4	1
Clapen	4		Davie	19	
Clark	3-6	21	Davis Q	27	1

Name				Name			
Dawson		(3)		Fitton		(28)	
Denn		26		Floodgate		18	
Dennison		1	[11]	Foley		26	
Despie		28		Fowler		7	[5]
Dickson	Q	5-6	5	Fullerton		6	12
Diggins		26		Gaines		30	
Dingwell		19	1	Gale		1	
Dobbs		3	19	Galston		6	12
Dobson		23		Galvin		11-30	
Dodd			19	Garran		2	
Doggart		6		Garth		6	
Douglas		5-6	13	Garvey		12	1
Drew			11	Gaw (Gall)		6	4
Drummond		4	4-9	Gawdy (Gowdie)		6	12
Duggin		5	23	Geddes		6	
Dwiggan		20		Gibson	Q	4-5-6	21
Eager		30	21	Gilbert	Q	5	22
Eccles		3	17	Gilfillan		6	9
Echlin		5-6	7	Gill (Mc)			22
Edwards		2	14	Gilmore	Q	5	2
Elder		1-5	1	Gillis		3	24
Elliott		11	20	Glashan (Mc)			5
Ellis		1	15	Glasson			5
Erlane (Mc)		3	12	Gordon		3-5	17
Erwin	Q	3		Gore		7	
Fawcett	Q	3		Goss		12	
Fee (Mc)		8	6	Goudy		6	15
Fenton		3	5	Gracy		7	
Fearn		7		Graham		2	
Ferguson		5-6	21	Granger		3-6	17
Ferron		4		Graves			
Ferry		3	5	Gray	Q	3-5	17
Filson		6		Greame		11	
Finnie		6	1	Greer	Q	4-5	21
Fish		11	17	Gregg	Q	4-5	21

Name	Q	(4)	[21]	Name	Q	(4)	[22]
Grierson		(4)	[21]	Hindshaw	Q	(4)	[22]
Gruder (Mc)			4	Hines		2	
Gugan (Mc)			22	Hodkinson	Q - Lancashire, Eng.		
Guinly (Mc)		1		Hogg		4	17
Gunn		30		Holland		2-6	12
Gurke (Mc)		4-6		Hollingsworth	Q	5	Eng.
Haddock	Q	4-5	11	Holmes		3	12
Hall	Q	3-5	17	Home		7	17
Haliday		6	21	Hood		3	
Haig		4	15	Hook		6	21
Hamill		29	12	Hooper	Q	3-5	
Hamilton		5	11-13	Hope		6	21
Hancock	Q	3-5		Horner		2-6	22
Hanna	Q	1		Horne		7	22
Hansard		1		Houston		2-3	13
Harrison		7		Hoole		6	
Harper		2	12	Huddleston		6	21
Hart		1	15	Hughes	Q	3	12
Hartley	Q	3		Hull		6	
Harvey		2	15	Hunter		2-3-6	12
Hasleton		3		Hutchieson		3	22
Hastie		3	9	Hutchins		12	12
Hatton		28	6	Hyde		27	
Hay (Hayes)	Q	3-5	12	Irvine		6	1-21
Healy				Irving		6	1-21
Hemphill		2	12	Jackson	Q	3-5-6	11
Henderson	Q	5-7	7-21	Jamieson		6	1
Henry		2-4	7-12	Johnston		4	11-21
Herbert			9	Karnes		18	
Hepburn		22	24	Keag (Mac)		6	
Hickson				Kee (Mc) (Mackay)		1	23
Higgenbotham	Q	3-5		Kelleher		6	Scotch
Hill	Q	3-5	1	Kenzie (Mc)			23
Hillard		30		Kerr	Q	5	24
Hilton		1	17	Kiedy			30

Kim (Mc)		(2) Clann Frazier
Kindelan	12	
Kennedy	3-6	[12]
Kinsell	1	
Kirke Q	3	21
Lander	5	
Lane	2	1
Laird		17
Lamb Q	3	17
Lambert	11	17
Leddy (Liddy)	22	
Lindsey	4	11-12
Linton	6	20
Little	6	21
Logan	3	12
Loudon	3	12
Lourie	6	
Lowdon Q	3	12
Lowrey	6	21
Lutterell	12	
Lusher		
Lyndsey	4	11
Machett	5	
Maglaughlin	3	9
Mahaffy	1-8	
Maithland	7	11
Maly	9	21
Mangan	30	
Mansfield	1	
Master (Mac)	3-28	21
Maston	18	
Maybury	26	
Meldrum	13-14	7
Menzes	8	11
Mercer Q	3	4

Meredith Q	(3)	
Metcald	18	[7]
Middleton	26	1
Milhouse Q	2	
Millar	2-3-4	21
Millikin Q	3	11
Mills	3	
Minehan	26	7
Moynihan	26	
Moffitt		13
Moore	5	12
More	11	12
Morrison	1-3-18	
Montgomery	2-6	11
Mottley	21-28-32	
Mulholland	1-2	
Mullady		
Mullen (Mc)	6	
Mure		10
Murdock	2-3	12
Murray (Mc)	6	
Munsell	18	
Musgrave	6	
Napier	3-6	11
Nelson	3	11
Neff (Mc)		
Nesbitt	4-11	20
Ness (Mc)		
Nesmith	2	17
Newland		18
Nevin	3	12
Nichol (Mc)		Skye
Ninn (Mc)		
Nixon	1-7	Cumberland
Norton	18	

Name		Col1	Col2	Name		Col1	Col2
Norris		(27)		Ralston		(11)	[11]
Nutt (Mc)		1-2		Ramsey		2	7
Nutterville		12		Rankin		2	12
Orr		6	[22]	Rea		2	1
Oxburogh		24		Reen		27	
Palmer		6	11	Reid		6	12
Park		2-3	17	Religh		28	
Parker		3-6	4	Riddle		6	11
Parsons		4	20	Ridgway		4	
Patterson	Q	3	11	Ritchie		3	7
Patty		6		Robertson		6	11
Paxton		6	17	Robins		27	9
Pay		29		Robinson		6	11
Perkins		1		Roe		4	
Perry		27	1	Rogers		2	11
Person	Q	5		Rolan		2-3-6	1
Phelps	Q	6		Rolleston		5	
Pherson (Mc)		6		Rooth		29	
Piersin	Q	5		Roseman		6	
Pinkerton		2	11	Ross		3-6	12
Pinner		11		Russell		1-11	11
Piper		4	1	Rutleidge		11	
Pippard		9		Ruth		29	
Pittarre		7		Say		5	
Pollock		4	12	Scot		3-6	7
Porter		6	11	Selkirk		6	11
Potts		8	15	Shanebane		28	
Pringle		4	20	Shanks		6	13
Purly		6		Sharp		3	4
Quade (Mc)		6		Sherlock		8	
Quedman (Redman)		6		Shine		26	1
Quigley		2		Short		4	21
Quill		27	30	Sibb		7	
Quoid (Mc)		6		Skiddy		6	
Racken (Mc)		6		Skilly		1	

Slattery	(30)		Tobyn	(23)		
Sloan	2-3	[15]	Todd	3-6		
Smelhome	7	11	Tom	2		
Smiley	3	15	Toulan	3		
Smith	2-3-6	1	Trail	3-7	[7]	
Smyth	14	15	Traill	3-7		
Spillane	26		Trant	18		
Speir	3	9	Trent	18		
Spens	6	7	Trumble	6		
Stanhawe	5		Trymble	6		
Starrat	3		Turk	3	11	
Steel	1	11	Tweed	26	1	
Stephonson	1	12	Tyler	3		
Stewart	1-4	20	Upton	3		
Stirling	3-4		Urie	4	1	
Stitt	6	21	Ury	4		
Straight	6	4	Vance	2		
Stratton	5	17	Vaughan	1		
Strickland	6		Vans	2-8	23	
Sutler	2		Vernor	2-3-4	11	
Swan	4		Wagner	26		
Swarnbeck	6		Waldron	11	English	
Syminton	6	13	Walker	1-3-6	15	
Taggard	3-4	21	Waller	18		
Taggart	3-4	21	Wans	1		
Tafe	9		Ward	7	English	
Tate	5	15	Wagner	26		
Taylor	3-6-11	15	Wallace	1-3-6	12	
Tayt	3	15	Warrington	18		
Teat	6		Waterson	5	11	
Teling	12		Watson	4-6	10	
Telling	12		Watt	5	1	
Templeton	6	12	Weir	2-3-6	24	
Thomb	3	11	Whitelaw	5		
Thompson	2-4	11	Whyte	3		

Wingfield	(4)	
Williams	5	[18]
Willoughbie	4	
Wilson	1	1
Winston	28	1
Wirrall	11	
Whitcurch	5	
Whitty	28	
Whiteside	3	
Whorter (Mc)	3-5	Scotch
Williamson	6	18
Wilson	2-3-4-8	
Windron	3	15
Wirling	6	
Woodburn	2	12
Woods	6	
Woodside	37	12
Worth	27	
Wray (Ray)	1-2	
Wright	3	
Wylie	3	12
Wily	3	12
Young	3	7

MAJOR SCOTCH CLANS, 1500 A.D.

In later times when the Clan system was broken up in
Scotland, many clan members took English names, thus
becoming subclans of those listed here. See map on page
143.

CLAN NAME	SCOTCH COUNTY		
BAIN	[31]	LINDSAY	[3]
BUCHANAN	[10]	LIVINGSTON	[4]
BUTTER	[4]	LOBAN	[31]
CALDER	[1]	LYON	[3]
CAMERON	[15-30]	MACALISTER	[26]
CAMBELL	[4-5-6-42]	MACAULAY	[6]
CHISHOLM	[5-31]	MAGREGOR	[6]
COLQUHOUN	[6]	MACIAIN	[30]
CUMMIN	[43]	MACINTYRE	[6]
CUNNINGHAM	[10]	MACKAY	[33]
DAVIDSON	[5]	MACKINNON	[29-32]
DEWAR	[4]	MACKINTOSH	[5-42]
DRUMMOND	[4]	MACLAY	[6]
DUNBAR	[43]	MALCOLM	[6]
ERSKINE	[1]	MACNAGHTIN	[6]
FARQUHARSON	[1]	MACQUARIE	[29]
FORBES	[1]	MATHESON	[31]
FRASER	[5]	MENTEITH	[10]
GAILBRAITH	[9]	MENZIE	[4]
GAYRE	[31]	MERCER	[3]
GORDON	[1]	MONC	[4]
GRANT	[5-43]	MONCREIFFE	[4-7]
GUNN	[34]	MORRISON	[36]
HALDANE	[41]	MUNRO	[31-33]
HAMILTON	[25]	MURRAY	[4-33-41]
HAY (le Hay)	[43]	Mac ARTHUR	[6]
INNES	[43-44]	Mac ASKILL	[32]
KEITH	[34]	Mac BETH	[27]
LAMONT	[6]	Mac CAULAY	[10-36]
LEITH	[1]	Mac CLEAN	[27]
LESLIE	[43]	Mac CODRUM	[38]

Mc CORQUODALE	[6]	ROSS	[31]
Mac CRIMMON	[32]	SHAW	[5]
Mc CULLOCH	[31]	STIRLING	[41]
Mac DONNELL	[5-26-27-31]	SUTHERLAND	[33]
Mac DONALD	[32]	SPAULDING	[4]
Mac DOUGALL	[6]	STORMONTH	[3]
Mac EACHERN	[26]	STEWART	[4-6-9-10]
Mac EOWAN	[6]	SINCLAIR	[34]
Mac FARLANE	[6]	STUART	[25-43]
Mac FERGUS	[6]	URQUHART	[31]
Mac INNES	[30]		
Mac LAREN	[4]		
Mac LAVERTY	[27]		
Mac LEAN	[30]		
Mac LEOD	[31-33-36]		
Mac MARTIN	[5]		
Mac MILLAN	[6]		
Mac NAB	[4]		
Mac NEISH	[4]		
Mac PHERSON	[5]		
Mac PHUN	[6]		
Mac QUEEN	[5]		
Mac RAE	[31]		
Mac NOBLE	[10]		
OLIPHANT	[34]		
OLLIPHAONT	[4]		
OGILVY	[3]		
ORDON	[44]		
RATTRAY	[4]		
ROSE	[42]		
ROBERTSON	[4]		
ROLLO	[8]		
RUTHVEN	[3-4]		
RAMSEY	[3]		
Clan RANALD	[5]		

THE TERRITORIAL DIVIDIONS OF IRELAND

PROVINCES: Four; Connaught, Leinster, Munster and Ulster.
                 In early times Meath was a separate province.
                 Provincial boundries as well as those of the
                 smaller political units have changed from time
                 to time.

BARONIES: More than 150 independent clan-kingdons exis-
                 ted in Ireland in the pre-Norman period.Follow-
                 ing the Norman invasion some of these kingdoms
                 began to be called Baronies. A similar adminis-
                 trative unit in England was the "Hundred".

THE COUNTY: Originally called the "Shire" in Anglo-Norman.
                 Some of the smaller Irish kingdoms were renamed
                 shires. The shire of Dublin was established about
                 1197. Prior to 1606 all shires had been renamed
                 counties.

THE PARISH: In it's Ecclesiastical terminology the Parish
                 was an extension of church administration over
                 territory rather than a built up community. The
                 present day boundries of the Catholic Church and
                 The Church of Ireland do not co-exist.

TOWN LAND: The BALLIBO, PLOUGHLAND and TATE became Townlands
                 under the English. This term is not related to a
                 built up community. The name is derived from the
                 old English, "TUN", meaning walled or enclosed.

IRISHROOTS

part

three

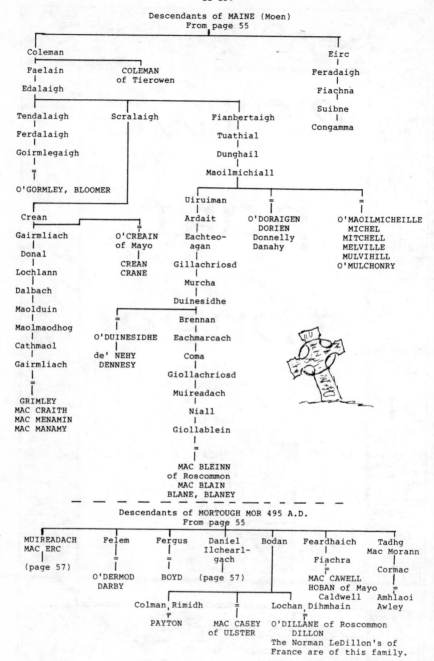

Descendants of MAINE (Moen)
From page 55

Coleman

Faelain   COLEMAN
         of Tierowen

Edalaigh

Eirc

Feradaigh

Fiachna

Suibne

Congamma

Tendalaigh   Scralaigh   Fianbertaigh

Ferdalaigh   Tuathial

Goirmlegaigh   Dunghail

Maoilmichiall

O'GORMLEY, BLOOMER

Uiruiman

Crean   Ardait   O'DORAIGEN   O'MAOILMICHEILLE

Gairmliach   O'CREAIN Eachteo- DORIEN   MICHEL

Donal   of Mayo   agan   Donnelly   MITCHELL

Lochlann   CREAN Gillachriosd Danahy   MELVILLE

Dalbach   CRANE Murcha   MULVIHILL

Maolduin   Duinesidhe   O'MULCHONRY

Maolmaodhog   Brennan

Cathmaol O'DUINESIDHE Eachmarcach

Gairmliach de' NEHY Coma

        DENNESY Giollachriosd

GRIMLEY   Muireadach

MAC CRAITH   Niall

MAC MENAMIN   Giollablein

MAC MANAMY

MAC BLEINN
of Roscommon
MAC BLAIN
BLANE, BLANEY

Descendants of MORTOUGH MOR 495 A.D.
From page 55

MUIREADACH Felem Fergus Daniel Bodan Feardhaich Tadhg
MAC ERC   Ilchearl-   Mac Morann
                    gach   Fiachra
(page 57)   Cormac
        O'DERMOD BOYD (page 57)   MAC CAWELL
        DARBY   HOBAN of Mayo
                                    Caldwell Amhlaoi
                                                  Awley

Colman Rimidh   Lochan Dihmhain

PAYTON   MAC CASEY O'DILLANE of Roscommon
           of ULSTER   DILLON
                      The Norman LeDillon's of
                      France are of this family.

THE SURNAME INDEX

NOTE: Not all surname forms in the charts are indexed.

BARTON   144 (7-2)
De Bartun   [24]

BASSINGHAM (De)
 English   132

BATES   14% (9-12-18)
De Bathe
 English

BAYLY   134 (3-18)
Baille
 Bailey from Yorkshire
 Bayley

BAXTER   144 (3) [4]
Mac an Bhacstair
 Scotch

BEALE   69 (3)
Beatley
BEARGA   72
BEARNACH   51 (7)
Mac Bearnaighe
 of Fermanagh

BEATTY   138 (12)
Betagg
 Betty
 Scotch

BEAUMONT   122 (9)
De Beaumont 129
De Bellomont
De Buamonn

BECK   17 (3-6)
O'Beice
 also English
BECON   72
BEDDY (O')   15 (14)

BEDELL   141 (11)

BEDFORD   144 (25)
 Scotch   [11]

BEECHER   144 (27)
Becher
 English

BEGG   144 (12) [15]
Small
 Norman-Scotch

BEIRNE (O') 84 (15)
 of Roscommon
 O'Beirn

BELESME (De) 124
            126 (17)
BELL   144 (3-6)
Mac Ghillechluig [21]
 Scotch

BELLEW   144 (12) [1]
De Belleau

BELSCHE   137 (3-6)
Belaisis
Belases
Belshies
Belshaes
Belshes
 Also Scotch

BELTON
 See Weldon

BEMISH   (26-27)
 Norman

BENNETT   86 (8-9)
Benedict
 Assumed Anglo-French
             name

BENNY   54 (3)
Bineid

BENSON   123 (3-6)
 English   144 (6) [15]

BENTON   6 (3)
 Scotch   130 (27)

BERGIN   37 (20)
O'hAimheirgin
Berrigan

BERMINGHAM (De)
 Norman   117 (19-21)
One branch
took surname Mac Corish

BERRAN   51 (14)
O'Bearain

BERREEN (O')   (14)
O'Birin
 See Birne (O')
BERRI (De) 115 (27)
 Barry of Cork

BERRIGAN
 A variant of Bergin

BERRY   35 (20)
O'Bearra   144 (6-11-
Anglo-Scotch   19)
Bury   [7]

BERTRAM   144   [15]
Beartram
 Anglo-Scotch

BEST   144 (3-5-13)
 Scotch-English [15

BETTY   144 (7) [21]
Mac an Bhiadhtaiche
Bettie

BIDDLE   144 (1)

BIDDY (O') 127

BIGGIN   144 (5)
O'Bigin   [13]
Beggan

BIGOD   125 (32)
Norman

BIGOT   129 (6)
 of England

BINLEY   54
O'Binnigh
Benny

BIRCH   59 (20)
Mac Buirche

BIRKES   136 (23)

BIRNE (O')   95 (14)
O'Beirn

BIRNEY (Mc) 35 (3-6)
Mac Biorna   51 (7)
Burney   144 (4) [15]
 also Scotch

BIRREN (O') 35 (6)
O'Biorain
Birrane

BISET   129 (3)
Bissett   Scotch
Mac Eoin   142 (3-6)
Mac Keon
Owen

BISHOP   60 (4)
an assumed name
 See Anaspie (Mac)

BLACK   135 (3)
Mac Ghilledhuibh
See Kilduff 144 (3) [13]

BLACKHEAD 127 (26)
O'Ceanduibh

BLACKER   109 (18)
Blacaire
Norse

BRANNON   67 (20)
O'Braonan
Brenahan
Banon
  See Brannan

BRASSILL (Mac)
Maoilbreasal 48 (28)

BRASSILL (O')46 (28)
Bresal (O') 47 (28)
O'Breasail   52 (28)
O'Brazil

BRAWLEY   55 (2)
O'Brolaig
Bradley
Bralley

BRAY   142 (11-18)
De Bri   Norman
  of Cornwall
Bree

BRAZIL   46 (28)
  of Waterford
Brassil

BREARTY (Mac)
Mac Briartaig
               26 (1)

BREEN (Mac)   20 (23)
Mac Braoin   51 (7)
Mac Brine   64 (29)
Brean   99 (24-29)
Bruen

BREEN (O')   54 (15-20)
Brain (O')
O'Braoin
Bruen

BREDIN   35 (4-7)
O'Bradain
Braden

BRENERTON   121 (23)
Breartun   Norman
Brerton
BRENHAM   67
BRENNAN   18 (12-26)
O'Braonain   49 (19)
O'Brenane   65 (7)
Brannan   75 (19)
              78 (19)

              98 (7)
             103 (29)

BRENNAN (Mac) 96 (24)

BRESLIN   47 (1-7)
O'Brislaine   67 (1-7-14)
Breslann   98 (14)
Brislane

BREWS (De)   125 (29)
De Berewa

BRICE (O')   43 (1)
  Bryce

BRICK   43 (26-28)
Bric (O')   52 (28)
Badger
  of Galway

BRIDE (Mac)   21 (1-14)
Mac Giolla Bhrighde
              145 (6)

BRIEN (Mac)   20 (23)
Mac Braoin
Mac Bryan

BRIEN (O')   19 (32)
O'Briain   21 (23-30)
              57
              59
              81 (22-23-
             120   30)

BRIGHT   14 (16)
O'Lunin   51 (7-11)

BRINE (Mac)   88 (7-15)
Mac Braoin
Mac Bryan

BRIONIS (De) 133 (14)
Bryan of Kilkenny

BRIONNE (De) 112
  Norman   118

BROCK   50 (9-21)
Mac Broc   52 (28)

BRODER   39 (27-29)
Bruadair
Brouder

BRODERICK   10 (19-27)
O'Bruadair   39 (27)
Broder

BRODERICK   58 (1-14)
  of Ulster
Mac Bradarain
Brothers

BRODIGAN   (9-12)
O'Bradagain
O'Bradigan

BRODY   75 (11)
O'Broduibh
O'Briody

BRODY (Mac)   23 (22)
Mac Bruaideada
Mac Brodie   84 (10)
Mac Brodin

BROGAN   27 (14)
Brocain (O') 64 (14)
O'Brogain   68 (20)
Brohan

BROHAN   143 (1-20)
O'Bruachain
Banks
Brougham

BROIN (O')   64 (25)
O'Braoin   104

BROLLAGHAN (O') (1-2-4)
O'Brolcain
Desc. from Suibhne Meann
Brallaghan
BROLLY   21 (2)

BROOKE   133 (12-32)
             136 (6)

BROTHERS   39 (27)
              58 (1)
BROWN   133 (32)
De Brun   142 (2-3)
             145 [17]
Norman-English-Scotch

BROWNLOWE   145 (1-9)

BRUCE   122
DeBrus -
  French   124
and Scotch   142   [19]
             145

BRUEN (O')   88 (15)
O'Braoin
Breen

BRUODIN   84 (22)
Mac Bruaidin
A branch of the Brodys

BRYAN   131 (29)
  Norman

BRYAN (Mac)   88 (7)
Mac Braoin   99 (24-29)

BRYANT   21 (22)

BUAIN (O')   102

BUCHANAN   61 (3-6)
  an assumed name
O'Bocainain 145 (4) [9]
  Scotch

BUCKLEY   100 (20-23-
O'Buachalla   27)
  English

BUDDY   127 (1)
O'Buadhach

BUGLAR   (22-32)
  English
  From Devonshire
Bolger
BUHILLY   100 (6)
BULLOCK   145 (5)
  Scotch   [10-18]

BURDETT   129 (8)
Bourdet
Burnett

BURDON   31 (6)
De Burdun
Verdon
Warden

BURGESS   17 (3-6)

BURKE   87 (14)
De Burg   92 (15)
De Burca   120 (19-14-4)
  Norman   124 (4)
             133 (19)
             140

BURLEY   145 (7)

BURNELL   136 (12-22)
  Anglo-Norman

BURNETTE   44 (8)
Also a branch of
  Burnell

BURNS   44 (8)
Mac Conboirne 67 (19)
O'Conboirne 72 (7-15)
Burn   79 (14)
Burne   104 (5-6)
O'Beirnes
Bourns
  A Scotch name
  assumed by the Irish
Byron

BURNSIDE   145 (2-4)
                [9]

BURNY
  See Birney (Mac)

BURRIS   (3-5-6)
Buirgeis   English
Burrowes

BURY   35
Also an assumed Norman
           name

BUSBY   145 [11]

BUTCHER   121 (28-32)
  of Essex
  See Boucher

BUTLER   119 (23-29)
Le Buitleir

BYERS   145 (6) [24]
  From East Lothian
  English
Byre

BYRNE (O')   64 (25)
O'Broin

BYSET   47 (6)
Bissett

C

CABE (Mac)   109 (10-11)
Mac Caba
  Norse

CADDELL   142 (18-19)
Cadwal
  The Welsh name of
  the Blakes

CADIMN (O') 19 (11)
Mac Aidin
O'Cadimn
Caden

CADDEN (Mac) 44 (5)
  of Armagh

CADEN   135 (2-3)
Mac Cadain

CADIGAN   (27)
O'Ceadagain

CAFFELLY (Mac) 32 (6)
  of Down
Mac Eachmhilidh
Mac Caughley
Mac Cawley

CAFFERTY (Mac) 69 (1-2)
Mac Eacmarcaig

CAFFREY (Mac) 51 (7)
Mac Gafraidh

CAFFY (O')   78

CAGNEY   53 (27)
O'Cainighe
O'Caingne

CAHAN (Mac) 57 (22)
Mac Cathain

CAHAN (O')   61 (2-4)
O'Cathain   69 (1)
O'Caine
Cain

CAHILL (Mac) 6 (1-11)
Mac Cathail 75 (1)
  Scotch

CAHILL (O') 38 (26)
O'Cathail   50 (6)
             55 (19-26)

CAICHDOMHAIN (O')
             53

CAIG (Mac)   6 (19)
Mac Thaidhg

CAIL (Mac)   47 (1)
CAINE O'Cahan 61 (14)
CAIRN (Mac) 50 (3-5-6)
Mac Ciarain

CAISIN   22 (24)

CALDWELL   56 (4)
  Scotch   145 (1-3)
                [11]

CALEY   14 (12)
O'Caoile   129
Keely
Kiely
Kiley

CALPIN (Mac) 44
  See Mac Alpin

CALUM (Mac) 11 (8)
Mac Colum
Mac Callum

CALL (Mac)   (19)
Mac Tail
Corless

CALLAGHAN (O') 15 (27)
O'Cellachain 16 (22)
Callighan   63 (15)
             79 (14)

CALLAN   54 (3)
O'Cathalain 65 (6-8)
Culhane   127 (8)
Cahalane

CALLANAN (O') 45 (19)
O'Callanain
Callinan

CALLAWAY   145
  Scotch

CALLEN (Mac)   44   (2)
Mac Calpin
Mac Allan
  See Alpin (Mac)
  See Allen
  Caley   129
CALLEY   145 (3) [7]

CALLIGHAN (O')
  of Erris   72 (22)
O'Ceallachain

CALLION (Mac) 6 (1)
Mac Cailin   Scotch
Mac Callan

CALLISTER (Mac)
  See Mac Allister

CALLUM (Mac) 6 (7-16)
Calum   11 (18)

CALLUM (Mc) 130 (27)
Mac Chaluim 145 (1-2)
Mac Colum   Scotch [12]

CALMONT (Mac)
  A branch of the
  Scotch Clann
Buchanan

CALVERT   145 (7) [7]

CAMERON   46 (14)
O'Cumarain 145 (14) [7]
Cameron of Mayo
Camshron

CAMP   6 (1)
Mac Cathmhaoil
              57 (4)

CAMPBELL   6 (1-3-4)
Mac Cathmhaoil
Camphill   43 (1-4)
              55

CAMPBELL   51 (4-7)
  of Tyrone
An assumed name

CAMPION   87 (24-29)
An assumed name
Norman

CANAVAN (O') 35 (19)
O'Canajan   86 (15)
O'CeannduBhain
Whitehead

CANDLESS (Mc)
Mac Cuindlis 145 (6) [23]

CANE
  A branch of O'Cahan
CANN (Mac)   19 (5)
Mac Canna
Mac Cana
Mac Kann
O'CANN   53

CANNADY   58   [12]
  From Ayr   Scotland
Kannady
Kennady

CANNELL (Mc) 145 (6) [6]

CANNIFF
  See Cunniffe
  See Mac Adoo

CANNING (O') 72 (22)
O'Cainin   79 (17)
O'Coinin of Westmeath

CANNON (O')   39 (1)
O'Canannain   45 (22)
Canning   52 (1)
  Also Scotch 70 (1)
              71 (1)
              78 (19)

CANNY   (14)
O'Caitmad
  See Mac Cann

CANTON
  See Condon

CANTRELL   (24)
  A Quaker family from
England about 1600

CANTY (O')   16 (27)
O' an Chaintighe
             127 (27)

CAOMHLONSIGH (O')
             12

CRACKEN (Mac)   (3)
  the Antrim branch of
the Mac Naughton family

CARBERRY (O') 14 (7)
  of Ulster
O'Cairbre   50 (7)
O'Clonlonan

CARBINE   102 (14-19)
O'Corbain
Corbett

CARDLE (Mac) 17 (8)
Mac Ardghail
Mac Ardel

CARDWELL   17 (3)
  A branch of Mac Mahon

CAREW   116 (23-27)
De Carrun   142 (31)
Carey

CAREY (Mac)   46 (12)
Mac Cearnaigh

CAREY (O')   52 (14)
O'Cairaighe

CAREY   18
O'Ciaradha   75 (12-17)
O'Cearry
Carry
Karey

CARLAN   53 (2-4)
O'Caireallain

CARLTON   32
O'Carelon   65 (3)
Carleton

CARMICHAEL   (3)
  A branch of the
  Scotch Stewarts

CARN (Mac)   (8)
  See Mac Carron

CARNES   145
  English

CARNEY   45 (12)
Mac Cearnaigh
Catharny (Mac)
Mac Caharney

CARNEY   64 (12-20)
O'Cathiarnaighe

CARNS (O')   50 (1)
O'Cairn
Karns

CAROLAN (O') 50 (11-14)
O'Caireallain 57 (2-4)
O'Carlain   58 (1)
Karlin
Carlin

CARON (Mac)   (17)
Mac Carrghamhna
Mac Crony
Mac Carron
Mac Carn of Monaghan

CARPENTER   37 (5)
Mac an jSaoir
Mac Ateer

CARR   116 (30)
  A branch of the Crews
  See mac Elhair

CARR   145 (4) [9]
Kerr   Scotch

CARRICK (Mac) 9
De Carraig   122 [12]
Rock

CARROL (O') 26 (8)
O'Cearbhaill 50 (9)
81 (11)
119

CARRY (O') 16 (10)
O'Cearry
Carey
  See Carew

CARSON 145 (3-4)
[22]

CARTAN (Mac) 33 (6)
  of Down 46 (2)
Mac Cartain
Mac Cartan
  of Lough Foyle
Mac Carten
Carton

CARTER (Mac) 16 (27)
Le Carter
Carty

CARTER (Mac)
  See Arthur (Mac)

CARTHY (Mac) 16 (26-27)
Mac Carthaigh
Mac Cartaig
Mac Cartie

CARTNEY (Mac)
Mac Cartaine
Mac Artney 145 (6) [22-
Scotch 23]

CARTY (Mac)
  See Carthy (Mac)

CARUTHERS 145 (4-5-6)
Caruth [21]
  Scotch

CASAUBON 141 (21)

CONCHATHASAIGH
Casey 53 (7-14-15)

CASEY (Mac) 56 (8)
Mac Cathasaigh

CASEY (O') 19 (22)
O'Cathasaigh 27 (19)
Casie 47 (14)
72

CASH 22 (23)
O'Casain 52 (32)
Cashin
Cass
Cassin
Keshin

CASIE (O') 26 (5)
  of Breagh

CASKILL (Mac) 6 (2)
130 (27)
CASSIDY (O') 18 (7)
O'Caiside
Cafsada
Casady
Casedy
Casseday

CATHCART 135 (2-3)
Scotch 145 (4-7)
[11]

CAUFIELD 6 (11)
  of Donegal Scotch
CAULFIELD See Gaffney
CAUGHLEY
  See Caffelly (Mac)

CAUGHY
  See Mulkahy

CAUGHY (Mac) 30 (4)
Mac Caughey
Mac Eachaioh

CAULEY (Mac)
  See Mac Auley

CAVAN
O'Caomain
  See Keevan

CAVINISH 97 (32)
  A branch of Kavanagh

CAW (Mac) 44 (11)
  of Cavin
  See Mac Adam

CAWELL (Mac) 55 (1-4-7)
Mac Cathmhaoil
Mac Caphull 56 (14)
Colwell
  Assumed names
  Campbell
  Caulfield
  Kemel

CAWLEY (Mac) 32 (7)
  See Mac Awley
  See Caffelly (Mac)
34 (13)

CAYLE 129 (12)
Cailey
Caley
Kayle
CEALLAGH (O') Kelly 104
CEITIN (O') 127

CELL (O') 22

CHALMERS 145 (4-5-6)
Scotch [12-13]

CHAMNEY 51 (7)
Le Champag
An assumed name

CHANDLER 143 [17]
Scotch

CHAPLIN 141 (11)
Chapelin

CHAPMAN 143 (5) [4]
Scotch

CHARTRES 141 (27)
French

CHEEVERS 132 (32)
Norman-English

CHERRY 74 (6)
O'Cherigh 143 (6) [12]

CHIDEOCK 131 (18)
Chaddock 137 (7)
Chadwick English

CHISHOLM (3-5-6)
De Cheseholme
Chisim [20]
  from Roxburgh
  Scotland
CHRISTY 143 (6) [7]
CIARAGAIN (O') 35
O'Ciarrovan
CIARROVAN (O')
O'Ciardubain 35 (9-19)
Kirwan

CILLAN (O') 22 (22)

CINEACHAN (O') 64 (27)

CLANCY 9 (8)
Mac Flanncaid 10 (10)
  of Monaghan 22 (22)
  of Leitrim 49 (22)

CLAPEN 145 (4)

CLARE (De) 118 (32)
De Cleir 125 (28-29)
Clear 134 (29)

CLAREN (O') 17 (30)
O'Cleireachain
CLARK 27 (11)
Mac an Chleirich
Mac Clery 76 (23)
O'Clery 145 (3-6)
  Also Scotch [21]

CLAUSSON 120 (4-14)
Mac Nioclais
Mac Nicholas
Classon

CLAVIN 72 (20-24)
O'Claimhin
O'Glaimin
O'Claimin
Cleevan

CLAYTON   123 (27-28)
De Cleatun   150 (27)
  English

CLEARY (Mac)   27 (11)
Mac Giollarraith
Mac Leary
  See Clark

CLEARY (O')
O'Cleirig   76 (19)
O'Cleirigh   77 (1-11-14)
O'Clery   87 (15)

CLEAVE (Mc)   145   [23]

CLEBOURNE   131 (15)
Cliborne
Cleburne

CLELLAND (Mc)
Mac Lellan   135 (3-6)
Leland

CLENAGHAN (Mac)
Mac Leannacain
               27 (2-3)

CLEMENT   (2)
  A branch of the Scotch
  Clann Lamont

CLERNON (Mc) 145 (6) [4]
Mac Giolla Earnain
Lernon

CLIFFE   136

CLIFFORD   95 (27)
O'Clumhain   134
  English

CLIFTON   145   [15]

CLIMONT (Mac)
Mac Lagmainn   63 (10)
Mac Clement
CLINCH   9 (21)
Clinse
CLOSKEY (Mac) 61 (2)
  of Derry
Mac Bhloscaidh
Mac Bloskey

CLOUD (Mac)   6
  Scotch   130 (18)

COACH   145 (6)

COATES   145 (4-6)

COBERT   145 (6)
  Scotch   [10-11]

COEN   72 (14)
O'Comhdhan

COEY (O')   61 (1-4)
  of Ulster
O'Cobthaigh

COFFER
  See Coffey

COFFEY   9 (27)
O'Cobthaigh   39 (9-10)
O'Cowhig   76 (1)
Cohey
Cowie
  See Durning

COFFIELD   73 (3-4-8)

COGAN   55 (19)
De Cogan   115 (27)
Coogan
Goggin
Norman

COGHLAN (Mac) 24 (20)
Coughlin
COHALAN A branch of
  Mac Coughlan   II-24
COHAN   74 (14)
Cohen
Coen
COIMIN   72 (22)
COININ (Mac)   72 (14)
Rabbitson

COKLEY   145 (26-27)
Mac Caochlaoich
Copley
Coakley

COLCHESTER (De)
  Norman   121
Coldwell See Colvin
COLE   116 (7)
  English

COLEMAN   52 (1-7)
O'Colmain   56 (4-15)
O'Columhain   65 (12)
Colman   95 (27)

COLGAINE (Mac)
Mac Colgan   98 (2)

COLGAN (O')   49 (20)
Mac Colgan   94 (2)
Colgahan
Coolacain
  See Culligan

COLHOUN   131 (3-6)
Colquhoun
  Scotch

COLLERAN (O') 45 (14)
O'Challarain
Challarain

CLURE (Mac)   (3-6)
  A Scotch family from
  Galloway

COOLEY   129 (12)
De Culeio
  Took the surname of
  Wellesley

COLLINS   22 (6)
Mac Coileain

COLLINS   14 (36)
O'Coilean   127 (27)
O'Cuileain
Collin
Coilea
Culean

COLLIS   134 (26)

COLLOPY (O')   21 (30)
O'Colpta

COLLVIN (Mac) 70 (1)
Mac Conluain
Colavin

COLLY   83 (15-19)
O'Coileaigh

COLSON   55 (2-3)
Colmson (Mac)

COLTHART   145 (6-9) [22]

COLTSMAN   36

COLUM   33 (16)
Mac Coluim

COLVIN   65 (13)
Mac Collvin 145 (5) [9]
Mac Conluain
Coldwell

COMANE (O')   98 (14-22)
O'Comain
  Hurley - of Clare

COMB (Mac) 145 (3) [23]
Mac Thom

COMISKEY (Mc)
Mac Cumascaigh
  Scotch   145 (8) [12]

COMISKEY (O') 43 (8-11)
Cumuscaigh

COMMINS   127 (14-28)
O'Comain
Commane
Cummins   (28)
Hurley   (22)

COMMON   77 (32)
  of Wexford
O'Cuimin
Cowan

COMMONS   52 (14)
O'Cuimin

CONAG (O') 104 (25)

CONAK (O')   14

CONAL (O') 127

CONALL (O') 49 (2)
  of Derry

CONAING (O') 19

CONARY   64 (27)
O'Conaire
Connery
CONAHA (O') 104
CONCHATHAISE (O')
Concagh   53 (19)

CONCANNON (Mac)
Mac Conceannain
             86 (19)

CONCANNON (O')
O'Concheanainn
             21 (19)

CONCUAN (O')104 (20)

CONDON   142 (27-28-
De Cauntoun   30)
Canton

CONEELY   14 (19)
Mac Conghaile

CONING   21 (19)

CONLAN   53 (15)
Conlian   63 (14)
Conleath
Connellan

CONLOGUE   69 (1)
Mac Connellogue

CONNAGHTY   104 (11)
O'Conatta

CONNALL (O') 14 (26)
O'Congaile   15 (26)
Connell
Connelly

CONNALLY   19 (12)
O'Coingheallaigh
CONNARY See Conroy 24 (19)
CONNEELY   72 (23)
O'Congaile
Kennelly

CONNELL (O') 15 (26)
O'Conaill   42 (26)
              53 (26)

CONNELLAN (O')63 (14-15)
O'Caoinleain
  See Kendellan (O')

CONNELLY (O') 15 (15)
O'Congalaig   32 (7)
O'Connell   64 (19)
CONNICK   104 (16)
Mac Conmaic

CONNIRY   45 (11-17-
O'Conaire   26)
O'Connery
  of Tralee

CONNOLLY   101 (19)
O'Conghaile

CONNOR (O')   88 (15)
O'Conchubhair 124 (15)

CONNOR (O')   37 (27)
  of Cork
  and Scotland

CONNOR (O')   53 (1)
  of Donegal

CONNOR (O')   94 (20)
  of Faley   117 (20)
O'Conchobhair
Failge

CONNOR (O')   35 (26)
  of Kerry

CONNOR (O')   25 (2)
  of Ulster

CONNULAY (O')101 (8)
O'Conghaile
Connolly

CONOLLY (O') 96 (20-24)
O'Congalaigh

CONRICK (O') 63 (19)
Mac Annraic

CONROY   24 (19)
Mac Conroi   64 (19)
Connary
King
CONSISINE (Mac)
  of Clare   20 (22)
O'Consisin

CONWAY (Mac) 64 (30)
Mac Congamhna 73 (14)
Mac Conmeadha 132 (30)
Conmey
Convey

COOK   120 (19)
Mac Coog

COOK (Mac)   46 (3-6)

COOKE   145 (3) [17]
  Cooke of Carlow
  is from Norfold, England

COOLACAIN   49 (19)
COOLEY   47 (3-6)

COOMBE   19 (5)
Combes
Mac Tomair

COONAN   53 (13)
Cuanain (O')

COONEY   26 (4-15)
O'Cuanaige   95 (22)
O'Cuanda   102 (4)
O'Cuana

COOPER   145 (26) [7]

COPE   145

COPELAND   95 (14)
Copling (O') 143 (16)
                 [11]

CORBETT
  See Carbine

CORCACHLANN Corkland 80
CORCORAN   25 (7)
O'Corcrain   26 (7)
Corcran
COREY   24 (4)
  See Curry
Corry

CORISH (Mac)   (21)
Mac Fheorias
  See De Bermingham
CORKINDALE (Mac) 130 (27)
  A br. of MacLeod
Corkindall

CORLESS
  See Mac Call

CORMACK (Mac)
Mac Cormaic   18 (7)
Cormac   25 (7)
               53 (29)
               68 (7)

CORMICK (O') 138 (26)
O'Cormacan
CORNAN   102 (28)
O'Cuirnin
Corneen

CORNICK   141 (29)

CORQUODALE (Mac)
               6 (3)
               62 (1)
Mac Torcadail Scotch

CORREY (Mac) 50 (22)
  See Godfrey

CORRIDAN   134 (22)
O'Corradain

CORRIGAN   50 (7)
O'Coraidheeain

CORRY   54
Mac Cairre

CORRY (O')   52 (7)
Correy

COSGRAVE   19 (25)
O'Cosgridhe   34 (19)
O'Coscraigh   101 (8)
Mac Oscar

COSGROVE   63 (25)
O'Coscraigh   101 (5-8)
Cosgrave

COSNAMAIG (O')
Mac Conmhaigh
Cono   74 (15-19)

COSNEY (O')   104

COSTELLO (Mac)
Mac Oisdealbhaigh
              135 (14)

COTTER   125 (27)
Mac Oitir

COTTON   142 (25-27)
De Cotun

COUEY   39 (27)

COUGHLAN (Mac) 24 (20)
Mac Cuthbreith
Cohalan
COUGHLIN (Mac) 23 (20)
Mac Cochlain

COULTON   76 (4-8)
O'Comhailltain

COURCY (De)   133 (3-6-
De Cursa   27)
  Norman   140 (6-27)

COURT (Mac)   48 (5-9)
Maolcuairt
Courtney

COURTNEY   136 (3)
De Courtenai   145 (26)
Mac Court   French

COUTTS   145 [1-15]
  Scotch

COVELL   55 (1-4)

COVERT   141 (27)

COVEY (Mac)   39 (6-9)
Mac Cobhthaigh
Coffee

COWAN (Mc)   145 [12]
  Scotch

COWELL   55 (4)
  of Scotland
Mac Cathmhaoil
Campbell
Mac Cawell

COWELL (Mac)   53 (4-7)
Mac Catmaoil
Mac Call
Mac Hall
Howell

COWLEY (Mac)   47 (1)
Mac Auley

COX   83 (15)
O'Coiligh
O'Coileaigh

COY (Mac)   39 (19-30)
Mac Aodha   51 (7)
Mac Cue
Mac Cooey
Mac Ahoo
  See Hughes

COYNE   63 (1-4)

CRACKEN (Mc)   145 (1)
  Scotc   [22]
See Naughton
                   [22]

CRAIG   9
De Craig   130 (27)
               145 (3) [17]
CRAITH (Mac)
Mac Crait
Mac Rait
  of Donegal   10 (1)
  of Kerry   15 (26)
  of Letrim   83 (10)

CRAMER   141 (29)

CRAMER   (27)
Von Kramer
  A German family

CRAMTON   99 (18)
O'Criomthain
Crampton

CRANE   56 (14)
O'Creain
  of Mayo
Crean

CRANN (Mac)
  See Rinn (O')

CRANOR (Mac)   (3-4)
  See Traynor

CRANSTON   145 [15]
  Scotch

CRAOIBHE (O') 47 (2)

CRAWFORD   134 (1) [12]
De Crafort   145 (3) [17]
  Scotch

CRAWLEY
  See Crowley

CREADY 18 (2)
Mac Conriada

CREAGH 19 (22)
Craobhach 47 (5)
Creaghe

CREAGHAN 78 (4)
O'Crocan
O'Criocain, Creigh
CREAN 56 (14)
Cregan
CREATH (Mac) 39 (27)
O'Croidheain, Crehan
CREAVY (Mac)
Mac Greevy, Mag Riabaigh
CREDHAN (Mac)
of Wicklow 104 (25)

CREED
O'Croidhen
Mac Criodain
Creedon

CREEHAN 48 (19-22)
O'Criochain

CREGHAN 75 (14)
O'Cridheain
O'Crean

CREMIN 16 (19)
O'Cremin
O'Creimin

CRENNAN (O') 10 (24-29)
O'Crionain

CREW 116 (27)
De Carrun
De Carron
Carr

CRISPIE 145 [26]
Scotch

CROFTON 142 (13-15)
De Croctun Yorkshire

CROHAN (Mac) 15 (27)
Mac Criomhthainn

CROIZIER 141 (7)

CRONAN 17 (30)
O'Cronain

CRONIN 15 (23)
O'Cronain

CRONIN 127 (27)
O'Cronan
Croinin

CRONELLY (O')
O'Cronagain 32 (9)
O'Cronghaile
Cronley

CROOKE 33 (3)
Croke

CROSBIE (24)
Mac an Crosain
Crossan
Cross
A br. of O'Moore II-30

CROSKEY (Mc) 145 (6)

CROWE (3-23)
MacConchradha
Mac Enchroe
  English in Ulster
  Irish in Thomond

CROWLEY 87 (15)
O'Cruidhlocha
Crolly

CROYDON 55 (27)
O'Croidhen

CRUISE 133 (12)
De Cruis
Cruys Norman
CRUPE 134
Crumpe, Crump - Norman
CUAGAIN (O') 55
CUAN (O') 63
CUCOGRY 77
CUDAHY 21 (27-29)
O'Cuidihthigh
  of Kilkinney
Mac Cuidithe
  of Cork

CUDBERT 145 (6-18)
  Scotch [21]

CUDDY 145 (6)
  Scotch [21]

CUE (Mac) 51 (7)
Mac Aodha
Mac Coo
Mac Coy
  See Mac Hugh

CUFFIE 90 (1)
A mistranslation
  of Duirnin
CUILY 129
CUIN (O') 72
O'Cuinn

CUINN (Mac) 35 (26)
  of Kerry

CUINN (O') 23 (22)
O'Quinn of Tyrone
  35 (4)

CUIRNIN (O') 10 (10)
O'Curneen

CULEAN
See Collins (O')

CULHANE
See Callan

CULKIN 57 (4)
Mac Uilcin
Quilkin
Gilkinson

CULLAGH (Mc) 135 (3-6)
Mac Culloch Scotch
Origin uncertain. Name
used by both Mac Donalds
and Mac Sweeneys.

CULLEN 14 (21-31)
O'Culhang 95 (21)
O'Cuileain
O'Qullayne
Quillan

CULLEN (Mac) 22 (8)
Mac Coilin 120 (14-27)
Mac Collin
  Also a branch of
  Burke

CULLENANE (O')
O'Cuileannain
Cullinan 32 (23-27)

CULLIGAN 25 (22)
O'Colgan
Quilligan

CULLEY 47 (4)
Mac Cullagh
Cully

CULLOCK (Mc) 145 (1) [22]
  Scotch

CULLY 145 (5)
O'Colla 129 (6)
Culey
Culai
Cuilys

CULLY (Mc) 145 (6) [5]
  Scotch

CULM (Mac) 63 (10)
Mac Coluim

CUMISKY 43 (8)

DAVITT (Mac) 96 (32)
Mac David

DAVORAN   14 (22)
O'Davoren   17 (22)
O'Dubhdabhoirenn

DAVY   52 (3)
Davys   97 (13)
Damer
Davis

DAVYMOR (Mac)   (32)
 A branch of the
 Mac Morroughs

DAWSON   97 (32)
Dasan   146 (3)
 English

DAY   101 (22)
 of Linster

DAY   23 (22)
O'Deadaid
O'Dee
 See Detty

DEA (O')   101 (22)
 of Linster
O'Deaghaidh
Day

DEANE   70 (1)
Mac an Deaghanaigh
Mac an Deagain
Mac Adegany
Mac Digany
 Also assumed name of
 the O'Donnell's and
 O'Gallaghers
  See Dane (O')

DEE (O')   23 (22-23)
O'Duibhginn
O'Deegan

DEELEY   75 (1-2)
O'Duibgiolla
DeVilly

DEENEY (Mac) 61 (1)
O'Duibhne
 Peoples

DEERING   14 (24)
O'Dirigh
 English
Deery - an assumed name

DEEVY (O')   101 (24-29)
O'Dubuide
DeVoy

DELAHUNTY   27 (20)
Dulchaointigh (O')
Dulanty
Hunt

DELANEY   141 (18)
O'Dubslaine

DELARGY (O') 72 (14)
O'Duibhlearga

DELMORE   131 (17)
De Lamare
Delmer
Mac Herbert Norman

DELPHEY See Duffy
DEMPSY (O')   96 (24)
DENISON
 See Donogh (Mac)
 Also a branch of the
 Mac Donagh's of
 Renfrew, Scotland

DENN   146 (26)

DENNESY   56 (15)
De Nehy

DENISON   (13)
 See Donogh (Mac)

DENNIS   16 (3)
O'Donngusa

DENNISON   146 (1) [11]
Dennistoun Scotch

DENNY   18 (26)
 of Kerry
 See Danahy (O')

DENRATHAY   59 (14)
O'Dubhionrachta

DERMOND (O') 54 (1-10)
O'Duibdiormaig

DERMOTT (Mac) 54 (1-4-15)
Mac Diarmada 87 (15)
              89 (15)

DERMOTT ROE (Mac)
 of Galway   87 (19)

DERRICK   72 (15)
O'Deirg
O'Derrig

DERRY (O')   14

DESPIE   146 (28)

DETTY   23 (22)
O'Deaghaidh
O'Deady
O'Dea
Day

DEVAN (O')   27 (15)
O'Damain

DEVANEY   58 (3)
O'Duibeannaig
Deveny

DEVEREUX   131 (32)
Deabrus   137 (32)
 Norman   142

DEVANE   38 (7-26)
O'Daimin
Devine
Davin
 See Dubhain (O')

DEVITT (Mac)   69 (1-2)
Mac Daibeid

DEVLIN (O')   57 (14)
O'Dobailein   (4-14)

DHRDAIN (O')   53

DIAMOND   70 (1-2)
O'Deamain

DICKEY   101 (3-6)
O'Dicneidhe   Scotch
Dickins

DICKSON   146 (5-6)[5]

DIFF (O')   21 (14)
O'Doithe
O'Duib
 See Duff

DIGGINS   146 (26)

DILLON   56 (15)
O'Dillane
 of Roscommon

DILWORTH   141 (27)
De La Cour
O'Dubhluachra
O'Dwlougherie
Delohery

DINAN   64 (22-27)
O'Dagnain
Dinen

FILSON   146 (6)

FINAGHEY
 See Fenton

FINELLY (O') 16 (29)
O'Fionnghalaidh
O'Fennelly

FINN (O')   95 (25-27)
O'Finn

FINNEGAN   53 (8)
O'Fionnagain 63 (15-19)
Finnagain
FINNEN (Mac) 16 (26)
FINNIE   146 (6) [1]
Finny   Scotch

FINNIGAN   72 (6-11)
O'Fionacain

FINNOC (O')   45

FINTON   49 (26)
O'Fionnachta
O'Finaghty

FIONNELLAN   21 (17)
O'Fionnelan
O'Fionnelan

FIRBISH (Mac)73 (13-14)

Forbis in Clare (22)

FISH   146 (11)
              Scotch [17]

FITSMORRIS 116 (26)
 of Kerry
mac Muiris
Mac Pearce

FITTON   146 (28)
              English

FITZGERALD
Mac Gerailt   60
 Norman   116 (26-27)
             117 (21)
             118 (26-27)

FITZGIBBON 115 (30)
Mac Giobuin Norman
             117 (30)
FITZGRIFFIN 116

FITZHENRY   114 (23)
Mac Einri
Mac Henry

FITZPATRICK 105 (24-29)
Mac Giolla Padraig
 The only native Irish
 name beginning with Fitz

FITZSTEPHEN 116 (14)
Mac Stofain

FLACK   135 (3)
Auchinleck   Scotch

FLAHEARTY (O')37 (19)
O'Flaithbheartaigh
O'Flaherty   51 (1-4)
O'Flaverty   57 (1-4)
Flarridee   71 (1)
Laverty   85 (19)

FLAHERTY   35
 of Munster

FLANAGAN   9 (7-8)
Mag Flannagain
              73 (14-22)

FLANAGAN   22 (22-19)
O'Flannacain
See Hanagan   27 (4)
              50 (8)
              65 (7)
              86 (15)

FLANLAOIS (O') 12

FLANN (O')   47 (7)
FLANNAGAIN (O')25 (23)
FLANNERY   15 (26)
O'Flannabra   (30)
              72 (14-19-
                      22)

FLATTERY   18 (20)
O'Flaitile
Ua Flaithri

FLAVIN   (27)
O'Flaitheamhain
O'Flavahan
 A branch of O'Sullivan

FLOOD   22 (27)
O'Maoltuile   35 (11-26)
Mac Atilla   57 (14-7)
 of Calvin   99 (14)
Mac Tully   103 (18)
 See Hurley

FLOODGATE   146 (18)

FLORENCE   16 (27)

FLYNN (O')   10 (6)
O'Flionn   22 (22)
O'Fhloinn   47 (3)
O'Lynn   82 (15)
             128 (8)

FOGARTY (O') 16 (27)
O'Fogartaigh 47 (22)
              50 (7)
              52 (4)
              67 (20)

FOLEY   146 (26)
O'Foghladha

FORAN   58 (1)
O'Fuarain   95 (28-30)
O'Foranan
O'Furadhrain

FORBES   37 (3-4)
 Scotch Clann in Ulster
 See Berbis (Mac)
              73 (15)

FORBIS
 Of Clare
 See Firbish (Mac)

FORD   83 (18-19)
Mac an Ata
 See Anawe (Mac)

FORHAN   53 (27)
O'Furadhrain

FORTUNE   16 (27)
Fairsing

FOWLER   146 (7) [5]
              Scotch

FOX   19 (22)
Sionnach   52 (4)
              64 (20)
              66 (12-20)

FOY   49 (14-18)
O'Fiaich   57 (11)
Foy of Cavin
O'Fee

FRAME   128 (6)
Freame   English

IRVINE   147 (6)
Irving   [1-21]
  Scotch

IVER   109 (4)
Mac Iomair
  Norse

J

JACKSON   60 (3)
  Scotch   147 (3-5-6)
                  [11]

JAMIESON   147 (6) [1]
Mac Shevmais
  Scotch

JAQUES   141 (15)

JASPER   128
  Dutch
JEFFREY   51 (17)
Jeoffrey

JEFFERSON   122
  (U.S.A.)

JENKINS   60 (28)

JENNINGS   120 (14-19-27)
Sedinin (Mac)
Mac Seoinin
  A branch of Burke
  See Shoneen (Mac)

JERETY   86 (17)
Mac GeraGhty

JEROME   141 (29)

JOHNSON   52 (4)
             147 (3-4)
                  [11-12]

JOHNSON   60 (5)
of the Fews

JOHNSTON   147 (4)
                  [11-21]

JOINER   37 (27)
Siuineir
  Assumed name
JORDAN (Mac)
Mac Siortain
             133 (14)

JOSLIN   135 (12)

JOYCE   138 (19)
De Jorse Norman-Welsh
  originally from
  Brittany in France
Joye
Joist
De Seoig

JUDGE   37 (14)
Mac an Bhreiteamnaig
Brehen

K

KALOHAR   19
  See Kelleher

KANE (O')   61 (2-4)
O'Cathain
  Also see O'Cahan

KENEELY   14 (19)
O'Kinneally
Kennelly

KANN (Mac)
  See Mac Cann

KAREY
  See Carey

KARNES   147 (18)

KARR   116 (19)
O'Carra
  See Caren

KASSHINE (Mac)
  See Cash

KASSIDY
  See O'Cassidy

KAVANAGH   74 (19)
CaomHanach   97 (32)
  An assumed 119 (32)
  name

KAVILL (Mac)
  A branch of Mac Call

KAY   83
Key

KAY (Mac)   50 (3)
Mac Aodha

KAYLE
  See Cayle

KEADY   76 (19)
Ceadach

KEAG (Mac)   147 (6)

KEANE   61 (2-4)
  See Mac Cathain
O'Kane

KEARN (O')   38 (25)
Kearon?
KEARNAN (O') 102 (13)
O'Ceirin

KEARNEY   18 (23)
  of Cashel
O'Cearnaigh

KEARNEY (O') 63 (14)
O'Cearnaig

KERNEY   53 (1-7)
  of Ulster
Mac Cearnaigh

KEARNS   50 (7)
O'Ciarain
O'Kieran
Kiran
O'Kearn
Carns

KEARTAN (Mac)
  See Mac Curtin

KEARY   18 (8)
O'Ciardha
Mac Aree

KEATING   116 (23-26-27)
Ceitinn   131
Kethin   133 (32)
  Norman-Welsh
  Also an assumed name

KEAVILL   55 (14-15)
O'Cibhil

KEE (Mac)   51 (1)
MacKay   147 (1) [23]
Mackey
  Scotch

KEEFE (O')   126 (27)
O'Caoimh

KEELY   14 (22-30)
O'Ceile
O'Cadhla
Kealy
Caley

KEENAN (O') 50 (7-8)
O'Caoinain   52 (3-6)
Kinahan   (20-24)

KEEN   61 (1)

KEEVAN   10 (27)
Va CiabhAin   (26)
Kevane   See Cavan

LANNEN   48   (14)
Lannin
 See O'Lynan

LAPP (De)   141 (7)

LAPPIN   141 (7-14)
O'Lapain
De Lapp

LARISSY   72   (14)
O'Learghusa
Laresy
O'Laryse

LARKIN (O')   15   (32)
O'Lorcain   52   (19)

LARMOUR   50   (3-6)
O'Labnairmor
Lawlor
Armour

LATHOM   137 (23)

LOUGHLIN (Mac)
O'Melaghlin   62   (1-3)
Mac LacLainn
Laflin

LAURIE   52   (3-6)
Laury   138 (4)
 Scotch

LAURY (O')   50   (3-6)
O'Labhradha
Lowry

LAVERTY (Mac)
Mac Fhlaithbheartaigh
               46   (14)
               57   (1)

LAVERTY (O')
O'Laithbheartaigh
Lafferty   77   (14)
 See Flaherty (O')
 and Armstrong

LAVERY   136 (3-6)
 Scotch

LAVIN   51   (14-15)
O'Flaithim   59   (4)
O'Lamhain

LAWLESS   86   (18-19)
O'LuaChlais

LAWLOR (O') 32 (18-24-32)
O'Leathlobhair
Lalor   50   (3-6)

LAWSON   15   (27)

LAWTON   26   (27)
Lachtnain (O')
Lachtan

LEA (Mac)   64   (2-4)
Mac Leigh
Mc Leay

LEA (Mac)   102 (18)
O'Mac Liaigh
Lee of Linster
Mac Alee

LEAMY   18   (23)
O'Leime

LEAN (Mac)   95   (2-3)
Mac Giollacain
Mac Clean

LEARY (O')   10   (14)
O'Laoghaire   11   (8)
 of Roscommon12 (10)
 of Ulster   63
 of Leitrim   127 (27)
 of Cork

LEAYS (Mac)   62   (9)
Mac Dunsleves
Levens

LEE   19   (8-25)
O'Laoidhigh
Leech

LEE (Mac)   (2-4)
Mac an Leigh
 A Scotch family from
 Dumbarton   [10]

LEE (O')   84   (19)
O'Laidihigh

LEENEY
O'Laighen
 See Lyons

LEGER (Saint)
 Norman-English
               137 (29-18)

LEGER (Saint)
Saileastar   119 (29)
Sailingeir   137 (29-18)
Lister
Sallinger
Devonshire, England

LEHAN   13   (27)
O'Fechan
 A branch of
 Lyon

LEHY   52   (29)
O'Laochdha
Leahy

LELAND
 See
 Mac Clelland
 GilFillan

LELLAN (Mac)
 See Mc Clelland

LEMON   49   (3-5)
O'Lomain   60   (1)
Lemmon   141 (18)
Lowman

LEMORE (Mac)
Mac Eachainn
 A branch of Clann
 Mac Lean from Scotland

LENNON   51   (7)
Mac Lonain   76   (5-18)

LENNON (Mac)
 from Scotland
Mac Giolla Adamnain
 Said to be from Ross

LEOD (Mac)   6   (3)
 Scotch 130 (27)

LEONARD   51   (1)
Lennan   71   (1-7)
Lynegar   77   (27)
Loonin
Lunin

LESTER (Mac)
 See Mac Allister

LEVELLE
 See MulFoyle

LEVER   63
Lefroy
(HuGuenot)
Liver

LEWIS   6   (3)
 Scotch   130 (27)

LEYDEN   62   (14)
Ladhmainn (Mac)

LEYDON   37   (19-22)
O'Loideain

LICANC (O')   63   (9)

LIDDY (O') 23 (22)
  of Clare 37 (19)
O'Lideadha 148 (22)
Liohda
Liddane
Leddy

LIERAN 78

LIGHTFOOT 137 (4)
  English

LILLY (Mac) 51 (7)
Mac Ailghie

LINDSEY 18 (19)
Mac Ghille Fhionntaig
Lyndsey 123 (2)
       148 (4)
       [11-12]

LINNAHAN 19 (27)
O'Lenaghan
O'Luingeachan
Linnehan

LINNEEN
O'Lennan
  of Cork

LINNEGAR 71 (7)
  See Lunin (O')
Linneen

LINNON 96
O'Laitile

LINTON 148 (6) [20]
Lyntoun
Mac Clinton

LISTER 119 (29)
  See St. Leger
    Devonshire, England

LITTLE 148 (6) [21]
Mac Ghillebhighe

LIVER 63
O'Libhoir
Livroy

LIVINGSTONE 62 (5-9)

LOANE 79 (8)
O'hUain
  See Lamb

LOCHLAN (Mac) 62 (1-3)
Mac LacLainn
O'Maoilseachlainn

LOCKE 87 (15)
  assumed name

LOCKHART (17)
Lockhard
Locard
  and Anglo-French
  family

LOFTIS 142 (32)
  English
De Loctus
De Lofthouse
  originally of
  Yorkshire England

LOFTUS 64 (14)
Loughnane 72 (14)
Mac Loughlin 128 (14)
            (18)
            132 (32)

LOGAN 126 (27)
O'Leoghain 148 (3) [12]
Scotch

LOHAN 126 (19)
O'Leochain
Loghan

LONERGAIN (O')
O'Longargain 19 (23-27-28)

LONG 13 (27)
O'LongaDh
O'Longseach

LONGAHAN 102 (14)
Mac Longachain
Lanigan

LONGAN (O') 52 (1)
Longain
Long

LONS (Mac) 70 (1)

LOONAN
Looney
  See Lunin (O')
LOPEZ 115
  Italian
LOSCAN (O') 95
LOUDON 148 (3) [12]

LOUGHLEN (O') 35 (22)
  of Clare
O'Loughlin

LOUGHLIN (Mac)
Mac Lochlinn 59 (1-2)
            67
  Some Loughlins are
  O'Melaghlins
            87 (15)

LOUGHLIN (O')72 (22)
O'Lachtnain

LOUGHNEY (Mac)
  See O'Malony

LOUGHRAN (O')
O'Luachain 24 (4-5)

LOURIE 148 (6)
Lowrey

LOVAINE (De) 121

LOVE 27
  See Gara (O')

LOWDON 148 (3) [12]

LOWELL 63 (27)

LOWMAN 49

LOWNEY 15 (27)
Leamna
  A branch of O'Sullivan

LOWRY 138 (4)
  See Laury (O')
Laurie
Laurey

LOWTHER 128 (7)

LUMLEY 103 (27)
O'Loimthuile
De Lumley (English)?

LUNIN (O') 51 (1-4-7)
O'Luinin 90 (1-7)
O'Luan
Leonard
Linnegar
Lynegar
Lennon
Loonan

LUNNY (O') 126 (27)
  of Munster
O'Lunigh

LUSHER 148

LUTTERELL 148 (12)

LYDON 39 (14-19)
Liodan (Vi)
LYNN (O')
LAGNAIN (O') 48 (14)
O'LaGnain
Lannen
Lynam

MAINE (O') 19 (17)
O'Manny 95 (32)
of Westmeath

MAINY 74 (14-24)
Meany

MAITHLAND 148 (7) [11]
Scotch

MAKEON (3)
A Branch of the
Bissetts

MAKEY
Mac Aoda
Mackey
  See MacKay

MALCOM 55 (3-5)
Mac Maolcoluim
Malcolmson

MAYLAN 86 (19-22)
  of Connacht
  Milan
Moylan
De Moleyns
Mullen

MALIN (O') 127 (8)
O'Maoilfhinn
O'Maolin

MALLANE (O')98 (27)
O'Maolain

MALLEN
See O'Mullen
Mellon

MALLETT
  See Mullette

MALLEY (O') 80 (14)
O'Maille
Mailey

MALLON 17 (4)
O'Meallain 98 (5)
Mellon

MALLONE (O')
O'Maoileoin 88 (20)
            98 (20)

MALONE 44 (18-22-
Magiollaeocain   32)
O'Maoileoin
O'Mullone
Melone

MALONY (O') 18 (22-24)
O'Maolohomhnaigh
Molony 22 (22)
Mac Loughney

MALY 148 (9) [21]

MAMON 141 (29)

MANAHAN (O') 32
  of roscommon
O'Mainchin 84 (27)
Manachan
Manni

MANAMY (Mac) 56 (15)
Mac Meanma

MANDEVILLE 120 (3-23)
De Moinbiol
  Appears to Branch
  from Burke as well as
  other families.
Some took the name
Mac Quillan

MANGAN 148 (30)
O'Mongain
O'Managain

MANNING 31 (27)
O'Mainnin 98 (27)
Mongain

MANNIX 32 (26-27)
O'Manahan
O'Muineug

MANSFIELD 148 (1)
Moinbiol

MANUS (Mac) 51 (7)
Mac Maghnuis 88 (15)
Mayne of Co. Antrim

MAOLMONY (O')70 (1)
MARCAN (O') 104 (22)
MARKEY
O'Marcaigh 50 (8-9)

MARKHAM (22)
O'Marcachain
  See Rider

MARKS 104 (24)
O'Marcan

MARLEY (O') 58 (1-14)
O'Mearlaigh

MARRIES (DE) 119 (23)

MARSHALL 97 (32)
Marascal 118 (32)
Le'Marechale 121 (18)
MARSON Norse 111
MARTIN 35 (1)
Mac Giollamartin
Kil Martin 46 (3)
GilMartin 58 (8-18)
Mac Martin 133 (3)
  of Ulster

MASON 37 (12-18)
  Assumed Name

MASSEY 129 (6-30)
De Masci
Maci

MASTER (Mac) 84 (7)
Mac an Mhaighstir
Masterson 148 (3-28)
  Scotch   [21]

MASTERSON 66 (10-11)
Mac an Mhaighistir
Master (Mac)

MASTON 148 (18)

MATHEWS 20 (22)
        50 (8)

MAUGHAN 35 (19)
O'Machain
Manghen
Mahon
Mochan
Mohan
Moan

MAURICE (Mac) (14)
  A Branch of Pendergast

MAXWELL 123 (3-6-18)
  Scotch

MAY 103 (8)
  of Orgilla
O'Maadhaich
O'Maith

MAYBURY 148 (26)

MAYNE (3)
  See Mac Manus

MEAD 98 (12)
O'Cumeid
O'Meid
Meade

MEADE 98 (27)
Maigh 125 (27)

MEAGER 26
  See Mahair

MEANY 55 (14)
O'Meannaighe
O'Maonaig
Meanny
Mooney
MEARA (O') 19 (23)
O'Meadhra
MEARN (O') 127 (5-8)
O'Meargan
O'Marron
MEEGAN (O') 16 (9-10)
O'Maothagan
O'Miadhagain
Meeghan
  Branch of McCarthy

MONAY (O') 104
O'Maonain
Money?
MONCREIFF 44 (6)

MONGAIN 126 (30)
O'Mongain

MONK 32 (7-22)
of Clare and
Fermanagh
O'Mainnin

MONROE (2)
Mac an Rothaich
A Scotch Clann in
Co. Derry

MONTAGUE 49
O'Taidg
See Mac Tique

MONTCHENSY (DE)
Norman-English
From Wales 121

MONTFORT (DE)
De Domfort 126 (19-27)

MONTGOMERY 109 (3)
117
136 (3-6)
148 (2-6)

MOONEY 52 (1)
O'Maonaigh 74 (14)
O'Maghna 76 (17)
98 (1)
99 (14)

MOONEYHAM
Moneyhan
Moonahan
Monihan
See Monaghan

MOORE (O') 30 (24)
O'Mordha 148 (5)
[12]

MOOREHOUSE 129 (18)

MORAHAN 54 (10)
O'Murchadain

MORAN (O') 35 (14)
O'Mograin 77 (22)
Morann 80 (15-19-
See Murran 26)

MORDIE (Mac) 67 (3-6)
Mac Maolmoroha
Mac Murdy

MORFI
See Murphy

MORGAN 95 (21)

MORIARTY 13 (26)
O'Muirceartaig
Murta 88 (15)
Mac Morrisy
See Murtaigh

MORISH (Mac) (26-14)
Mac Muiris
A Branch of Fitzmaurice
and Pendergast
MORISSY 65 (5)
O'Muirgheasa
Morris, Morrison
MORLEY 58 (1)
O'Murtuile
O'Murgaile
Morrally

MORONEY (O') 87 (22-26)
O'Maolruanaid

MORRAINN (Mac)
Mac Murcain 80 (19)

MORRIN (Mac) 91 (7)
Mac Mugroin 97 (32)
Mac Murcain

MORRIS (Mac) 65 (14)
O'Muirgis 87 (15)
Morrison 116 (26)
Norman

MORRISON 87 (1-2)
Mhic Gille Mhoire
148
(1-3-6-18)

MORRISSEY 74 (14)
O'Muirgheasa 87
also Norman

MORROUGH 97 (32)
Mac Murcada
Morrow

MORTIMER
De Moirtimeir
Norman 120 (12)
134 (27)

MOTTLEY 148
English (21-28-32)

MOYLAN (O') 15 (22-23-
O'Maolin 27)
O'Maoilean See Malin

MOYNAHAN 72 (26)
O'Muimhneachain
Moynihan 98 (27)
Moynehan

MUGHRON (O') 79
O'Mughron

MULCONRY (O')72 (15)
O'Maolchonaire
Melconor (O')

MULDERRY (O')71 (1)
O'Maoldoraid
Muldory

MULDOON 52 (7)
O'Mulfover 67 (12-29)
O'Maolduin 74 (15)
See Meldon 77 (14-22)
98 (7)
MULEN (O') 15 (27)
MULFOVER (O')
See Muldoon

MULFOYLE 53 (1)
O'Maoilfabaoil
Mulfaal
Fall
Levelle

MULHOLLAND 148 (1-2)
See
O'MAOLCHALANN

53 (30)

MULKAHY 30 (4)
Mulcahy
Caughy

MULKERRIN(O')94 (15)
O'Mulkieran 98 (15)
O'Maoilchiarain

MULLADY 49 (19)
148

MULLALLY (19-27)
O'Maolalaidh
See Lally

MULLAN (O') 60 (4)
Maoilin 61 (2-22-
Mullen 27)
Mullin
See Malin

MULLANY 10 (13-14-
O'Mailfhina 15)
O'Maoileanaig

MULLEADY (17)
See Melody (O')

MULLEN (Mc) 86 (3)
Mac Maoilain 148 (3-6)
Scotch

MULLEN (O') 17 (2-3)
O'Maolain
Mullane See Malin

MULLETTE 80 (32)
Mallett
Millett
 A Branch took the
 name Hogan
  Heuguenot

MULLIGAN
O'Maolacain 50 (1-8-14)
O'Molaghan 70 (1)
 Also see Tigue (Mac)

MULLINS 134 (26)
 A Branch of the
 Scotch Mac Millans

MULLOY (O') 87 (15)
O'Maoil Aoda
O'Maolmhuaidh
Molloy 93 (15)

MULQUEEN 24 (22-30)
O'Maolcaoin

MULRENNAN 87 (15)
O'Maoilbreanainn
MULRENIN 75 (15)
O'Maoilbhreanainn
MULROONEY 51 (7)
O'Maolruanaidh
MULROY 70 (1-14)
O'Maolruaidh
Mulrey 128 (14-16)
MULRYAN (O')96 (23)
O'Maoilriain, Ryan
MULVANEY 50 (2)
O'Maoilmheana
Mulvena 54 (1)
MULVEY 36 (10)
O'Mulmhiaigh
Mulvy 67 (12)

MULVIHILL (O')
O'Maoilmhichil
Melville 56 (22)
of Clare 81 (15)

MUNCHAIN (O')
 13

MUNSEL 116 (18)
Munsell 118 (27)
 148 (18)

MURDOCK (Mac)
 Scotch 46 (3-6)

MURDOCK 26 (12)
Mac Muirceartaig
Mac MhurchaiDh
 Scotch 148 (2-3)
Murtagh [12]

MURE 148 [10]
MURIARTY 13 (26)
O'Muircheartaigh
 See Moriarty
MURIOS (O') 86
MURLEY 18 (27)
O'Murtuile 22 (27)
O'Murilly 58 (1)
Hurley
MURPHY 86 (10-15)
O'Murchadha
O'Murcada
Murry
Mulrey
Murphys in Linster may
 be Mac Murroughs

MURPHY 96 (32)
O'Moirchoe 101 (32)
O'Moroghe 125
Morfi

MURRAN 48 (7)
O'Muireain
O'Miurain
 See Moran

MUIRIR (Mac) 53 (6)
Murray

MURRAY 44 (6)
O'Muiredaigh 58 (7)
 in Linster 101 (32)
O'Muireadhach
 in Ulster

MURRAY (Mac) 84 (6)
Mac Mhuirich 148 (1-6)
 Scotch

MURRIHY (O') 100 (22)

MURRONEY 19 (32)
O'Murruanaid

MURRONIE (O')19 (27)

MURROUGH (Mac)
Mac Murcada 96 (32)
 Some took 101
 surnames Kavanagh,
 Kinsella, Hendrick and
 Murphy

MURROW 97 (32)
 Branch of
Mac Morrough

MURRY (O') 72 (1)
O'Muireadhaigh
Murray 73 (13)
 86 (15)

MURTA(GH) (17)
Murtaigh
 See Moriarty
 Some in the North are
 Scotch MURDOCKS

MURTAGH 26 (20)
Mac Muirceartaigh
Mac Moriarty 88 (15)

MURTY (Mac) 26 (3)
 of Antrim
 See Mac Brearty

MUSGRAVE 148 (6)
 From Co. West
 Moreland

MUSSENDEN 141 (6)

MYNAHAN 79 (26-27)
O'Muimhneachain
Minahan
Moynihan

N

NABB (Mac) (10-13)
Mac ANABADA
 A Branch of Scotch
 Clann Mac Kinnon

NAGHTEN
 See Norton
Naughten

NAGLE 135 (17-27-
De Angulo 28)
De Nogla
 Some took the surname
 Mac Costello

NAHEY 54
Mac Conbheathadh

NAMARA (Mac) 22 (22)
Mac Conmara

NAMEE (Mac) 64 (14)
Mac Conmidhe 69 (1-4)

NAMER (Mc)
 See Namara (Mac)

NAPIER 148 (3-6)
Napper [11]

NARGHAILE (O')53

NASH 135 (26-30)
De Nais
Naish
Nashe
NASSEY 135 (26)

NAUGHTON 45 (15-19-
NechTan (O') 22)
O'NeacTain 49 (5)

NOWLAN (O') 42 (26-31)
O'Nuallain 95 (21)
Nolan

NUGENT 88 (15)

NULLY (Mac) (3-6)
 of Ulster
Mac Con Uladh
A Branch of the
Scotch Mac Cullaghs

NULTY (Mac) 63 (1-9)
Mac an Ultaigh
Mac Anulty

NUNAN (O') 21 (22-23)
 See Noonan
O'hIoninaineain

NUNN 140 (32)
 English

NUTT (Mc) 149 (1-2)

NUTTERVILLE 149 (12)

O

OAKS 46 (3)
 Scotch

OAKES (3)
 See Darragh

OATS (5)
 See Quirk
 assumed by a
 Branch of the Quirk
 family

OBIN 141 (5)
Hobin

ODANE 127 (15)
O'Deaghain

ODELL (30)
Major John Odell
granted castle of
Ballingarry, 1667

OGILVY 88 (15)
O'Giolla Bhuidhe
O'Gilby
Gilboy

OKEY 101 (27)
Mac Onchuin
 See Onkey (Mac)
OLIVER (30)
S. Oliver brought German
Palantines to his property
at Glenosheen, Co. Limerick

OLIS (10)
 A Clann in Leitrim
who assumed the name
Mac Raghnaill

OLLIVER 49 (9)
ONED 130 (27)
O'NED Br. of Mac Leod
ONKEY (Mac) 101
Mac Onochie

ORALY
 See Reilly (O')

ORCACHT 86 (19-22)
Mac Orachta
Mageraghty

ORMSBY 141 (13)

ORPEN 134 (26)
 A literary 141 (26)
 family

ORR 149 (6)
 Scotch [22]

ORROURKE
 A Branch of the
 O'Shaughnessys

OSCAR (Mac) (27)
 See Cosgrave

OSWALD (3)
 See Hussey

OTTER 115 (3)
Mac Oitir
Norse

OUGHTER 120 (14)
Jochtar

OWENS 16 (26)
O'Eoghain 19 (22)
 27 (3)
 84 (7)

OWEN (3)
of Ulster
 See Biset

OWEN (AP) 118 (27)
Welsh

OWEN (Mac) 44 (6)
Mac Eoin 52 (3)
 Scotch

OXBUROGH 149 (24)

P

PADDEN 20 (29)
Mac Phaidin 64 (14)
Patten
Patison
 See Fadden (Mac)

PARK 149 (2-3)
 Scotch [17]

PARKER 149 (3-6) [4]
 Scotch

PARKS 116 (3-4-6)
 Norman

PALMER 149 (6) [11]
 Scotch

PARNELL (16-25)
Originally from
Cheshire, England

PARROTT 132 (27)
Perrott

PARSONS 47 (3)
Mac an Phearsain
 Scotch 149 (4) [20]

PATRICK (Mac)
 A Branch of De Courcy
 Also a Branch of the
 Scotch Clann Lamont

PATTERSON 149 (3) [11]
 Scotch
PATTEN 20 (23)
PATTON
O'Petain
O'Pattane
Payton
Peyton

PATTY 149 (6)

PAXTON 149 (6) [17]
 Scotch

PAY 149 (29)
Pey

PAYTON 56 (15)

PEARCE (Mac) (26)
Mac Piarais
Pearse
Pierce
 See Fitzmaurice
PENDER 119 (3)
PENDERGAST 119 (23)
De Pendergast
Prendergast
Pender
Mac Maurice of Mayo

PENN   128 (27)
 of Buckingham
 England
William owned Castle
Macroom

PENNYFEATHER
                 15 (3)

PEOPLES   61 (1)
 See Deeney (Mac) (O')

PEPARD   135 (3-18)
Pepper

PERKINS   23 (22)
Mac Peaircin 149 (1)
Perkinson
PEPPER   135 (3)

PERRIMAN   134
 From Devon, England

PERRY   149 (27) [1]
 Scotch

PERRY   138 (4-18)
Peere
 Welsh

PERSON   149 (5)
 See Pherson (Mac)

PETIT   136 (12)

PETTITT   132 (26-32)
Petit
Petty
Little

PEYTON
 See Patton

PHELAN (O') 100
 See Felan (O')

PHELAN (O') 43 (23-28-
O'Fialain   29)

PHELPS   149 (6)

PHERSON(Mac)47 (3-18)
Mac an Pearsuin
                 149 (6)

PHILBIN
 See Philson

PHILLIPS   (1)
 of Donegal
A Branch of the
Mac Donalds in
Scotland

PHILPOT   135

PHILBIN (Mac)120 (14)
Mac Filiin
Philbin
Philson

PICKINS   (11) [1]
 of Cavin
 came from
Aberdeenshire, Scotland

PICKLEY   86

PIERSIN   149 (5)

PILKINGTON 132 (17)
 English

PIMS   140 (18-24)
 of Lancashire
England

PINEAU   141 (14)

PINKERTON 149 (2) [11]
 Scotch

PINNER   149 (11)

PIPER   149 (4) [1]
 Scotch

PIPPARD   149 (9)

PITCHFORD 141 (12)
De Pitche
Norman-English

PITTARRE   149 (7)
 of Salisbury, England
PLANTAGENT 125

PLUNKETT   20 (12-18)
O'Pluninceid
Pluingcead

POE
 of Cavin
Ancestors of the poet
lived at Kildallon, Co.
Cavin

POLLOCK   149 (4) [12]
 Scotch

POOLE   87 (15)
 assumed name

PORTER   149 (6) [11]
Le Porteur
Norman Scotch

PORTIS   (29)
Porteous
 Scotch   from 1570

POTTER   (18)
Le Poter
 1250 Norman

POTTS   149 (8) [15]
 Scotch

POWELL   (27)
Mac Giolla Phoil
AP Howell Welsh

POWER   124 (28)
Le Poer
Some took the surname
 Mac Shere

PRAER   121 (16)

PRATT   142 (30)
De Prato
De Prat   English

PRESTON   121 (12)
 English
De Preastun

PRICE   114 (18)
AP Rhys
 See Rice
            Welsh

PRINGLE   149 (4) [20]
Hoppiringle
 Scotch

PRIOR   35 (11)
Mac an Phriora

PRYOR   109 (3-30)
Mac an Prir
Prior
Norse

PUGH   (13)
 Welsh
AP Hugh

PURCELL   46 (23-29-
Puirseil   18)
 Also an assumed name of
a Branch of the
Mac Sparrans

PURDON   130 (3-6)

PURLY   149 (6)

Q

QUADE (Mc) 149 (6)
Mac Quoid
Quedman
Redman

QUEDMAN 149 (6)
(assumed name)
Redman

QUEEN 62 (3)
Mac Shuibhne

QUIGLEY 79 (1)
O'Cigilgh Scotch
O'Coigigh 149 (2)
Twigg

QUILEY 23 (11)
O'Caollaidhe
O'Queally

QUILKIN
See Culkin

QUILL (O') 15 (26)
O'Cuill 149 (27-30)

QUILLAN
See Cullen (O')
Also Mandeville

QUILLIGAN
See Culligan

QUIN 35 (16)
O'Cuinn 62 (5-8)

QUIN (Mac) 23 (22-23-
Mac Cuinn 30)
O'Cuinn 64 (26)

QUIN (O') 53 (4)
O'Cuinn 55 (4)
73 (22)

QUINAN 50 (23)
O'Cuinneain

QUINCEY (De) 122
Norman-French
Scotch

QUINLAN 63 (22-23-
of Linster 30)
O'Caoindealbhain
Kindellan

QUIRK 19 (23)
O'Cuirc 37 (22)
O'Quirke 103 (23)
Kirke
See Oats

QUISTON (Mac)51 (7)
Houston

R

RABBIT 50 (1-10-
O'Caoinain 13)

RABBITSON 72 (14)
See Coinin (Mac)

RABE (5)
Mac Robb
A branch of Scotch
Clann Mac Farlane

RACKIN (Mc) 149 (6)

RADUBHAN (O')72

RALEIGH 137 (23-30)
De Raileig
Rawley

RAGNALL 35 (10)
See Reynolds

RAHILLY (O') (26)
O'Raithile
an assumed name
See Reilly (O')
Br. Cenel Eoglain

RAINEY
A Branch of Reynolds
Also an English family
in Ulster

RALSTON 149 (11)
Scotch [11]
Rolston

RAM 10 (8)
O'Reighe

RAMSEY 149 (11) [7]

RANCAN 54 (1-7)
O'Rancain

RANKIN 149 (2) [12]
Mac Fhraingein
Branch of Scotch Clann
Mac Lean of Duart

RANNALL (Mac)47 (3-9)
Mac Raghnail167 (3-9-10)
Reynolds 109 (30)
See Olis

RAPPAN (O') 104

RATTIGAN 49 (15)
O'Reachtagain

RAVERTY (Mac) (1-5)
Mac Robhartaigh
Rafferty
Keepers of the Battle
Book of the O'Donnells

RAY
See Rea
A Branch of Scotch Clann
Mac Raith
Also from the Irish
Reavy family.

RAYMOND (Mac)120 (19)
Mac Reamoin
Mac Redmond

REA 149 (2) [1]
Scotch

READY 18 (29)

REARDAN 26 (27)
Raiardan (O')
Riordan

REARDEN 16 (27)
O'Riogbardain
O'Riordain 25 (27)

REDDIN 102 (22)
O'Ruadhin

REDDINGTON 67 (14-19)
of Galway

REDMAN (3)
See Quade (Mc)

REDMOND 97 (32)
De Raymond 116 (1-26-27)
Reamonn
Rodman

REED 137 (3-6)
English
Reid

REEN 146 (27)
Some Reens became
Ring

REEVY (Mac) 30 (15)
Mac Riabhaigh
Mac Greevy

REGAN 19 (22-27-
O'Riagain 28)
of Clare
Reagain
Riggins
Rogan

REGINALD
See Reynolds

REID   149 (6) [12]
↓
REID   (4-7)
Mac Riada
Mc Redy

REILLY (O') 83 (11-12)
O'Raghallach
O'Rahilly
Raleigh - assumed name
Reille
Oraly

REITHE (O') 10

RELIGH   149 (28)

RENYARD   64   (21-25)
An assumed French
name

REYNOLDS   10   (10)
Mag Ragnaill
Rainey   35   (10)
Reginald   47   (3-6)
            67   (32)

RICE   114 (32)
AP Reys
Price   Welsh
RIAIN See Ryan
RICE of Ulster
                (5-8)
A name assumed by
the O' Maol Craoibes

RICHARDS   135 (4)
English

RICHARDS (Mac)
Mac Risteaird
            61   (2-3)
            119 (28)

RICHARDSON
of Ulster
Usually a branch of
Clann Sinclair of
Scotland
Also a branch of the
Burkes

RIDDLE   149 (6) [11]
De Riodal   142 (30)
Ruddle

RIDER   50   (8-9)
O'Marcaigh
Riding
Ryder

RIDER   21   (22)
O'Markahan
Ryder

RIDGWAY   149 (4)

RIGGINS
See Regan

RILEY   83   (11-12)
North American form of
O'Reilly

RING   14   (27)
O'Rinn

RINN (O')   12   (10)
Mac Bhroin
Mac Crann

RINTOUL   137 (2-3-
De Rintoul   4)
Scotch-Huguenot

RIORDAN   26   (20-23)
See Reardan

RITCHIE   149 (3-6) [7]
Scotch

ROBERTS   48   (3-5-6)
Mac Robeartaighe
Robertson
ROUARC (O') 83   (10)
See Ruairc (O')

ROBERTSON   44   (3-5-6)
Mac Raibeirt 149 (6) [11]
Scotch

ROBINS   149 (27) [9]

ROBINSON   149 (6) [11]

ROBUCK   78   (11-12)

ROCHFORT   132 (21-28-31-
De Rupe Forti   32)
De Rochfort

ROCK   9   (19)
Mac Concairrge

RODDERY   115 (32)
Norman

RODDY (O') 67   (14-15)
O'Rodaig

RODMAN
See Redmond

ROE   60   (4)
O'Ruaidhe   149 (4)
Rowe
English

ROGAN   23   (5)
O'Ruadacain 50   (5)
O'Ruadhagain 52 (3-6)
O'Ruagain
Some Regans took this
name

ROGERS   46   (3-6)
Scotch   149 (2) [11]
Mac Rory

ROLAN   10
Scotch   149 (2-3-6)
Rowland   [1]
See Rowley

ROLLESTON   149 (5)

RONAN   52   (14)
O'Ronain
Ronayne

ROOKE
A branch of
O'Rourke
            19   (25)
ROONEY   50   (6)
O'Maolruanaidh
Mulrooney   51   (7)
O'Ruanaidh 79   (1)
Mulroy   87   (15)
Rowney

ROOTH   149 (29)
Rut
See Ruth

RORISON   46   (3)

RORY (Mac) 34   (15)
Mac Ruaidri 46   (2-4)

ROSEMAN   149 (6)

ROSS   11   (6-8)
Rois   149 (3-6)
                 [12]
ROTHE   121 (29)
Rut
Ruth

ROWAN   46   (3-6)
O'Roghain
Rohan

ROWAN   23   (22)
O'Ruadhain 76   (15)
O'Ruane

ROWE   132 (28)
English

ROWLEY   10   (14)
O'Rothlain
Rolan

IRISH COATS OF ARMS

HERALDRY IS THE SCIENCE OF DESCRIPTION AND MANAGEMENT OF
SYMBOLS CALLED "COATS OF ARMS". IN ANCIENT TIMES HERALDS
WERE APPOINTED TO VISIT HOLDERS OF ARMS FOR PURPOSES   OF
RECORDING AND TAXATION. IN THE BEGINNING ARMS WERE CRUDE
UNREGULATED DESIGNS SIMILAR TO THOSE ON THE FOLLOWING PAGE.
PROBABLY FRENCH CRUSADERS WERE FIRST TO MAKE EXTENSIVE USE
OF ARMS. WHEN WILLIAM BECAME KING OF ENGLAND FRENCH BECAME
THE OFFICIAL LANGUAGE OF THE COURT. EVERY NEW ART SOON DEV-
ELOPES IT'S OWN DESCRIPTIVE LANGUAGE. THE TECHNICAL TERM
COVERING THE DESCRIPTION OF THE VARIOUS PARTS OF A COAT OF
ARMS IS "BLAZONRY". THE LANGUAGE IS OLD FRENCH AND REQ-
UIRES SOME STUDY FOR A CLEAR UNDERSTANDING. DESCRIBING THE
HOGAN ARMS WILL PROVIDE AN EXAMPLE. IN OLD FRENCH;"SABLE ON
A CHIEF OR THREE ANNULETS OF THE FIELD". A FREE TRANSLATION:
"A BLACK(Sable), SHIELD(Chief), WITH GOLD STRIPE ACROSS THE
TOP(Field), WITH THREE BLACK RINGS(Annulets)".

ARMS ARE OFTEN SHOWN WITH A SCROLL   BELOW THE SHIELD.THE
ORIGINAL PURPOSE WAS TO DISPLAY THE MOTTO OF THE OWNER. NOW
DAYS A CARDINAL RULE OF BLAZONRY IS VIOLATED BY REPLACING THE
MOTTO WITH A FAMILY NAME. JUST AS A WESTERNER IN OUR EARLY
HISTORY COULD RECOGNIZE THE OWNER OF A CATTLE BRAND, EUROPEANS
MEMORIZED THE ARMS OF FRIENDS AND NEIGHBOURS.

MANY OF OUR ANCESTORS ATTACHED SMALL VALUE TO THESE SYMBOLS.
WHEN RICHARD DURNING BUILT A FREE GRAMMAR SCHOOL FOR THE CHIL-
DREN OF BISPHAM IN CO. LANCASHIRE HIS SHIELDAT THE PEAK OF THE
ROOF BORE ONLY HIS INITIAL AND THE DATE. MANY SCOTS AND OTHERS
UPON MOVING TO IRELAND FAILED TO REGISTER THEIR ARMS. IN THIS
CASE IT WILL BE DIFFICULT PERHAPS IMPOSSIBLE TO FOLLOW THE
SCOT ARMS TO IRELAND.

FEW OF THE ORDINARY FOLK IN IRELAND POSSESSED ARMS IN THEIR OWN
RIGHT AND NOT MANY USED THE ARMS OF THEIR CHIEF. FEWER STILL
UPON ARRIVAL IN THE NEW WORLD GAVE ANY THOUGHT TO ARMS   AS A
STATUS SYMBOL. NEAR THE END OF THE LAST CENTURY WHEN MORE THAN
ONE IRISH PERSON HAD GAINED WEALTH AND POSITION DID OUR ANCES-
TORS BEGIN TO THINK ABOUT STATUS AND POSITION. FOR MOST OF US
THE PAST IS STILL GUARDING THE SECRET OF OUR HERITAGE.

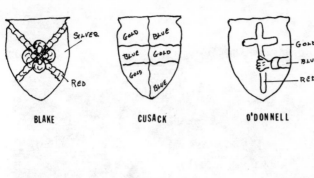

BLAKE

CUSACK

O'DONNELL

FITZGERALD

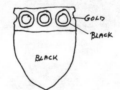

POWER

TIERNEY

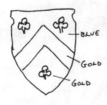

HOGAN

LYNCH

CLONMACNOIS